DogLife ❧ Lifelong Care for Your Dog®

SIBERIAN HUSKY

Donna Beckman

SIBERIAN HUSKY

Project Team
Editor: Heather Russell-Revesz
Copy Editor: Joann Woy
Indexer: Dianne L. Schneider
Design: Patricia Escabi
Series Design: Mary Ann Kahn, Angela Stanford

T.F.H. Publications
President/CEO: Glen S. Axelrod
Executive Vice President: Mark E. Johnson
Publisher: Christopher T. Reggio
Production Manager: Kathy Bontz

T.F.H. Publications, Inc.
One TFH Plaza
Third and Union Avenues
Neptune City, NJ 07753

Printed and bound in China

11 12 13 14 15   1 3 5 7 9 8 6 4 2

Library of Congress Cataloging-in-Publication Data
Beckman, Donna.
  Siberian husky / Donna Beckman.
      p. cm.
  Includes index.
  ISBN 978-0-7938-3611-6 (alk. paper)
  1. Siberian husky. I. Title.
  SF429.S65B43 2011
  636.73--dc22
                           2010035749

This book has been published with the intent to provide accurate and authoritative information in regard to the subject matter within. While every reasonable precaution has been taken in preparation of this book, the author and publisher expressly disclaim responsibility for any errors, omissions, or adverse effects arising from the use or application of the information contained herein. The techniques and suggestions are used at the reader's discretion and are not to be considered a substitute for veterinary care. If you suspect a medical problem consult your veterinarian.
Note: In the interest of concise writing, "he" is used when referring to puppies and dogs unless the text is specifically referring to females or males. "She" is used when referring to people. However, the information contained herein is equally applicable to both sexes.

The Leader In Responsible Animal Care for Over 50 Years!®
www.tfh.com

CONTENTS

INTRODUCTION

INTRODUCING THE SIBERIAN HUSKY

Nearly as long as man has existed, the human–animal bond, too, has existed. Through oral histories, cave paintings, and archeological and anthropological findings, there is proof of the longtime relationship between humans and canines. Serving as helpers, partners, and companions, domestic dogs have been a significant part of human life for thousands of years.

Until recently, the prevailing theory was that the most ancient breed of dog was the Saluki from Africa. However, the findings of the canine genome mapping project, published in 2005, caused this theory to be modified. The work conducted under the auspices of the National Institute of Health looked at 85 breeds of domesticated dogs and wild canids. In mapping the genes of these canines, the study divided the dog breeds into eight groupings based on genetic similarities.

The Siberian Husky was grouped with the Asian and African Primitive dogs, sharing their heritage closely with the wolf. Siberian Husky fanciers, and anyone who has ever watched Siberians interact in groups, have known this for years. In addition to their similar appearance, Siberians show many of the same behaviors observed in packs of wolves in captivity and in the wild.

Even with these new findings, as well as with archeological and anthropological study, there are still a number of schools of thought regarding when these ancient or primitive breeds were originally domesticated. The prevailing theories range from between 10,000 and 15,000 years ago. However, based on skeletal remains from a site in Africa, there is some belief that this domestication may have occurred even earlier, perhaps as long as 30,000 years ago. Regardless of the exact time and place, it is obvious that mankind has relied on the dog for help and companionship for a very long time.

THE HISTORY OF THE SIBERIAN HUSKY

The story of the domestication of one of these primitive dog breeds begins in the area known as Siberia. Siberia comprises 10% of the land mass of the Earth. It is the northern portion of Asia, beginning in the west at the Ural Mountains (the dividing line between Europe and Asia). It is bound on the north by the Arctic Sea, on the south by the countries bordering the Russian Federation, and in the east by the Bering Sea and Pacific Ocean.

The Chukchis of Siberia are responsible for the development of the Siberian Husky.

Siberian Dogs

The peoples who were responsible for the domestication of the dog known to us as the Siberian Husky are the Chukchis from the far northern and eastern corner of Siberia. This is the land mass closest to Alaska, and connected to it during the winter by the frozen Bering Strait. This part of Siberian is known as the Chukchi peninsula. It is bordered in the southwest by the Anadyr River, and spans the land north to the Chukchi Sea and east and south to the Bering Sea.

This area is a desolate one, known for harsh winds off the water, mountains, and permafrost tundra. There is little vegetation— only small bushes and no trees; in short, it is a frozen desert. It is on this peninsula that the Chukchi people have lived for 30,000 years. And during this time, their Siberian dogs (the forebears of the modern Siberian Huskies) aided in the survival and life of the Chukchis.

Due to the land and its climate, Chukchi society was not agrarian; the Chukchis survived by hunting, fishing, and trapping. To help in this semi-nomadic life, the Chukchis utilized teams of dogs for transportation. Because of the harsh living conditions, these Siberian dogs needed to be easy-keepers and capable of traveling long distances over varied terrain to support the survival of the Chukchi peoples— which they did most capably. Over time, some trade occurred between the Chukchis and other Asian peoples, as well as with their close Western Hemisphere neighbors in Alaska. With the expansion of the Chukchi's world, the world of the Siberian Husky also expanded.

The first Europeans to settle in the Alaskan territory were Russians, significantly due to the close proximity of Siberia to Alaska. These Russians encountered a number of native peoples, including the Inupiat, and found the lives of these native populations similar to many in Siberia, relying on dog teams for transportation in the cold, northern climate. With the purchase of Alaska by the United States in 1867, and the subsequent appointment of a governor in 1888, Alaska became a US territory. This event coincided with the discovery of gold in Juneau.

By 1896, gold was also discovered near Dawson in Canada's Yukon territory. It was soon clear that the gold followed the path of the Yukon River, across the border into Alaska and all the way across the Alaskan territory to Nome and the Bering Sea. This northern gold rush prompted the need for additional dog teams to help transport the influx of people to the area.

These native Alaskan village dogs were quite large, resembling Greenland dogs or Alaskan Malamutes in size. And, as one can imagine, where people, dogs, and money came together, sled dog racing soon followed. With time, racing became more formalized, and the All-Alaska Sweepstakes, a race of over 400 miles (644 km) in the Nome, Alaska area, was started.

The Influence of Sled Dog Racing

About this same time, upon hearing of the extraordinary speed and stamina of the Siberian dogs, trader William Goosak brought the first team of Siberian Huskies to Alaska. These dogs were significantly smaller than the native Alaskan dogs, and were ridiculed for their size. However, Goosak entered this first team of Siberian dogs in the second All-Alaska Sweepstakes race. These "Siberian rats,"

as they were referred to due to their relatively small size, did quite well in the race. Their accomplishment captured the attention of a Scottish nobleman in the area, the Honorable Fox Maule-Ramsay. Ramsay organized his own expedition to Siberia to bring back 60 of these Siberian dogs.

Subsequently, Ramsay entered three teams in the 1910 All-Alaska Sweepstakes, and his teams placed first, second, and fourth. The first-place team, driven by John "Ironman" Johnson, set the record for a race at this distance (400 miles [644 km]), and this record held until 2008. These Siberian Huskies were proving themselves on the trail in Alaska, as well.

In 1913, Norwegian explorer Roald Amundsen, the first man to the South Pole, began to plan an expedition to the North Pole. He enlisted help from his friend, Jafet Lindeberg, called the "Founder of Nome," to help plan this adventure. Lindeberg enlisted the help of Leonhard Seppala, another Norwegian, to procure and train dogs for the upcoming

The 1910 All-Alaska Sweepstakes winning Siberian Husky team.

Leonhard Seppala's 1925 Serum Run team of Siberian Huskies.

venture. As the result, a call went out to find the best Siberian Huskies for the expedition.

Seppala trained teams of Siberian Huskies for Lindeberg and Amundsen, and while doing so, he entered and won the All-Alaska Sweepstakes races in 1916 and 1918. Unfortunately, with the rapid onset of World War I, Amundsen's expedition was cancelled, and the All-Alaska Sweepstakes races were also curtailed. Seppala, however, continued working with his Siberian Huskies, and the name Seppala would become forever tied to the Siberian Husky.

The Serum Run

In the winter of 1925, an outbreak of diphtheria occurred in Nome. The life-saving serum needed to get from Anchorage to Nome, if there was any hope in saving the children of Nome. But, the waterways were frozen, and the weather was too bad for flight. The serum could be sent by train from Anchorage to the railway end in Nenana, but this was some 600 miles (966 km) short of its goal: Nome. It was decided that a dog team relay was the best

solution to convey the serum the rest of the distance.

Twenty mushers and 150 dogs participated in this life-saving relay, which began on January 27th. For five and a half days, teams of mushers and dogs crossed Alaska through the harshness of an arctic winter, while the world followed their progress by telegraph and newspaper. The longest and most difficult leg was run by Leonhard Seppala and his team of Siberian Huskies, led by Togo. They began in Nome and raced to Shaktoolik, a distance of 170 miles (274 km), over the frozen Norton Sound, to meet the team with the serum. Then, with the serum, they ran another 91 miles (146 km) from Shaktoolik back to Golovin, in temperatures of –30°F (–34°C) and wind chill temperatures of –80°F (–62°C).

On February 1st, the serum arrived in Nome, in a sled driven by Gunnar Kaason and his lead dog Balto. None of the serum was damaged, and by that afternoon, it was thawed and ready for use. In all, the serum traveled 674 miles (1,085 km) by dog sled in a record-setting five days and seven hours, through blizzard conditions.

The accomplishment made the mushers and their dogs famous. Leonhard Seppala and Togo and Gunnar Kaason and Balto traveled to the continental United States on tour. Although all Siberian fanciers consider Seppala and Togo the real heroes of the Serum Run, a statue of Balto was erected in New York's Central Park late in 1925. This monument bears the inscription:

Dedicated to the indomitable spirit of the sled dogs that relayed the antitoxins 660 miles over rough ice, across treacherous waters, through Arctic blizzards from Nenana to the relief of stricken Nome in the winter of 1925.

Endurance • Fidelity • Intelligence

After the publicity tours, Leonard Seppala settled for a time in Poland Springs, Maine, where he established a kennel with Elizabeth M. Ricker (Nansen). Ms. Ricker had imported some of the last dogs from Siberia. The ship importing the dogs became stranded for the winter, and only four of the dogs survived. Among these dogs were Kreevanka and Tserko.

Seppala and his Siberian Huskies competed in a number of races in New England during this time. Upon his return to Alaska, Seppala left his dogs with Mrs. Nansen and Harry Wheeler in Québec, Canada. Every registered Siberian Husky can trace his lineage directly to these dogs, original imports and a few of their direct descendants.

RECOGNITION OF THE SIBERIAN HUSKY IN THE UNITED STATES

The success of these early Siberian teams in New England contributed to their popularity. These dogs captured the interest of Milton and Eva B. "Short" Seeley of Chinook Kennels in Wonalancet, New Hampshire; Lorna Taylor (Demidoff) of Monadnock Kennels in Keene, New Hampshire; and Dr. Roland Lombard, a veterinarian from Wayland, Massachusetts, and owner of Igloo Pak Kennels. These individuals were instrumental in the popularization of these Siberian Huskies.

This fledgling group of Siberian Husky fanciers in New England raced their dogs in the winter. Wanting something to do with the dogs in the summer, they sought recognition for the breed with the American Kennel Club (AKC). They wrote the first breed standard based on those original imports and their offspring, and AKC recognition of the breed was achieved in 1930. Approximately 20 years after the first Siberian Huskies arrived in Alaska, their descendents competed in their first AKC dog shows. In 1938, this group of Siberian enthusiasts formed the Siberian Husky Club of America, Inc. (SHCA), the AKC-recognized parent club that serves as the guardian of the breed standard—a written description of the ideal Siberian—for Siberian Huskies.

INFLUENTIAL PEOPLE AND KENNELS

The Siberian Husky is a strikingly beautiful dog. The athleticism, appearance, and demeanor of the breed soon captured the hearts of many who encountered them. Their popularity as sled dogs, show dogs, and companions grew. Those early kennels in New England, Chinook, Monadnock, and Igloo Pak, were soon making their marks in every aspect of the dog world.

Chinook Kennels

In addition to their Siberian Huskies, Milton and "Short" Seeley raised a number of breeds of sled dogs, including Alaskan Malamutes and some of Arthur Waldon's Chinooks. They worked their dogs, and some trained for Arctic and Antarctic expeditions. Chinook Kennels produced the foundation stock for many of the prominent kennels in the United States and abroad. Two of Mrs. Seeley's dogs won Best of Breed at the first and second National Specialties of the Siberian Husky Club of America in 1940 and 1941. These were Ch. Laddy of Wonalancet and Wonalancet's Baldy of Alyeska. In addition to the dogs she bred, "Short" Seeley became a popular AKC judge, and was very active in the Siberian Husky Club of America, Inc., having been named Honorary Life President in 1959, a title that remained with her until her death in 1985.

Monadnock Kennels

Any Siberian Husky fancier the world around recognizes the name Monadnock—it is that much a part of the history of the Siberian Husky. Named for a mountain in New Hampshire, Lorna B. Taylor (Demidoff) founded Monadnock Kennels, which became one of the most influential Siberian kennels in history. In the first 23 SHCA National Specialties, dogs bred or owned by Mrs. Demidoff won Best of Breed fifteen times and Best of Opposite Sex seven times. Her Ch. Otchki of Monadnock, CD, won Best of Breed at four national specialties and Best of Opposite Sex once.

Arguably the two most famous Monadnock dogs were father and son, Ch. Monadnock's Pando and Ch. Monadnock's King. Both National Specialty winners, it is King's head that was immortalized in the logo of the Siberian Husky Club of America. King was the first Siberian Husky to win Best in Show in the continental United States in 1961. Ch. Monadnock's Pando won five consecutive Best of Breed awards at the Westminster Kennel

Club shows, and was the number-one ranked Siberian in 1961 and 1962. Pando's fame really grew as a stud dog. Pando's offspring were to become the basis for many Siberian kennels throughout the world.

Igloo Pak

Dr. Roland "Doc" Lombard earned his fame in the sled dog world a bit differently than his contemporaries. Although he bred and showed his Igloo Pak Siberians, once winning Best of Breed at a national specialty with Igloo Pak's Anvic, his true love was sledding. Over the years, "Doc" competed in many sled dog races, and his rivalry with Alaskan native George Attla is legendary in the sled dog racing world.

Alaskan-Anadyr Siberians

In the 1930s, in Lake Placid, New York, a young girl named Natalie Jubin was exposed to some of the Siberians Leonhard Seppala left in New England. Natalie grew up and moved with a few Siberian Huskies and Alaskan Malamutes from Chinook Kennels to Alaska, where she met Earl Norris. Earl and Natalie married and founded the premier Siberian sledding kennel in the world. Their Alaskan-Anadyr Siberians have been succeeding on the trail ever since. Both winning dog drivers themselves, the Norrises had the first Siberian Husky to win Best in Show at an all-breed show, Ch. Alaskan's Bonzo of Anadyr, CD. Bonzo, like the other Anadyr dogs, was a working sled dog. For over 60 years, the Norris' dogs have competed in a number of notable races, including the North American World Championships and the Iditarod. And others have made their marks on international trails.

The Iditarod

The world famous Iditarod Trail Sled Dog Race commemorates the 1925 diphtheria

Ch. Kontoki's E-I-E-I-O ("Donald"), bred by Thomas "Tommy O" Oelschlager and Marlene DePalma, holds the record for having won the most all-breed Best in Show awards; he is pictured with Tommy O.

serum run. Begun in the 1970s, the Iditarod is run every winter from Anchorage to Nome, Alaska, a distance in excess of 1,049 miles. It is most fitting that almost every year a team of purebred, registered Siberian Huskies is entered in the Iditarod Trail sled dog race, commemorating the accomplishments of Seppala and Togo with his team of Siberian Huskies—the forebears of today's teams.

Other Notable People

As the Siberian gained fame, others acquired Siberians and founded kennels throughout the country. Some of these notable people included Lyle and Peggy Grant's Marlytuk Kennels in New Hampshire, the Forsberg's Savdajaure Kennels in Massachusetts, and Charles A. Carolyn Posey's Yeso Pac Kennels

in Virginia and later New England. In the Midwest, Donna and John Foster founded Frosty Aire Kennels, and Bob and Dorothy Page's Chotovotka (pronounced "shot of vodka") Kennels flourished.

In Colorado, the Clines were famous for their Baltic Siberians, along with Janis Church (Stadler) and her Siberian Huskies of the Midnight Sun. Frank and Phyllis Brayton's Dichoda Kennels in Northern California, and the Martha Lake Siberians in Washington state helped popularize the breed on the West Coast.

Kennels that moved around the country and are still quite active and successful today are Norbert and Kathleen Kanzler's Innisfree Kennels and Judith M. Russell's Karnovanda Kennels.

More recently, Thomas Oelschlager and

The only Siberian Husky to win Best in Show at Westminster is Ch. Innisfree's Sierra Cinnar, shown here with Patricia "Trish" Kanzler.

Marlene DePalma's Kontoki Kennels in Pennsylvania, and Dr. David and Sheila Qualls' Indigo Kennels in Florida have been extremely successful and influential.

In the sledding world, in addition to the Norrises' Alaskan-Anadyr Siberians, Indiana-to-Alaska transplants Wayne and Chris Curtis's Stormwatch Siberians have taken the Iditarod trail to Nome a number of times, as has Canadian Karen Ramstead with her North Wapiti Siberians.

MEMORABLE DOGS

Any history of the Siberian Husky would not be complete without mentioning some significant dogs. The list, of course, begins with those dogs who appear in nearly every pedigree of today's Siberian Huskies. This group begins with Togo, whose feats as a lead dog make legends, and his sire Suggen. Two of Elizabeth Ricker's imports, Kreevanka and Tserko, are also among this list. Another dog with significant pedigree influence is the leader, Fritz.

As is the case with dogs, all Siberians of the past have been memorable to their owners and friends. But, a few Siberians should be noted for their place in the breed's history. Some of these dogs have been mentioned, as their accomplishments were so much a part of their breeders' and owners' contribution to the breed—dogs such as Togo, Kreevanka, Pando, and Bonzo. But other great dogs have also added to the breed's history.

The first Siberian Husky to complete an American Kennel Club championship was the Shattuck's white bitch, Ch. Pola. The first Siberian Husky to receive all AKC titles available during his lifetime was the Garretts' Ch. Chornyi of Kabkol, UDT. In addition to his Championship, Chornyi was the third Siberian to finish his CD, the first Siberian to finish his CDX, the first Siberian to finish his UD, and the first Siberian to finish his Tracking title. Chornyi and his accomplishments were honored in a memorial trophy for High in Trial at the SHCA national specialties. A Best of Breed winner at two SHCA national specialties, Peggy Grant's Ch. Marlytuk's Red Sun of Kiska was also an influential stud dog. A Pando son, Ch. Savdajaure's Cognac, bred and owned by the Forsbergs also won two national specialties.

In the Midwest, Arthur Piunti's Ch. Frosty Aire's Banner Boy was a very influential stud dog, and a significant influence in his day. And, on the West Coast, the Brayton's Ch. Dichoda's Yukon Red had significant success and influence, and won best of breed at a National Specialty.

In the show ring, a few Siberians have achieved notable accomplishments. Only one Siberian has ever won Best in Show at the Westminster Kennel Club Show, the Kanzler's Ch. Innisfree's Sierra Cinnar, handled by Trish Kanzler. Ch. Kontoki's E-I-E-I-O, known as "Donald," bred by Thomas "Tommy O" Oelschlager and Marlene DePalma, holds the record for having won the most all-breed Best in Show awards. These two dogs, in addition to their remarkable show records, were also quite influential stud dogs.

The two "firsts" in companion events include the first Siberian to achieve an Obedience Trial Championship, OTCH Storm King of Siberia, owned by Weldon Fulton. Storm also went High in Trial at the 1977 SHCA national specialty. The first dog to achieve the Agility MACH title was MACH Jasper Wild Thunder Mitchell, owned by Tim Mitchell. Currently, the highest MACH title for Siberians is MACH5! And, the first, and to date only, Siberian to complete his Champion Tracker title is CT Savitar's Pipe Down Otis, owned by Carol Clark from Kansas.

In today's sledding world, two notable dogs, a male and a female, come to mind. Monte, Ch. Stormwatch's Montana, SDO, an accomplished sled dog who raced in multiple Iditarod races, was an AKC champion of record, completed all three of the Siberian Husky Club of America's Sled Dog titles, and won Best of Opposite Sex at a national specialty. The female, Alaskan's Yakut of Anadyr, although she never finished her championship, was an accomplished lead dog, having raced in three Iditarod Trail Sled

Dog races and the Hope Race (from Siberia to Alaska), and she was presented with an Award of Merit at a National Specialty.

All of these people and dogs have had great influence on the world of the Siberian Husky. Whether through their individual commitment, their breeding contribution, or their remarkable achievements, all have played a role in shaping the breed, and are appreciated for it. However, as anyone who lives with a Siberian Huskies will tell you, Siberians living in everyday homes contribute so much to their families' lives that all of them are notable and very special.

Whether your Siberian is a champion like the author's Ch. Karnovanda's Your Teddy Bear ("Ted") or a family pet, he's sure to bring joy to the whole family.

PART I

PUPPYHOOD

CHAPTER 1

IS THE SIBERIAN HUSKY RIGHT FOR YOU?

Before bringing a dog into your home, it is important to look at your family, location, and lifestyle, in order to determine what type of pet is most suitable. All breeds have natural behavioral traits, plus requirements for space, exercise, and other factors that must be met for the animal to thrive. These requirements should coincide with your life and family in order to make a successful team. For example, a dog requiring a lot of exercise may not be suitable in a small apartment with a family too busy for a daily walk or run. Likewise, a small dog with short legs or difficulty breathing might not be the best choice for a runner's pet. The worst thing that can happen is to select a dog breed solely based on appearance, without knowing if the puppy has a chance of fitting with your home and family.

If you are considering adding a Siberian Husky (or for that matter, any breed of dog) to your family, it is a good idea to research the breed thoroughly. First, we'll take a look at some of the typical behavioral traits of the Siberian Husky, then cover the physical aspects of the breed. The last section covers environmental needs, energy level, exercise requirements, health and genetic predispositions, lifespan, grooming, and training challenges.

BEHAVIORAL TRAITS OF THE SIBERIAN HUSKY

To prepare yourself for a Siberian Husky, never lose sight of his history and purpose. Keeping this in mind will help you meet the challenges of owning this beautiful breed. Remember that these are team dogs, used to working together. They are long-distance endurance runners, and they are highly intelligent. At the onset of dog ownership, this seems to be a wonderful group of qualities—and it is. However, when incorporating a Siberian into your life, these wonderful qualities may come with some challenges.

Welcome to the Team

As a team dog, the Siberian Husky is friendly and should get along well with people and other animals. However, there are a few things to consider. First, you'll need to come to terms with the fact that *you* will become a member of your Siberian's "team," and therefore it will be up to you to determine each family member's place in the hierarchy of that team. Although this may not be as apparent when bringing a puppy into your home, as that puppy grows (or if you adopt an adult dog), his humans will need to establish their place as leaders of his team.

Siberians are very intelligent animals, with an established pack structure of dominance and submission. As the human member of this pack, you must secure your role within it. Unlike some other breeds, Siberians do not automatically see their humans as pack leaders; humans are just members of the team, and possibly not even the most important ones. Do not forget that, for the survival of the team, sled dogs on the trail must have personalities strong enough to disobey the musher's commands if they will put the team in danger. If you are not prepared for it, this intelligence and independence may be a bit of a challenge. Siberian owners need to appreciate this intelligence and independence—even

cherish them as hallmarks of the breed—as their Siberian inevitably refuses to come when called.

Inquisitive With a Dash of Silliness

Although they are quite agreeable companions, Siberians can also be very inquisitive and determined. They will want to explore everything—often something you do not want them to. And, they tend to be tenacious in overcoming any obstacle you might put in front of them. They seem to enjoy the challenge of outsmarting us.

Siberians also seem to have a great sense of humor. Although they can be very dignified and even regal at times, they can also be quite silly. You will find their behavior humorous and occasionally frustrating. So, Siberians require owners with a great capacity to laugh at themselves and their dogs' antics.

On the Run

The most important trait that a Siberian owner must take quite seriously is the breed's desire to run. The Siberian's desire to run, combined with his intelligence, inquisitiveness, and sense of humor, can often get him into serious trouble. Siberians must be properly controlled in an adequately fenced yard or on a leash at all times. An open door or gate can mean a Siberian's first dash across the street, and his last. Although your Siberian may love you, his desire to run, to see what's around the corner, and to have you chase him can be very dangerous. Although all dogs should be kept adequately controlled on a leash or in a fenced yard, this is even truer for the Siberian; anyone considering this breed must understand this.

PHYSICAL TRAITS OF THE SIBERIAN HUSKY

The typical Siberian Husky is a medium-sized working dog. People are often surprised at how

Siberian Huskies are bred to work as a team.

relatively small Siberians are; they think that sled dogs must be big and bulky—in a word, *husky*. Actually the word "husky" has become a somewhat generic term for a northern-type sled dog, but it does not describe the dog's build; these are not husky dogs. Rather, the word "husky" is thought to be a corruption of the word Eskimo, or "esky" dog; again, indicating a northern dog.

Overall Build

The Siberian Husky is significantly smaller than the Alaskan Malamute. Remember that the first Siberian dogs brought to Alaska were referred to as "Siberian rats," due to their smaller size. But, like marathon runners, size and bulk are not beneficial in endurance running. The job of the Siberian Husky is to carry a light load at a moderate speed over great distances.

These dogs originated in a fairly inhospitable land, where there was no excess nourishment available; they had to manage to do their job on a relatively small amount of food. The breed's size, structure, and metabolism help in

By the Numbers

- 21 to 23½; 45 to 60: Siberian Husky males are from 21 to 23½ inches (53 to 60 cm) in height at the withers and weigh between 45 and 60 pounds (20 and 27 kg).
- 20 to 22; 35 to 50: Siberian Husky females are from 20 to 22 inches (51 to 56 cm) in height at the withers and weigh between 35 to 50 pounds (16 to 23 kg).

achieving this efficiency. Any excess—in height, weight, bulk, structure—keeps the Siberian from doing his job efficiently. For this reason, Siberians do not have heavy bone and excess bulk. Rather, they are the marathon runners of the sled dog world, and their build reflects this.

The Siberian Husky (left) is significantly smaller than the Alaskan Malamute (right).

Height and Weight

Fully grown, these medium-sized dogs weigh between 35 and 60 pounds (16 and 27 kg), with the females on the lower end of that range, and males on the higher end of the range. Siberians stand between 20 and 23 1/2 inches (51 and 60 cm) at their shoulders; again with females on the smaller size and males larger.

A Siberian Husky is a dog who most adults could pick up, if necessary. He is a bit too large to be a lap dog, although he might just try to fit!

Coat

In every way, the Siberian coat reflects his northern heritage. He is well-furred with a double coat—a dense undercoat that supports a straight, somewhat medium-length outer coat of coarser fur. This double coat keeps the Siberian dry in snowy conditions.

His coat comes in any variety of colors and markings, from pure white to black, and everything in between. Although the Siberian breed is known for its beautiful markings, color and markings are not as important as the length and thickness of the double coat that is required for survival.

Ears

His medium-sized, triangular ears with slightly rounded tips are set fairly high on the head.

Eyes

His eyes are almond-shaped and obliquely set. They are any shade of blue or brown, one of each, or multiple colors within one eye. The expression is intelligent, friendly, and mischievous—as if he is thinking of starting trouble.

Neck and Head

The Siberian has a medium-length neck that is gently arched from the withers to the head,

The Siberian's coat comes in any variety of colors and markings, from pure white to black, and everything in between.

and is carried proudly erect. The well-balanced muzzle length and tapering skull form a head in balance with the rest of the dog.

Tail

His head is balanced by a fox-brush tail that can be carried over the back in a sickle curve, dropped, or trailing—that is, whenever it is not wagging!

LIVING WITH A SIBERIAN HUSKY

Now that you have a better understanding of the Siberian's general temperament and physical characteristics, it's time to look at the other factors that will influence living with the breed. As you may have already discerned, the Siberian Husky is not the right dog for everyone. The breed of dog you end up choosing should fit your life, your personality, and your view of the proper relationship between humans and canines.

Before looking for that dog, make a list of things that are important to you and your life. This list should include where you live, if you have a fenced yard, if you enjoy physical activity like jogging, if there are children or other pets in the house, if you have time for a lot of grooming, what size of dog you want, and more. Consider all of these aspects of pet ownership before you fall in love with that adorable puppy. Because by then it will be too late!

Environment

If you are considering a Siberian Husky, know that they are fairly adaptable to many environments, but fitting them into your home may still require some work on your part. Whatever the location, it requires commitment on your behalf to make sure the dog is safe and content. The bottom line is that a Siberian will

A securely fenced yard may be no match for a bored Siberian—he can and will find creative ways to escape.

thrive in a safe environment where he is well controlled, but can get plenty of exercise.

Suburban

A suburban home with fenced yard and lots of family interaction can be ideal. But if the suburban owner doesn't have enough time to spend with a Siberian, the dog will get bored. And a bored Siberian will become creative—finding ways to dig under, climb over, or eat through that "secure" 6-foot (2-m) fence.

Urban

A city apartment with an owner who doesn't mind walks during the day and engages in a daily run with the dog can be a fine option. However, if a change in work schedule curtails those frequent walks, or inclement winter weather puts a damper on the daily run, a Siberian will find ways to entertain himself in inappropriate ways. Although not known for barking, Siberians can be vocal dogs. Their howling or "talking" can become annoying to neighbors.

Rural

A rural life, with ample places to run and play, might be seen as the best environment for any dog. However, remember that the Siberian was bred to run, and his curiosity could take him to the highway or to a local rancher's chicken coop. Both journeys could result in disaster.

Exercise

One of the biggest commitments you'll need to make to your Siberian is to ensure that he gets adequate exercise. While the need for real exercise varies from breed to breed, and even from dog to dog, finding a method to exercise a Siberian is a must.

Siberian Huskies are sled dogs, and as such are called upon to expend great amounts of energy while working, and to sleep and rest during the lulls. For this reason, Siberians often appear to have an amazing capacity for laziness, and it's one reason that such a "high energy" dog can succeed as a house dog. However, this does not mean that Siberians require little exercise. Exercise is very important to keep a dog fit and alert, and to keep him from getting into mischief. (This is especially true of puppies and youngsters.)

What's important to realize is that some of the more traditional ways to exercise dogs aren't so successful for Siberian Huskies. For example, many breeds (like Labrador Retrievers) will retrieve a thrown tennis ball for hours, thus providing an exercise method that is relatively easy on their humans. Siberians, as a general rule, are not very good at retrieving. They'll look at you as if to say, "Why did you throw it if you want it back?" Some breeds are able to be let loose for a run, but Siberians are definitely *not* one of those breeds. So, exercising a Siberian requires far more participation on behalf of the typical owner. Are you ready for this?

Before you even start looking for a Siberian, make sure you completely understand the breed's need for exercise and have an achievable plan that you are willing to stick with.

Sociability

Another consideration when selecting a dog is the social aspects of the breed. Is the breed good with children? Is it wary of strangers? Does it get along with other pets? Please realize that the answers to these questions can change

---

Multi-Dog Tip

One of the easiest ways to exercise Siberians is to allow them to play together in a fenced yard. Remember that these are pack dogs, with a structured society. Allowing them to interact is one way to reinforce that hierarchy, while giving them a good workout. Their games will include "chase," "attack," and sometimes "keep away." All of the games involve running, a Siberian's favorite thing to do, and are great exercise.

based on the age of the dog, and can vary among individuals. However, we can generalize about a breed's tendencies and temperament—especially with dogs purchased from ethical breeders.

With Children

No matter how "kid friendly" a breed may be advertised, you should always be cautious of animals around children. Puppies who have not yet learned manners can nip at children. Children can pull ears and tails, aggravating dogs and occasionally eliciting a poor response. Dogs can chase children as they run, believing it's all a game. Dogs may not differentiate between their toys and a child's toys, often resulting in a tug-of-war. You can easily see the danger when children wear the same type of fleece as the dog's toy. In short, allowing a dog or puppy to play unsupervised with a child is a recipe for trouble.

As a general rule, however, Siberian Huskies are very good with children. Remember that these are team animals and are bred to get along with others. The Chukchis kept their children and dogs with them, and the dogs were reported to be quite good with the youngsters. In fact, although Siberians are not known for being particularly possessive or protective, it is not unusual for one to be somewhat protective of the children in his family. If you have children, a slow and cautious introduction of the Siberian to the kids, with adult supervision, usually results in a strong bond forming between dog and children.

With Strangers

Siberian Huskies do not, as a general rule, possess guard dog tendencies. They are naturally inquisitive, and the gregarious nature that comes from being a team dog

Exercising a Siberian requires more participation on an owner's behalf than some other breeds.

does not make them suspicious of strangers. Their reactions to strangers usually range from curious to friendly to a bit aloof. In fact, aloofness is not unusual for the breed. However, aloofness should never be carried to the point of shyness or aggression. To help reinforce their natural tendencies, every Siberian owner should make sure to expose her dog to new experiences and people, so the dog feels comfortable in new situations. The more secure a dog is, the better pet he makes.

Siberians are gregarious dogs, and they thrive on the company of other dogs.

With Other Animals

As team dogs, Siberian Huskies do get along with other animals. However, there are some limitations to this statement. Siberians, as with most breeds of dogs, have a prey drive. This means they will chase small animals. Whether they see it as a game of chase or a potential meal, Siberians will go after small animals. And when "catching" the smaller animal with a pounce or grab, the dog could cause damage.

If you have a cat or small dog in your household, only consider bringing a Siberian puppy or an adult who is already "cat proofed" into your home. Puppies growing up with cats generally learn a healthy respect for them, and refrain from bothering the family cat (the neighbors' cats, however, are another story). Be very cautious when bringing a grown Siberian who was not raised with cats into a home with cats.

However, if correctly socialized with small animals, a Siberian puppy can grow up to enjoy the companionship of all animals and family members. They are gregarious dogs, and they thrive on the company of their pack. A bored and lonely Siberian is trouble waiting to happen. Although Siberians are very drawn to other Siberians or other Arctic breeds, they are generous enough to expand their families to include other breeds of dogs, too.

Grooming

If you cannot tolerate dog fur on anything and everything, you might want to reconsider your decision to bring a Siberian Husky into your home. In the canine world, there are two types of coats on dogs: hair and fur. Hair is similar to the hair on people's heads—it grows and has to be cut, but also occasionally falls out. (Examples of breeds with hair include Poodles, Bichons Frise, and similar breeds.) Fur, in contrast, grows only to a certain length, does not need to be cut, and periodically falls out (sheds). Siberian Huskies have fur, and a lot of it!

Shedding

As a general rule, Siberian Huskies shed their coat once or twice a year, and contrary to popular belief, this shedding does not always occur in the summer. Although temperature can affect shedding, so can hormones, food, and a number of other factors. (Including, as people who show dogs will tell you, the onset of a major show—or any other occasion when you want your dog to look his best!)

When a Siberian begins to shed, or "blow his coat," you'll be amazed at how much fur is on that medium-sized body! During the shedding process, a single Siberian Husky can fill several large trash bags with fur. And unfortunately, the shedding usually does not happen all at once. Rather, it can be a fairly lengthy process spanning several weeks or more. During this time, you will feel as if there is Siberian fur everywhere—in your yard and house, on your clothes, in the food you eat, and in the air you breathe.

Since the bulk of the Siberian's coat consists of undercoat, most Siberians shed mostly white or light-colored, relatively soft fur. This fur collects in corners of rooms and under furniture like giant "dust bunnies." The good news is that Siberian fur easily forms these fur "tumbleweeds," making it somewhat easier to collect than, for example, the single straight strands of a Labrador Retriever's fur. The bad news is that this fur is light and easily becomes airborne, and it seems to be drawn to carpets, furniture—and particularly dark-colored clothes. To combat this foe, you will need every available tool in your arsenal—vacuums, rakes, lint rollers, brushes, tape, just about anything you can think of—and you may still find it a losing proposition. When your clothing returns from the dry cleaner and still has fur on it, that's when you learn graceful surrender.

You can mitigate the process. Frequent grooming and bathing while a Siberian is shedding helps capture the fur as it is released, rather than waiting for your affectionate dog to rub against you and leave half of his coat on your dark suit. But this can be a lengthy and time-consuming process. Most Siberian owners do what they can to remove and capture as much fur as possible. The rest of the time, they

You'll have to accept shedding as a part of life if you become a Siberian owner.

just consider Siberian fur additional fiber in their diet.

Routine Care

The good news about Siberian grooming is that, other than during heavy shedding times, these dogs do not require excessive grooming. No trimming is necessary; in fact, trimming is actually detrimental. The Siberian's double coat is uniquely designed to be water-resistant and to insulate from both cold and hot temperatures—and it repels dirt. Altering that coat by trimming or shaving can put a Siberian in danger of heat distress, getting cold, or even having ice balls form in the coat.

Occasional baths, somewhat frequent brushing (once or twice a week when the Siberian is not shedding), and nail trimming are all that is needed to keep your Siberian looking good. And if you work with your Siberian from puppyhood, the grooming process becomes just part of life: Your dog will look forward to having your undivided attention during his grooming sessions. Once you have established a grooming routine, day-to-day coat maintenance is not an onerous task.

Health

Bringing a dog into your household is a long-term commitment. Depending on the average lifespan of the breed of your dreams, you are committing to anywhere from 7 to 17 years. And it is important to know what health issues you might expect from the breed during those years. Although health problems vary from dog to dog, some breeds are prone to certain genetic, congenital, and environmental health issues. Being prepared for any potential breed-specific problem, and knowing ways to prevent the occurrence of these problems, will make your pet's life as long and healthy as possible.

The average lifespan of the Siberian Husky is between 12 and 13 years, and Siberians are a relatively healthy breed. Their medium size keeps at bay many of the joint and structural problems seen in larger breeds. Their longer muzzles eliminate the breathing and overheating problems seen in the brachycephalic, flat-faced dogs, like Bulldogs. Although they can have blue eyes, their good pigmentation reduces the chance for the skin issues and deafness that are often seen in dogs without dark pigment. Their erect ears nearly eliminate ear infections. And they do not seem to present the symptoms of canine follicular dysplasia, an issue seen in other Northern breeds like Alaskan Malamutes and Pomeranians. However, Siberian Huskies do have some breed-related genetic health issues, as well as the potential for those health problems common to all canids.

Eye Problems

Siberian Huskies have a familial tendency toward some eye problems: progressive retinal atrophy, bilateral cataracts, and corneal crystalline opacities. As a general rule, these Siberian-specific eye problems do not cause blindness. More rarely, but also seen, are goniodysgenesis, glaucoma, and pannus.

Since the 1970s, ethical Siberian Husky breeders have been checking their breeding stock and only breeding from animals clear of these problems, so the incidence of eye problems has been dropping.

Want to Know More?

For more information about the health of Siberian Huskies, see Chapter 8: Siberian Husky Health and Wellness.

Hip Dysplasia

Siberian breeders have been routinely screening for hip dysplasia since the early 1970s, with great success. Since then, hip x-rays from over 16,000 Siberian Huskies have been sent for evaluation to the Orthopedic Foundation for Animals (OFA). According to the OFA, only 2% of those x-rays submitted were found to be dysplastic. These results rank the Siberian Husky 154th out of 157 breeds for prevalence of hip dysplasia. This may be the result of a natural tendency away from hip dysplasia for this athletic breed, or because a dedicated group of breeders have worked to eliminate this debilitating problem.

Other Issues

A number of other health issues have been found in Siberian Huskies, but these are not necessarily breed-specific. Some incidences of low thyroid function, seizure disorder, and skeletal, joint, and connective tissue issues have been reported. There have been some problems that produce coat and skin symptoms, including zinc-responsive dermatosis and hair follicle dystrophy. Siberians are known to have some allergies to grains and legumes. And, as is the case with many breeds these days, there seems to be an increase in the number of cancers afflicting the Siberian population.

Training

Training is one of the biggest challenges facing the owner of any dog, especially a first-time owner. All behaviors that are not instinctive must be taught, and Siberian Huskies may often add their own level of complexity to the training equation. These dogs are very intelligent, independent thinkers, and may not see you as the most important member of their pack. For these reasons, some find Siberians difficult to train. But I don't believe that this is the case.

Siberian Huskies have a familial tendency toward some eye problems.

As a general rule, Siberians learn behaviors fairly quickly. However, once learned, the Siberian owner may have a difficult time getting the desired response when asking her Siberian to perform on command. Depending on how important the behavior is to the Siberian, he may feel no reason to demonstrate what he has learned all the time, or at any time.

Siberian Huskies are the very best at what they were bred to do—run in front of a sled for a long time, over rough terrain. Never lose sight of the generations of reinforcement and selection on those traits important to the

Siberians are intelligent and independent, which makes training an extra challenge.

success of being a sled dog. Any lessons you wish to teach them that are related to that job should be fairly easy, and they will excel at these tasks. They should easily learn how to jog or run beside you as you bicycle, and they are naturals at pulling a sled or digging a hole for a "den."

If, however, any of the behaviors you want to train are in conflict with or vastly different from those related to their job, it may be a bit more challenging. If you wish to do something that is very different from "sled dog behaviors," such as retrieving a tennis ball, you will find that this takes much more

time for your Siberian to learn. And, in some cases, your Siberian may never be interested at all in "playing catch" with you. Siberians are much more inclined to demonstrate those behaviors that coincide with their heritage.

Training Success

Three factors will aid in training success with a Siberian.

- Be consistent. A consistent approach, using the same words, the same tone of voice, the same kind and fun approach, the same praise, etc., will lead to success. Consistent repetition will make sure that the message is delivered.

- Ask your Siberian to do things that coincide with his strengths; try not to ask him to do things that he will not really understand. Be patient if you are not successful in training him to do something that might be contrary to his nature. Thousands of years of selection for specific behaviors are difficult to change in a single generation.

- "WIIFM?" You can achieve success by finding the correct motivation for your Siberian, in other words: "What's In It For Me?" Praise helps reinforce good behavior, but with a Siberian nothing speaks louder than a treat. Siberians are very often highly motivated by food. So, use this to your benefit.

By using all three of these training tips, your Siberian will begin to see you as his "lead dog," which is necessary for his successful integration into your family. With the right approach, you will find that Siberians are as trainable as any breed; they just may require a bit more creativity from their owners. Intelligence and independence, those qualities

◎ *Training Tidbit*

When training Siberian Huskies, always keep in mind the breed's original purpose. You will find it far easier to train a Siberian to perform tasks similar to his original purpose (like jogging with you for long distances), than tasks contrary to his original job (such as retrieving a ball).

Siberian lovers cherish, also add complexity to life with these beautiful dogs. Siberian fanciers see it as a trade-off—one in which everyone wins. So, if you are looking for beauty and brains in one fascinating package, and are prepared for the challenges these traits bring, welcome to the world of the Siberian Husky. And once you become a true "Siberian Husky Person," all other breeds pale in comparison.

CHAPTER 2

FINDING AND PREPPING FOR YOUR SIBERIAN HUSKY PUPPY

Once you have decided that the Siberian Husky is the perfect dog for you, the next decision you'll need to make is whether to bring a puppy or an adult into your home. If you decide on a puppy, you'll need to research how to find your perfect Siberian. Then the fun truly begins as you prepare to bring a new puppy into your lives.

WHY GET A PUPPY?

The decision of whether to get a puppy or adult Siberian is tied to many factors. The first thing to consider is your existing family (both human and animal). If you have other dogs and/or cats in the household, it will be easier to introduce a puppy into the family. Puppies do not come with biases against other animals, and the prey drive of a puppy is not as highly developed as that of an adult—especially if the new puppy is initially smaller than the potential "prey." And, although all new dogs must be supervised with children, the smaller size of puppies can often make it easier for children to accept. A puppy, although equipped with sharp little teeth and nails, doesn't yet have the strength of an adult dog, and will be less able to jostle children in exuberance.

Although puppies require more time for training and socialization, they give you the opportunity of doing both. You can train your puppy right from the start, and will he not come with any pre-existing bad habits or problems caused by someone else's poor training. All dogs go through a series of developmental stages, mostly during their puppyhood, when they must be exposed to certain external situations and individuals, and when they form their personalities. By bringing a puppy into your home, you have the most influence possible on these developmental stages, and the best opportunity to help your dog to become the type of family member you want.

By getting your Siberian as a puppy, you will have the added benefit of your dog's company for his entire lifetime. Dogs live much shorter lives than people, but they still become important parts of their families' lives. By bringing a puppy into your home, you can maximize the time you share with him. With good genetics, nutrition, and care, you will have your Siberian for a long time, which will give him ample opportunity to become what you want him to be.

WHAT'S THE LIFE PLAN?

After you decide a puppy is right for your family, usually the next question people ask is whether to get a male or female. It turns out this question is tied to a bigger question: What are your life plans for this puppy? Your future plans for your Siberian just may dictate your dog's gender.

Show Versus Pet

For a variety of reasons, ethical breeders of purebred dogs usually divide their litters of puppies into two groups: "show/breeding-potential" puppies and "pet-quality" puppies. The show/breeding puppies are given full registrations with a national club like the American Kennel Club (AKC), which allows them to be shown in any AKC competition venue and allows registration of their offspring. A show/breeding designation means that the breeder thinks the puppy does not display any traits that would be detrimental to the breed. Show/breeding Siberians are of sufficient quality to be shown in the conformation ring. The breeder chose these puppies as the ones to watch while they mature because they have the possibility of being good enough to eventually be used for breeding.

A puppy who's been designated "pet quality" by a breeder is usually sold with AKC limited registration and a requirement for spaying or neutering. The breeder believes that these puppies possess some trait that would render them uncompetitive in the conformation show ring. The breeder does not want that trait to be passed along to any offspring—thus, the requirement for spaying/neutering. Often the "faults" of these pet-quality puppies are subtle aspects of the breed Standard apparent to breeders, but not even visible to most people. A pet-quality puppy is still an AKC-registered, purebred Siberian Husky, and he can compete in all AKC competitions—such as obedience, agility, tracking, and sledding—except the conformation ring.

To Breed or Not to Breed?

Breeding dogs is hard work. Breeders who want to produce the happiest and healthiest puppies possible must have experience with their breed, and must be willing to invest the time and money required to be successful. Breeders must be able to evaluate potential breeding stock and perform all the proper genetic testing. Breeders need to care for the dam while she is carrying the puppies and be able to help (if needed) during the delivery, including recognizing potential problems and seeking immediate veterinary help. After this, the work really begins! Breeders must care both for the dam and her puppies, providing them with a clean, healthy environment, as well as good food and veterinary care. Breeders must know about proper socialization of puppies and provide them with correct interactions at the correct times during their development. Breeders must find and screen potential puppy owners in order to place their puppies in the best possible homes. And, if those good homes cannot be found, breeders must be prepared to keep the entire litter. Most ethical dog breeders lose money on every litter they produce.

So, as you can see, your future plans with your Siberian will help determine not only show or pet quality, but also your choice of gender. If your plans are to show your Siberian in the conformation ring, look for a show/breeding-quality puppy. And if your plans are eventually to breed your Siberian, you will want a female. If you want to participate in other companion events (aside from showing), but are not interested in breeding, then you might prefer a male, as females cannot participate in these events when in season (although spaying can eliminate this problem).

If you are adding a beloved family pet to your home who will be neutered or spayed, the gender choice may not be so important. However, if there are other pets at home, it is a general rule that a male will get along well with a female. And if they are both altered, there will be no chance for unexpected arrivals! If your new puppy will be an only dog, then you could choose gender based on size, as females are generally smaller than males. Or, if size does not matter to you, go ahead and select your puppy based on personality.

WHERE TO FIND YOUR PUPPY

You have already made several important decisions: you want to add a dog to your family; you've chosen the Siberian Husky as the right breed for you; you've decided on a puppy rather than an adult; and you know if you're interested in a pet-quality or show/breeding puppy and if the gender is important to you. Now you are faced with one more extremely important decision: Where to find the puppy. With the inception of Internet, it is very easy to find an adorable Siberian Husky puppy these days. However, it is not as easy to find a good, reputable breeder.

The first thing you need to know is that not

Breed Standards

Each AKC-recognized breed has a parent club. In the case of the Siberian Husky it's the Siberian Husky Club of America, Inc. (SHCA). This is a group of experienced and dedicated Siberian fanciers who are responsible for their breed. One of the most important tasks for members of a parent club is writing a description of the "ideal" representation of their breed. This description is called the *Standard*. It is this written Standard for Siberian Huskies that Siberian breeders and judges use in evaluating dogs. Although no dog is perfect, breeders use the Standard to help determine the extent of a dog's faults, and whether or not that dog should be shown and used for breeding. To most people, these faults may be barely noticeable, and they will not affect the dog's ability to be great member of your family.

all "breeders" are alike. All it takes to produce a litter of puppies is to have a breedable female and find a stud dog—and you can call yourself a "breeder." Actually, becoming a *knowledgeable and ethical breeder* takes a lot of work and a lifetime commitment. This is the kind of breeder you are trying to find, and there are a number of ways to help you determine whether a potential breeder is knowledgeable and committed to the breed.

Ethical Breeders: What to Look For

The following list includes signs of an ethical hobby breeder:

The breeder is very involved in the breed and

An ethical breeder will introduce you to the litter's dam and other family members.

the sport of dogs, and is a member of both a local breed club and the national breed club. Good breeders frequently test their breeding stock through participation in dog shows, companion event trials, or races—or all of these.

- The breeder takes her love of the breed seriously, and can readily discuss in great detail the breed's history, purpose, and legends.
- The breeder is well known and respected with others involved in the breed and in the dog world. She has knowledgeable mentors and adequate experience and success with producing good dogs.
- The breeder approaches the breeding of dogs seriously and scientifically, carefully evaluating the sire and dam to assure that the offspring will be healthy examples of the

breed. She is able to explain the strengths and weaknesses of the sire and dam, why they complement each other, and what are the expectations for the puppies. She talks with you about different breeding approaches, such as inbreeding, line breeding, and out-crossing, when it's best to use a certain method, and what approach she used for this litter and why.

- The breeder does everything in her power to make sure your puppy is genetically sound, healthy, and of good temperament. She knows the hereditary diseases breed is prone to, and what tests are required to be assured that your puppy will have the best chance of being free of those genetic problems. She produces health certifications.
- The breeder is able to introduce you to the

litter's dam and other family members. (Do not be surprised if the sire of the puppy is not on the property—this is not a bad sign. In an attempt to produce a better dog or to expand the gene pool, a reputable breeder often breeds to stud dogs she does not own.) The grown canine family members should be friendly and interested in you, as should the puppies.

- All the dogs you meet at the breeder's are clean, groomed, and kept in a clean environment (either in kennels or other types of housing).
- The breeder asks you questions about your plans for the puppy, such as who will care for him, where he will be housed, and a number of other things about you and your lifestyle. This is to make sure that the puppy is wanted by your entire family, and that he will be well cared for.
- There is a waiting list for the breeder's puppies. Because of the care a good breeder takes with every litter, do not be surprised if you have to wait some time for your puppy.
- The breeder's puppies are on the higher end of the cost range in your area. A good hobby breeder spends money on producing and caring for a litter, and such puppies will cost a bit more.
- The breeder is not producing puppies to make money, and she is most likely not making a profit on the litters.
- The breeder registers her puppies only with the national registry in her country.
- The breeder discusses the difference between "show/breeding potential" puppies and "pet-quality" puppies, and to which group your puppy falls and why.
- The breeder clearly explains the terms of sale for the puppy, including the type of registration with the national club, any guarantees, and return policies.

- The breeder stands behind her puppies, and offers to replace or refund payment in case of problems.
- The breeder discusses puppy socialization, and at what age the puppy may go to his new home. Anything before 7 weeks is too early.
- The breeder informs you of permanent identification for the puppy, such as microchipping.
- The breeder provides a list of the vaccinations your puppy has received, and the recommendation for completing the vaccination schedule.
- The breeder explains what type of food is best for a Siberian.

Registries

A large number of groups "register" puppies and dogs. But in the United States, the only nonprofit registry that has "care and conditions" policies for its breeders, that conducts thousands of kennel inspections each year, that is concerned with the integrity of its pedigrees, that has donated millions of dollars to canine health and genetics research, and that supports dogs through many different charities, is the American Kennel Club (AKC). Reputable breeders register their dogs with the AKC. Although it's not an absolute guarantee of quality, it's a good indication. Most countries around the world have a national registry similar to AKC, and these registries have reciprocal registration processes.

Do not be surprised if there is a waiting list for your puppy—a good breeder's litters will be in high demand.

directory at www.shca.org. You can also get a referral from the local area clubs that serve the breed across the country. The SHCA's (and area club's) websites are full of information about the breed, ethical behavior for breeders, and other items of interest, such as upcoming events.

With the names of a few reputable breeders in hand, do some online research, starting with their websites—most good breeders have them. If you prefer a more traditional approach, go to the library or a book store and find books on Siberians, which also can help you research kennels and breeders.

Another place to meet breeders is at a local dog show. You can find information about dog shows across the country from the AKC's website (www.akc.org) and through the local show superintendents (a list of which is available from the AKC). Each superintendent has a website that lists upcoming shows. Find shows near you that include Siberians and attend them. If you a purchase a show catalog, it will include information about all the entries at the show, including names and addresses of all owners. Watch the dogs and note which ones you like the best. Then wait until *after* judging to approach the exhibitors. Prior to being judged, exhibitors are usually busy preparing their dogs and may be feeling nervous. By waiting until after judging, you will not interfere with their preparation, and you'll have more time to visit with a relaxed exhibitor.

• The breeder offers to provide you with advice and support throughout the life of your puppy.

How to Find an Ethical Breeder

So, where do you find such a paragon of breeding virtue? Not by doing a random Internet search for "Siberian Husky puppies" or by looking on Craig's List or in the local newspaper. The best place to begin your search is the parent club for your breed—in this case, the Siberian Husky Club of America, Inc. (SHCA). Check out the club's online referral

Contacting a Breeder

Now that you've narrowed the field, start contacting breeders. Interview them to see if they meet your requirements as breeders, using the bulleted list above to formulate appropriate questions. Keep in mind that a good breeder will also be interviewing *you* as a potential

Want to Know More?

If you decide a Siberian puppy might be a bit too much work, and you would prefer an adult, check out Chapter 5: Finding Your Siberian Husky Adult.

owner. You should also understand that ethical and dedicated hobby breeders usually have a wait list for their puppies, and/or the right breeder for you may not reside in your local area.

When have done your research and met breeders, keep this in mind: You *will* fall in love with any puppy you bring into your home. All Siberian puppies are beautiful and darling and a bit naughty—everything a puppy ought to be. Don't lose sight of the most important thing about getting a puppy: *finding the right breeder*. Don't fall in love with any puppy—fall in love with a puppy with the best chance of being genetically sound, healthy, and happy. This comes from finding a well-respected, knowledgeable breeder who will be around to offer advice and friendship.

Choosing the Right Puppy

Once you've found the right breeder, it's time to start thinking about your perfect pup. Many coat color, eye color, and marking combinations are possible with Siberian Huskies, but don't think you can place an "order" for your ideal combination. No breeder can guarantee that the next litter will have your ideal "look" for a Siberian. You'll need to be flexible, and realize that the most important thing is getting a genetically sound, healthy, well-socialized puppy with a good temperament.

Once the long-awaited litter has arrived, how

do you choose your own special puppy from those available? As we mentioned, coat color, eye color, and markings (although certainly a matter of preference) are probably not the best criteria for selecting your puppy. Far more important is finding a puppy who will fit in with your family and lifestyle.

The best way to choose a puppy is to rely on your breeder. You spent a great deal of time researching and interviewing potential breeders and finding the bloodlines you want. During this time, as you became better acquainted with your breeder, you shared your plans for the puppy's future. You know if you want your Siberian to be a show dog, a sled dog, a pet in an athletic family, or a companion in an apartment. You've told the breeder about the environment of your home, your family, and lifestyle. You've expressed your desire for a certain activity level and behavior. With these discussions, your breeder formed an opinion of your expectations and what type of puppy

By the Numbers

- 7 to 12 weeks: Most breeders let their puppies go to their new homes between 7 and 12 weeks of age.
- 2 days: Try to give yourself at least two days without other commitments when bringing a puppy home. That way, you can establish a schedule, and the puppy will have a chance to feel comfortable before you resume your life and other commitments.

would best meet them and be happiest in your home.

Although you will undoubtedly visit the litter on more than one occasion, it's the breeder who sees the puppies grow and develop every day. A knowledgeable breeder will be evaluating the litter in a number of aspects, including each puppy's potential as a show/breeding Siberian. She'll also be looking to see each puppy's personality traits—is the puppy fearless? Active? Snuggly? Dominant or submissive? Does the puppy like people? Children?

The point of this constant evaluation is to

The breeder will direct you to the best puppy for your home.

make sure the puppy is receiving the required socialization, and also so that the breeder can direct you to the best puppy for your home. A breeder's first concern is getting the right puppy in the right home. So, listen to what your breeder advises regarding the right puppy for you.

Once selected, continue to visit your puppy, so he begins to bond with you and your family. Then it's time to prepare for his arrival at his new home!

BEFORE YOUR SIBERIAN PUPPY COMES HOME

Although it might be difficult to wait, there is a lot to do before your puppy comes home, and the time will pass swiftly.

Puppy-Proofing

Most people, parents and non-parents alike, understand the concept of "child-proofing" a home. Take that idea and turn it toward the canine world, and it's called "puppy-proofing." Puppy-proofing means removing anything that the puppy might be able to reach that could harm him or that you do not want damaged. Realize, of course, that the puppy will initially have no manners at all, be fairly small (so he'll be able to fit through small spaces), be highly mobile, and be able to climb. With this in mind, begin looking at your yard.

Outdoors

Most likely, you will want your puppy to have access to at least some portion of your yard, since one of the first things you will begin teaching him is not to eliminate in the house. So, you will want to give him access to a place he can use as his potty area. Depending on a variety of factors (e.g., the size of your yard, the state of your landscaping, the strength of your fence, etc.), you may initially wish to restrict

Secure fencing is a priority for anyone interested in bringing home a Siberian.

your puppy to only a portion of the yard. You can do this by erecting a temporary fence or partition to block the puppy from the rest of the yard. Although the perimeter fence of a Siberian's yard should be 6 feet (2 m) tall, a temporary puppy enclosure may be shorter. Don't forget that a puppy can squeeze through a small space, so make sure that the slats or bars in the fencing will not allow the puppy to escape.

Fencing

Even if you plan on using a temporary outdoor puppy enclosure, you should still check the security of your entire fenced yard before your puppy comes home. If the fence is less than 6 feet (2 m) tall, replace it or extend its height. A 4-foot (1-m) fence presents little challenge for

a climbing Siberian, so make sure your fence is tall enough for a full-grown dog. Another option is to create a dog pen or run with secure fencing. If you choose this option, check the dog pen or run for security just as you would your yard fencing.

Check the security of the fence itself. If it is a wooden fence, check the solidity of the fence posts, then test each board to make sure it is secure. Check the boards by pushing and pulling on them, as well as trying to slide them from side-to-side. Secure or replace any boards that are weak or not fixed in place. If the fence is made of iron bars or other types of slats, make sure that the puppy cannot squeeze through the spaces. If you think there is any chance for puppy escape, temporarily secure the fence by placing a wire mesh on one side

Toxic Plants

Common poisonous plants include:

Almond	English holly	Rhubarb
Apricot	Foxglove	Spinach
Buttercup	Hemlock	Tomato vine
Castor bean	Jasmine	Yew
China berry	Larkspur	Wild cherry
Daffodil	Lupine	Wisteria
Delphinium	Mushrooms	

(Please note this list is not exhaustive)

of the bars or slats, which can be removed when the puppy reaches sufficient size to render him unable to fit through the bars. If the fence is chain link, make sure that there are no weak or rusted spots, and that the chain fabric is securely connected to the bars along the base. Over time, the wire ties can break and wear, so make sure they are secure. If you have any other type of fencing, please check it for stability and security.

Secure the base of the fence. Occasionally, landscaping or settling will cause the ground to recede from the bottom of the fence. Make sure that your fence meets the ground everywhere. If it does not, move some earth or add rocks or other fill to remedy this situation. Siberians are often creative in their escape abilities, so many Siberian owners often go to extremes to keep their dogs at home. If you doubt how easy it might be to dig under your fence, you may wish to consider a couple of alternatives.

Some owners will keep a dog from digging by burying wire mesh under the fence. Should their dog attempt to dig under the fence, he will encounter the wire, which he cannot penetrate. Occasionally, people set patio blocks, bricks, or concrete blocks at the base of a fence to dissuade digging. The only caution with this option is that you'll need to avoid creating a step that could help the dog climb the fence. Ask your breeder for other ideas on how to keep your yard secure.

Check the yard for anything that could be used as steps. Siberians can be so crafty you'll need to remain one step ahead of them. Look at any items that back up to your fence. Does anything create a natural "step" that your Siberian could use to climb to the top of the fence, roof, or garage, or to a low spot? If you're not careful, you may walk outside and find your puppy on the roof, because he used the patio chair, table, and outdoor barbecue as "steps." Move or remove everything close to the fence or roof that your dog could use to escape.

Secure your gates—an open gate is often an easy method of escape for a Siberian. Think about who will be using the gate to your yard. If children are going to be entering and exiting your yard, perhaps they could be encouraged to use an alternative door. At the very least, you must remind them to close and lock the gate. If the only access to the meter or the garbage cans is through the gate, consider building a second gate that your Siberian won't have access to. Check the latches. Determine if your gate could be opened by jumping at it. Also, consider adding a lock to each gate—the most secure yard is one where the gates are locked.

Yard Hazards

With the perimeter secure, look for any hazards in the yard itself. Do you have a swimming pool, hot tub, or pond? Any of these could prove dangerous to a puppy, so fence them off from the puppy's yard.

Look for poisonous plants in the yard. The reaction to ingesting toxic plants varies by amount ingested, part of the plant ingested, size of the dog, and the plant itself. Anything dangerous must be removed from the yard. A number of resources are available to help with identifying poisonous plants, including the AKC (www.akc.org), the American Society for the Prevention of Cruelty to Animals (ASPCA; www.aspca.org), or you can ask your veterinarian or an employee at a local nursery. Removing poisonous plants is the easiest and safest way to assure your puppy's safety in the yard.

You may have other toxic substances in your yard. Find and secure fertilizers, pesticides, herbicides, compost piles, or any other yard chemicals. Also, remove rakes, hoes, gardening claws, and other tools that could cause injury. It is also a good idea to secure hoses and sprinklers, and anything else that a puppy might find tempting to chew. Removing temptation is the most foolproof solution to keeping your puppy safe.

Indoors

Many of the same processes for puppy-proofing outside your home work inside as well.

Your first step is to look for any chemicals that might be toxic to puppies/dogs, and make sure they are safely locked up. These include household cleaners, furniture polish, pesticides, and items such as antifreeze, soaps, bleach, etc. found in many garages. Don't forget there are also toxic items in your house, including medications, nail polish and remover, alcohol, makeup, disinfectant, acetaminophen, and deodorant—just to name a few.

Next, take a look at what your puppy might be able to reach from "puppy height"—that is, things 1 to 2 feet (30 to 60 cm) off the floor, as well as things easily reachable by climbing onto a chair or couch. You will probably find electrical cords, glass objects, books, area rugs, pillows, and more. These things will all tempt a puppy, so try to remove them (at least temporarily). Your other option is to find a way to restrict the puppy's access to these dangerous items.

A puppy will get into anything and everything—it's up to you to keep him safe by removing harmful items.

Setting Up a Schedule

Now that your environment has been prepared for the newest family member, it is time to give some thought to your puppy's schedule. Much like small children, puppies need a set schedule: they do best when fed at the same time each day, exercised at the same time, put to bed at the same time, etc. If someone in the house is at home with the puppy each day, providing such a schedule is easy to follow. However, if this is not the case, the puppy's schedule may take a bit more coordination.

Start with the feeding times for your puppy, which your breeder will help you determine.

A properly fitted rolled leather collar, flat webbed buckle collar, or quick-release collar are all appropriate for your Siberian.

This will probably be two to three times each day. Then work from there to come up with a schedule. At least initially, your puppy will have little control of his bodily functions, so he will need to be taken out for potty breaks frequently—after eating, upon waking, and every couple of hours during the day. Going out after sleeping is especially important, and puppies sleep a lot, so there will be frequent naps—which in turn means frequent trips outside. Now add this routine to your family's waking and sleeping schedules, work schedules, school schedules, and figure out how it all goes together. WHEW—puppies are a lot of work!

You may find that initial puppy care is best handled during a vacation time or during good weather, which may help you determine when to bring your new puppy home. But usually, with a bit of flexibility on everyone's part, you will be able to develop a schedule that works both for the puppy and for other family members.

Supplies

As the time nears for your puppy to come home, make a list of the supplies you will need when he arrives.

Collar

A properly fitted rolled leather collar, flat webbed buckle collar, or quick-release collar are all appropriate for your Siberian, and these collars have the advantage of allowing identification tags to be added. During his lifetime, your Siberian will go through a few collars of varying sizes and purposes. As a puppy, a short, soft nylon collar is just perfect to start. These usually have a few holes, so the same collar can be adjusted as he grows.

Should you leave your puppy's collar on when he's inside the home? Collars can be dangerous. They can catch on things that could immobilize or injure a puppy. If they are too loose, they can be slipped off the puppy's head. However, properly fitted collars are a good "handle" to use to catch a puppy, and they are a place to attach identification. The best advice is to be careful if you leave a collar on your puppy when he is alone, and to make absolutely sure he is secure whenever you leave him inside without his collar. (Never put your puppy in a position where he really needs his identification and doesn't have it.) Most Siberian Husky owners are more concerned about losing their dogs than worried about the chance of a collar injury.

Crate

Crates are essential items for most dogs—but especially for Siberians. Siberians are denning dogs, and crates can help mimic a den, which they love. A crate is also a significant part of training your dog. Not only is his crate a safe place when you need your Siberian out of the way, it will be his bed and can help with housetraining. Crates are also the doggy equivalent of seat belts, so you must always crate your dog when he's riding in the car. This is the best way to assure his safety in the event of an accident.

Ask your breeder if she crate trains her puppies, because this can be a huge help when your puppy comes home. Before leaving for their new homes, some breeders have their puppies spend the night together in a crate. Although your puppy will not have his littermates when he comes to his new home, the crate will be familiar to him.

Three basic types of crates are available: those made of molded plastic or fiberglass, those made of wire mesh, and those made of fabric. Each of these crates comes in a variety of sizes for all breeds and sizes of dogs. Because

of their creativity, tenacity, and strength, foldable fabric crates are not recommended for Siberians. A Siberian, even a puppy, can generally chew a hole big enough to escape. The molded plastic or fiberglass crates (most of which are approved for airline travel) are fairly well enclosed and have a solid bottom that will contain spills or accidents. These are also relatively lightweight. Airline-approved crates are a good choice, especially if you ever plan on flying your dog, and they are good for puppies. However, because these types of crates are significantly enclosed, make sure there is adequate air exchange, especially in hot weather. The wire mesh crates are formed from heavy-gauge welded wire. Because they are mesh, they allow for good air flow. However, they do not have a solid base, so spilled liquids are not contained. Most wire crates will collapse for easy storage and transport, but they are also fairly heavy. Ask your breeder the approximate size your puppy is expected to grow and then decide which crate size will be best. The crate should be big enough to allow your Siberian to move, but not so big he'll use it to potty.

Look for International Air Transport Association (IATA)-compliant crates. Most male Siberian Huskies are best in a size 400 or 500 IATA-type airline crate, and females in a size 400. Or, start the puppy in a smaller

You may not want to invest in an expensive dog bed until your puppy grows up.

portable crate, like the ones Nylabone makes, and eventually graduate to the final larger size.

Dog Bed

Your new addition is both a Siberian Husky and a puppy, which means he's going destroy many things during his puppyhood. All puppies like to chew and shred things. So, you might want to hold off on buying that darling (but expensive) dog bed until your puppy grows up (or never, as some Siberians like to shred things till their dying day). However, putting an old towel or sheet in your puppy's crate is not a bad idea; it will make a comfortable bed, and you will not be devastated if it is destroyed. Plus, it will absorb any accidents, and it is easily laundered.

Ex-Pen/Baby Gate

Another method of controlling your puppy's environment is to use baby gates or exercise pens (ex-pens). You can use the same pressure-fit or free-standing gates that keep toddlers from stairs to keep your puppy from venturing into off-limits area of your home. Likewise, ex-pens made of a variety of materials, such as PVC pipe or heavy-gauge wire, can help limit your puppy's world to a manageable size.

Food and Water Bowls

Your puppy will need stable food and water bowls. For water, find a bowl that has a weighted bottom, so the puppy cannot turn it over easily. Stainless steel bowls are good as they clean easily and cannot break.

Grooming Supplies

You will need some initial grooming supplies. Small nail clippers and a brush will be fine for his puppyhood, and you can add more tools as he grows. You might also wish to purchase a good, gentle dog shampoo. Puppies always get into trouble, and you might find the need to bathe your pup after he finds some mud to wallow in.

Identification

Attach a tag with your Siberian's name and your phone number to his collar. You should add his microchip chip tag, too. In the past, the only way to identify your dog if he got lost was through a tag on his collar. Unfortunately, the collar or tags of a free-running dog can come off, which often left lost dogs with no identification. The advent of the canine microchip has solved this problem. A microchip is a very tiny electronic chip with a unique identification number. The chip is inserted under your dog's skin through an injection. Your breeder or veterinarian will usually insert the microchip in the back of your dog's neck when he is a puppy. You or your breeder will register your dog's unique chip identification number with a national registry. The chip does not emit any signal on its own, but when scanned by a chip reader, the unique chip number will display on the reader. Checking the chip number of a lost dog with a national registry provides contact information for the owner, which leads to a happy reunion. A registered microchip is also the way to prove ownership of a dog if there is any question. After your puppy is microchipped, don't forget to enroll the chip number in the AKC's Companion Animal Recovery (AKC-CAR) program, which is the most successful recovery group in the country.

Leash

You'll need a 6-foot (2 m), fairly lightweight leash for your puppy. As he grows, you will want to increase the strength of the leash, but initially a lightweight puppy leash is perfect.

Toys

Finally, add a toy or two for your puppy to play with, and your house will be just about ready. Make sure the toys are small enough for a puppy pick up, but not so small that they will be swallowed. And make sure at least one of the toys is made of hard rubber (like those made by Nylabone), which is safe and good for chewing—since there is a lot of teething in your puppy's future.

THE BIG DAY

It's the day of your puppy's homecoming. The supplies are purchased and you are looking forward to bringing that adorable ball of fur into your house—what fun! It is a good idea to try to pick up your puppy in the morning, on a day when family members do not have to go to work or school. Even better if that's the case for at least a couple of days—so picking up the puppy on a Saturday morning of a free weekend works fine.

Regardless of how much fun you will be,

What About a Harness?

You may think a harness would be a great fit for a dog with sled-pulling in his genes. But just because your dog is a Siberian Husky does not mean he needs a harness for daily walks. It's important for your Siberian to learn how to walk on leash, and in my opinion harnesses do not give you enough control to teach proper leash walking.

at some point your puppy will miss his littermates and breeder's house. By picking him up in the morning, he will have the maximum amount of time with you before he has to go to bed without the other puppies. And by giving him at least two days with you before you must return to your regular schedule, the puppy will have time to relax a bit, and you will have time to nap (just in case you lose some sleep during the night).

When you first bring your Siberian puppy home, the normal inclination is to show him off to everyone. After all, he is darling, and you are very proud of the newest family member. But try to avoid this if possible. Your puppy will have just left his siblings and the only world he has ever known. He'll thrive best on a set schedule, and the sooner you establish

his new schedule, the better. Introduce him to the house, his crate, the yard, and to his family. (However, you may want to wait to introduce him to any other animals or human babies, especially if he might be a bit overwhelmed.) Feed him on his new schedule. Start bringing him to his new bathroom area. Let him play with his toys. Keep the day as calm and normal as possible.

THE FIRST NIGHT

If your plan is to have your puppy sleep in his crate, make it a fun place for him. Try feeding him in his crate; give him puppy-safe Nylabone toys in his crate; give him treats in his crate. For short periods of time, close the crate door while he is in it, opening it only when he is quiet. Prior to bedtime, play with your puppy

Your puppy will be exhausted from all of the changes during his first few days.

and take him to his bathroom area—stay out there for a little while, trying to get him to eliminate. At bedtime, give him a puppy biscuit and a toy, and put him in his crate where you want him to sleep. If you have other animals, put his crate near the crates of the other dogs. That way, he may not be as lonely.

This first night might be difficult. Siberian Huskies are prone to drama, and he may carry on. If possible, try not to succumb. If you end up giving in to his cries, try placing the crate next to your bed. That way, you can talk to him when he fusses, and also pick up on when he needs a potty break. The first few nights may be difficult, but with time, he will adapt to his new life and become everyone's favorite family member.

THE FIRST FEW WEEKS

Within the first few days, you should take your puppy to his veterinarian for a checkup, microchipping (if it has not already been done), and to discuss his vaccination schedule. This would be a good time to individually register him with the AKC, and register his microchip with the AKC-CAR.

Your Siberian puppy will be getting used to his schedule, and your work as a trainer will begin. As he becomes more comfortable, he'll become more adventuresome. Siberians are very curious, and he will soon begin testing his

Multi-Dog Tip

When introducing a new puppy into a house with other dogs, do so slowly, especially if the existing dog is larger. Although the puppy will love the company, he might be initially intimidated by a strange, larger dog.

new environment. Do not leave your puppy unsupervised and uncontrolled in your house. A bored Siberian can be a destructive one, so make sure that nothing is left out that he can destroy or that can hurt him.

In fact, after the first few days with your puppy, you will need to re-puppy-proof your house and yard. Your previous attempt was fine—as far as it went. But now you know what your puppy is capable of doing, so it's a good time to rethink your puppy-proofing. Remove more temptations from his view. Resecure fences, gates, and latches. Expand or limit his area within the house and in the yard. In short, rededicate yourself to outsmarting your puppy.

And welcome to the joy of having a Siberian Husky in your life!

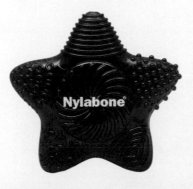

CHAPTER 3

CARE OF YOUR SIBERIAN HUSKY PUPPY

Congratulations on your new Siberian puppy! Your life is about to change, and with a little bit of help and support—along with a sense of humor—this change will be for the better. If you've never had a puppy before, you may find this time a bit trying, since everything will be so new. If this is not your first puppy, remember that you've survived puppyhood before! Experienced or not, you will get through the puppy months and end up with a wonderful new member of the family. Until then, keep a sense of humor about your new puppy's antics and enjoy them, because this time goes by very quickly.

FEEDING YOUR SIBERIAN PUPPY

Bringing a puppy home is a big change, so to make this time as manageable as possible, try to minimize the change he experiences. Start by feeding your puppy what he ate at his breeder's kennel and on the same schedule. Your breeder will either give you a small amount of food to take home, or inform you of the brand you should have on hand. She will also explain the quantity of food and the schedule for feeding your puppy. (Because puppies often eat in a communal bowl at their breeder's house, the quantity may be an estimate.)

Entering a new home is a big change for your Siberian puppy, and it may initially cause intestinal distress. A change in schedule or quantity of food, different water, or excitement and stress can all add to stomach upset. It will usually resolve itself in a day or two. If it does not, consult your veterinarian. Because puppies are fairly small, diarrhea puts them at risk for dehydration.

If a change in water and environment is capable of causing diarrhea, imagine what a change in food might do. It's important to avoid changing the quantity, composition, and frequency of your puppy's meals—at least at first.

Types of Commercial Puppy Food

There are probably as many theories about what to feed a dog as there are dog breeders. To help make your decision, you should understand the types of food available for puppies.

Kibble/Dry

The most common dog food is the dry type, generically referred to as kibble. Kibble is most common type of commercial food for a number of reasons: it is easily stored and transported, it has a long shelf-life, it is relatively inexpensive, and it still offers good nutrition. A large number of dry dog food options are available, including generic kibble, natural and organic brands, and exotic kinds made of duck or even ostrich.

Most breeders feed a dry food alone or in combination with other types of food, such as canned or raw meat, or supplements.

Semi-Moist and Canned

Other commercial dog food options are also available, including semi-moist packets and canned food. Few breeders recommend semi-moist foods, as they often contain less nutrition and high amounts of sugar, sodium, and dyes. However, they are convenient and do not have much odor. Canned food usually provides a palatable (and often odiferous) mixture of meat, vegetables, and grains. But canned food is largely comprised of water, which makes it heavy, expensive, and awkward to transport and store. However, a high-quality canned food can be used to tempt reluctant eaters into cleaning their plates.

Reading the Label

The US Food and Drug Administration (FDA) and the Association of American Feed Control Officials (AAFCO) requires standard labeling on dog food, which includes a list of ingredients, a "guaranteed analysis," feeding directions, and a calorie statement. You may find the first two items—ingredients and analysis—to be of most interest.

Ingredients show the main protein and carbohydrate sources in the food. As with human food, the package ingredients appear in descending order of composition. The item listed first is the largest component of the food, the second listed is the second largest ingredient, and so on. In a good-quality food, the first ingredient on the list should be a good protein source—meat, fish, or poultry. If you are interested in minimizing your dog's consumption of preservatives, artificial colors, and other non-organic ingredients, you can determine this from the list of ingredients. And, although not a common occurrence, Siberians occasionally develop food allergies. Should this happen to your dog, it is important to know what exactly he's been eating.

The guaranteed analysis section shows the percentage of protein and fat, among other

For the most part, Siberians cannot tolerate the volume of food that is recommended on the manufacturer's label.

things, in your dog's food. You will find that most commercially available puppy foods are "hotter" foods; that is to say, they are higher in protein and fat than many adult maintenance foods. Puppies grow fast and need a lot of nutrition, so a larger amount of fat and protein is necessary. Puppy foods usually range between 27% and 32% protein and 18% to 22% fat. It is also not unusual for puppy foods to be made of easy-to-digest proteins and grains, such as chicken and rice.

The calorie statement may be of some interest as well, although there are other, more direct ways to be assured that your dog is getting the correct amount of food for his level of activity.

Where to Buy

Most premium commercial dog food is available at specialty pet food or livestock feed stores, or occasionally from your veterinarian. The dog foods sold at grocery stores or warehouse stores generally do not contain the same nutrition or quality food sources as premium pet food products. Do your research, so you're knowledgeable about what your dog is eating. The manufacturer and where you purchase the dog food are not as important as what is inside the bag. Make sure to check your ingredients and the analysis—they are important to a growing Siberian puppy.

How Much?

Although you should look closely at the label on your puppy's food, one section you should ignore is the one recommending quantities to feed. In reviewing the feeding directions on a number of commercially available puppy foods, the recommendations for an 8-week-old Siberian Husky-size puppy ranged from 1/2 cup (4 oz) to more than 5 cups (40 oz) of food each day, and from 300 to 600 kilocalories per cup!

Non-Commercial Options

There is quite a growing interest in feeding dogs home-cooked meals or even completely raw diets. With both of these options, pet owners feel they are better in control of the food and chemicals their dogs ingest. The raw food proponents wish to avoid the vitamin and mineral loss caused when food is heated during processing. However, opponents to raw food are concerned about the bacteria introduced with a totally raw diet. Regardless of your school of thought, dogs need a balanced diet, so care must be paid in providing the necessary nutrition.

For the most part, Siberians cannot tolerate the volume of food that is recommended on the manufacturer's label. To understand this, you should look to the Siberian's past—where and how the Chukchis' dogs lived. There were few plants and no farming. Food was scarce and mostly comprised of fat and protein in the form of fish and game. From this genetic legacy, Siberian Huskies often cannot tolerate the large amounts of carbohydrates found in commercial dog foods. For a Siberian to get the amount of protein and fat he needs, he may have to consume too much commercial dog food. That large a volume of food contains far too many carbohydrates for him. If your Siberian needs more nourishment, increasing his kibble is probably not the best way to get him the food he needs.

In determining the quantity to feed your puppy, initially listen to your Siberian's breeder. From then on, watch for the two signs that indicate you need to change the quantity of food you are feeding: your puppy's stools and his body weight. If his stools are firm and well formed, he is able to tolerate the amount of food (including carbohydrates) that he is eating. If he is at a good weight, he is getting the nutrition he needs.

Proper Weight

It is important to keep puppies well-nourished but not heavy. Overfeeding puppies can lead to joint issues and other physical problems. Take the time every couple of days to assess your puppy's weight. Check his ribs, spine, and hip bones. If these bones are too pronounced, increase his feed. If these areas are well padded, slightly decrease the amount he is being fed.

If you wish to increase your puppy's feed, do so very slowly over several days, all the while watching the firmness of his stools. The minute his stools get loose, cut back a bit on the amount of food you fed at his last meal, and remain at that quantity until his stools get firm once again. Only then should you continue to increase his food, again watching for the firmness of his stools.

If your puppy is too thin and has diarrhea, it's probably because he cannot tolerate more kibble. If you have been slowly adding kibble, and each time you do, his stools get too loose, check with your vet to be sure that he is free of parasites. Then, make sure you are aware of exactly what you puppy is eating. Is he being fed scraps or too many cookies or treats? If all he is ingesting is his daily meals, your puppy may need more protein and fat in his diet, but not more carbohydrates. In attempting to get him the necessary protein and fat in his diet,

If your puppy is thriving on his existing food, you may want to stick with it.

the increase in kibble caused him to ingest an excessive volume of carbohydrates, which can cause digestive problems.

Instead of just increasing the amount of kibble, increase protein and fat in other ways. First, try to find a "hotter" food—one with higher protein and fat numbers than you are currently feeding your puppy. If you do this, please pay careful attention to how you switch foods (see the section "Changing It Up" below). You could also increase the protein and fat levels in his diet by adding meat or a canine protein supplement to your puppy's diet, along with some additional essential fatty acids. This, too, should be done slowly, and only after consulting with your breeder or veterinarian. Usually, with most Siberians, there is less intestinal upset when only slightly increasing protein and fat.

How Often?

You've been cautioned about making changes to your puppy's feeding routine. However, one feeding change you may wish to consider is to stop free-feeding. If your breeder kept a bowl of food available for the puppies at all times so they could free- or self-feed, you may wish to change to a set schedule. Siberians are usually quite motivated by food, so free-feeding can lead to overfeeding. Also, if your home has other pets, it is difficult to know who is actually eating the food. An established feeding schedule will also lead to a more established elimination schedule, thus making the process of housetraining easier.

So, once he has settled into his new home, consider feeding your puppy three times a day at scheduled times: breakfast, lunch, and dinner, for example. If he has been eating four times a day, once he is settled in, you may wish to reduce his feedings to three times a day. To do this, increase each meal

Multi-Dog Tip

Free- or self-feeding is not the best way to feed a puppy in a multi-pet home, as you will not know how much of the food each pet is actually eating.

by 1/3, and establish a new feeding schedule. If your breeder was feeding the puppy twice a day, there is no reason to increase the feedings to three a day—just keep his feedings the same.

No hard and fast rule dictates how many meals a puppy should eat each day and for how many months. Often, the puppy's schedule is determined by your own schedule. Puppies are generally fed more frequently than adult dogs. Due to their size and the amount of food they need to grow, it is often easier to feed a puppy more meals than you would an adult. Consult with your breeder and your veterinarian to establish the schedule. Or, try this one: feed three meals a day until the puppy is 3 to 4 months old; feed two meals a day until the puppy is 5 to 8 months old; then feed one meal a day or as you feed your other pets.

Changing It Up

Other than scheduled feeding, do not make any change to the type of food, quantity, or feeding schedule until your puppy has been in his new home for a time, has been given a clean bill of health by his veterinarian, and has firm stools. Then, and only then, can you consider making a change to his feeding regimen.

If you are interested in changing your puppy's food, the first question to ask yourself is: "Why?" If your puppy is thriving on his present food, it is readily available, and the expense is not excessive, there may be no real reason to change foods—if it isn't broken, don't fix it! If, however, there is a compelling reason to change his food, here are some ways to do it.

Find out the protein and fat content, grain base, and protein source of your puppy's current food. If there is a problem with the current food, you will not want to select a new food with the same main ingredients. If the current food is working fine, but you have other reasons for switching, try to find a very similar food. If you need to increase the protein and fat content, look for a food with a similar base, but with higher protein and fat percentages.

Once you have decided on a new food, mix it with your puppy's current food. For 1 week, feed 3/4 of the current food and 1/4 of the new food in each meal. If your puppy's stools are firm, change the ratio to 1/2 current food and 1/2 new food during the second week. Again, if all is okay, increase the new food to 3/4 and decrease the current food to 1/4. And, if all is fine after a week, continue with this ratio until the old food runs out. If at any time the puppy develops diarrhea, keep at that ratio longer (until the diarrhea stops) or step back to the previous week's mixture.

Treats

Finally, pay attention to the number of treats your puppy eats each day. A small

Get your puppy used to having his body touched by rewarding him with a tasty treat.

Siberian puppy eating several biscuits each day significantly increases the volume of food being consumed, most of which is carbohydrates. You can use pieces of his kibble as treats—they are the right size and nutritionally balanced. Refrain from feeding table scraps to your puppy. Not only does this change the composition of his diet, it turns him into a table beggar, and can start him on the road to becoming a finicky eater. A well-balanced, premium dog food will give him all the nutrition he needs, especially if you watch for the warning signs of over- or underfeeding.

GROOMING YOUR SIBERIAN PUPPY

Having handled your puppy's nutritional needs, it's time to look at his physical needs. The way you handle grooming your puppy lays the groundwork for grooming success throughout his life. It is important to start off on the right foot. Siberians who learn to tolerate (or even enjoy) grooming as puppies are much easier to groom as they grow up—and, as you know, Siberians need lots of grooming. So, start off right from puppyhood.

Once your Siberian accepts grooming, you'll both to enjoy this special time together. Grooming sessions are the perfect times to begin bonding with your puppy. Plus, routine grooming provides you with an established time for performing periodic health checks.

To help develop a good routine, try to understand what dogs do not like about grooming. As a general rule, dogs are not fond of being immobilized, which is necessary during grooming. They may not like being bathed, the sound and force of a dryer, or having their coats brushed (especially if there is any discomfort or pain). They often do not like having their teeth or ears touched during cleaning. And nearly all dogs do not

Training Tidbit

Getting your puppy used to grooming will pay off in the long run. He'll become accustomed to being touched all over his body, which prepares him for other types of handling, including veterinary examinations.

like having their nails trimmed or hearing the sound of the nail grinder. You'll need to begin desensitizing your puppy to these tasks, so he will learn to readily accept them as part of life.

Getting Started

The two grooming activities to start with are brushing or combing the coat and trimming nails. These two tasks get your puppy used to immobilization, give you a chance to do an all-over body check, and make for great first bonding opportunities.

Coat Care

Start with the least objectionable task from your puppy's prospective: brushing/combing the coat. Choose a fairly soft brush or a widely tined comb. You can sit on the floor or put your Siberian puppy on your lap. Start by petting him and getting him calm. Slowly add the brush or comb to the process. Keep the brushing gentle and restricted to the less sensitive parts of his body, such as his back, sides, or tummy if he rolls over to ask for a tummy rub. Initially, avoid those areas that might be tender, such as his head or tail. Talk to your puppy while you're brushing, telling him what a good boy he is. Praise him lavishly, and even offer a small treat. Although these

Routine nail trimming is an important part of grooming.

nails are fairly thin and soft, and they are small enough to hold. So, this is the perfect time to get him used to it.

There are a number of different styles of nail trimmers, including scissors-type, guillotine-type, and electric and battery-operated grinders. With a puppy, you can start with something even smaller, such as a human toenail clipper. You should also have some styptic powder on hand just in case you accidentally cut the quick (the blood vessel that runs down the center of the nail). The quick should be easy to locate if your Siberian has white nails. If, however, his nails are darkly colored, it will be more difficult.

To start, hold your puppy in your arms and quickly snip just the tip of each nail. By trimming just the tip, you will be in no danger of cutting through the quick, which could hurt and bleed. And if you do it fast enough, your puppy will never know what happened. Follow with praise and a small treat. As your puppy grows, you can graduate to larger nail trimmers.

sessions should be kept short, you'll still have the opportunity to run your hands all over his body, which will allow you to discover any injury, scab, tick, or other external problem with the puppy. (You can do this physical check any time—even if you do not have a brush or comb close at hand.) Brush your Siberian a few times each week, so it becomes a normal part of your relationship with your puppy.

Nail Care

The next task is to trim his nails. Puppy nails are usually sharp and pointed like little needles. Some puppies wear down their nails by running on a hard surface, such as concrete, or by digging. However, routine nail trimming is an important part of grooming. Nail trimming is less difficult for puppies, as their

Bathing

Puppies get dirty—this is a constant of life. And dirty puppies need baths. Initially, you may be able to wash your puppy in a large sink, but as he grows, you will need to find another place. Dogs have a different skin pH than people, so make sure to use a good-quality, mild dog shampoo on your puppy. Make sure you rinse all the shampoo out. You will probably be able to towel-dry your Siberian puppy, but as

Warning
Never use a human's heated hair dryer on a puppy or dog to dry his fur—it could cause burns.

an adult he'll need another solution, such as a blow dryer made especially for dogs. *Never* use a human's heated hair dryer on a Siberian, as this could cause skin burning.

HEALTH OF YOUR SIBERIAN PUPPY

Siberians are usually healthy dogs. However, your Siberian will need veterinary services over his lifetime, including periodic vaccinations and yearly checkups. Just as it was important to find a breeder you could rely on, your veterinarian will also be your partner in keeping your dog healthy and happy.

Finding a Veterinarian

Before you bring your Siberian puppy home, begin searching for a good veterinarian. If you have other pets and are happy with their veterinarian, your search is over. Otherwise, there are some things to consider when looking for a veterinarian.

You will want to find a local veterinarian with hours that are convenient to your schedule. The ability to schedule regular appointments around your work schedule or other time constraints is important. If evenings or weekends are your only free times, find a veterinarian who offers these hours. Location is important, because getting to your vet's office quickly is essential—especially in an emergency.

A number of resources are available to help you find veterinarians in your area. Each state has a veterinarian licensing board that provides information about state-licensed veterinarians. In addition, a number of professional veterinary organizations, including the American Veterinary Medical Association (AVMA), the American Animal Hospital Association (AAHA), and a variety of others, provide referral information.

Recommendations are another great way to find a veterinarian. If your breeder lives close to you, ask her for a recommendation. Ask friends and neighbors who have pets. Contact other Siberian Husky owners in your area. There are local websites that allow individuals to write reviews of local businesses; see if any veterinarians are mentioned. Recommendations are always helpful when you are faced with a long list of possibilities.

When you have narrowed down your list, it's time to ask more specific questions, which can be done initially by phone. Ask about:

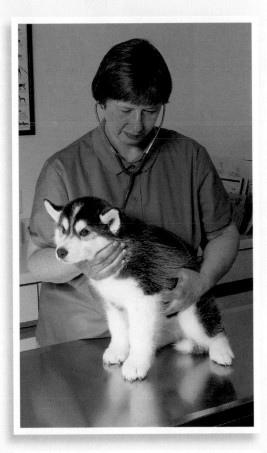

Within the first week of bringing your puppy home, take him for his first veterinary checkup.

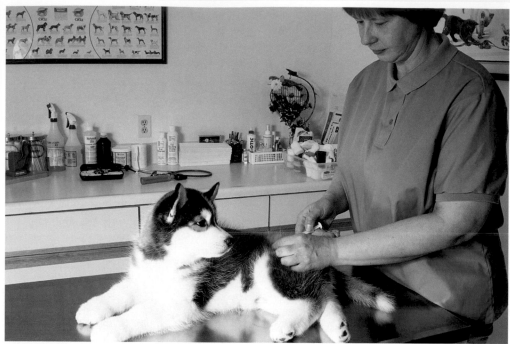

Ask your veterinarian about the most current vaccination recommendations.

- the hours of operation
- the number of veterinarians and technicians in the practice
- the services offered
- their plan for emergency care
- if they are staffed 24 hours a day
- if they have a breed specialty or preference
- pricing on normal procedures, such as vaccinations, office visits, and spaying/ neutering. (Although you will want to offer your Siberian the best possible veterinary medical care, it must be affordable.)

This telephone screening should give you a short list of good veterinary possibilities. The final decision should be made after a visit to the facilities. Make an appointment, asking for an opportunity to meet the staff and visit the facility. Look for cleanliness

and order. Meet the veterinarians and ask if they have experience with Siberian Huskies (or other Northern breeds). Siberians can be stoic about serious illness yet babies about small injuries, and their somewhat silly antics can annoy some veterinarians. Try to find a vet who appreciates Siberians as much as you do. Finally, find a veterinarian with whom you have a good rapport, someone you think is knowledgeable and that you can trust.

Once you have selected a veterinarian, if at any time you stop feeling comfortable with this vet and want to make a change, do not hesitate to do so. You are a consumer of veterinary services, and if you become dissatisfied with those services, find another vet.

Puppy's First Checkup

One of the first things you will do after bringing home your new Siberian puppy is to take him to meet his veterinarian. Your breeder will recommend a veterinary visit within the first week. When you arrive for this first appointment, bring all information from your breeder regarding vaccinations, wormings, and any health-related issues. You will want your veterinarian to meet her new patient and to examine him for his overall health. If the veterinarian discovers any problems, contact your breeder immediately. Most likely, though, your vet will find a healthy, happy Siberian Husky puppy.

Vaccinations

At birth, a puppy's immune system is not fully developed against disease. To ensure the survival of the species, Mother Nature enables a mother dog to pass along her immunity to her offspring through colostrum, or "first milk." This first 24 hours of milk from your puppy's mother passes along her antibodies, plus it is highly concentrated with vitamins and minerals, all of which will protect the puppy during the first months of life.

As your puppy grows, his body will be able to process additional antibodies between 6 and 18 weeks, and so your breeder began a regimen of vaccinations to prevent common canine diseases. Now that he's in your care, you will need to continue those vaccinations to make sure your puppy stays as healthy as possible.

While at the veterinarian's office, discuss completing your puppy's vaccination schedule. The AVMA frequently reevaluates vaccination protocols, so ask your veterinarian about the most current recommendations.

Canine vaccines can have side effects similar to those used in humans. There can occasionally be tenderness at the inoculation site, or a vaccinated puppy can become sleepy. On rare occasions, dogs may have additional sensitivities to vaccines, which although very rare, can be serious. Canine vaccines have also been as successful as their human counterparts, so most people have never seen the suffering caused by rabies, distemper, or parvovirus. Unfortunately, this success, along with the rare potential for side effects, has caused some to question the need for canine vaccination. For the sake of your Siberian, do not fall into this trap. Anyone who has ever seen an animal suffer from any of the diseases we can vaccinate against will tell you that protecting dogs from these illnesses is more than worth the slight chance of side effects.

Core

The AVMA has divided vaccinations into two groups: core and noncore. It is recommended that the core vaccines be administered to all canines every 3 years. The core diseases include canine distemper, parvovirus, hepatitis, and rabies. Many veterinary medical suppliers have combined most of these vaccines for these core diseases into a single vaccine. This way, rather than giving your dog five different inoculations, one shot covers distemper, hepatitis, parainfluenza, parvovirus, and adenovirus.

Distemper

Canine distemper is a virus similar to the one that causes human measles, and it can affect

Want to Know More?

For information on health of your Siberian, see Chapter 8: Siberian Husky Health and Wellness.

Puppies are particularly susceptible to canine parvovirus.

communicated via contact with feces, and it may lie dormant in inanimate objects. Since its discovery, CPV has changed, and various strains have emerged. Puppies are particularly susceptible to CPV, and some veterinarians believe they should receive their first vaccination at 5 weeks. The vaccination is highly effective and shows a low risk of side effects. CPV is part of the combination vaccination given at 6 and 9 weeks, between 12 and 16 weeks, at 1 year, and thereafter every 3 years, based on your veterinarian's recommendation.

Hepatitis

Canine hepatitis is a virus that attacks the liver. Initially infecting the throat, symptoms can appear similar to pneumonia, but the infection later moves to the eyes, kidneys, and liver, ultimately resulting in dehydration and seizures. Puppies are particularly susceptible to hepatitis. The vaccine is highly effective, with low risk. The disease is similar to the noncore adenovirus cough, and either vaccine protects against both diseases. The canine hepatitis vaccine is usually part of the combination vaccination given at 6 and 9weeks, between 12 and 16 weeks, at 1 year, and thereafter every 3 years, based on your veterinarian's recommendation.

Rabies

Rabies is virus that affects both humans and animals. It is transmitted through a scratch or a bite from an infected animal. There is a long incubation period, and three stages of the disease: nervousness and anxiety; restlessness; and the final paralytic phase, in which the dog salivates and chokes, eventually going into respiratory failure and death. There is no known test for canine rabies and no effective cure. However, the vaccination is highly effective, with some risk of side effects. Your puppy's first rabies shot should be given when

many organs. Symptoms include coughing, diarrhea, vomiting, and fever. This is a highly contagious disease with a high mortality rate. Modified live virus (MLV) vaccines are very effective against it and have a low risk of adverse side effects. Distemper is usually one component of the combination vaccine. Puppies should be vaccinated at 6 and 9 weeks of age, between 12 to 16 weeks of age, at 1 year, and then every 3 years, based on your veterinarian's recommendation.

Parvovirus

Canine parvovirus (CPV) is a highly communicable canine virus. Symptoms include vomiting, dehydration, and diarrhea, which may or may not be bloody. CPV is he is at least 12 weeks old or older, and the age may be mandated by local law. The second rabies vaccination is administered at 1 year, and thereafter every 3 years, based on your veterinarian's recommendation and local law.

Noncore

The noncore vaccines include bordetella and parainfluenza, coronavirus, leptospirosis and Lyme disease, and may be administered annually based on your veterinarian's recommendation. The information provided for the noncore vaccinations is based on current AVMA protocols. Please consult your veterinarian for local recommendations.

Bordetella and Parainfluenza

Parainfluenza and bordetella appear as a hacking cough most frequently in nonvaccinated puppies, and these diseases are often referred to as "kennel cough." There are two different methods of inoculation: intranasal and injectable, neither of which is highly effective, mainly due to the number of different strains of the disease. However, the risk of side effects is low. Try to prevent your puppy from contracting these diseases by keeping him away from kennels and large groups of dogs, where some may be affected. If your puppy is receiving a combination vaccine, parainfluenza may already be included. Consult your veterinarian for her recommendation.

Coronavirus

The symptoms of coronavirus are similar to those of canine parvovirus. Most adult dogs have a natural immunity to coronavirus, but

One method of controlling your dog's exposure to Lyme disease is to use tick prevention methods.

puppies are susceptible. Please consult with your veterinarian regarding the prevalence of coronavirus in your area, and if recommended, puppies should be vaccinated at 6 and 9 weeks, between 12 and 16 weeks, and possibly at 1 year of age.

Leptospirosis

Leptospirosis is a bacterial disease that affects both animals and humans, and there are many strains. Both a test and a treatment are available for affected dogs. The best approach is prevention—keeping your Siberian away from contaminated water and affected domestic or wild animals. The vaccination has a high incidence of side effects, and a large percentage of dogs may not respond to the vaccine. Please consult with your veterinarian regarding the prevalence of leptospirosis in your area, and if recommended, puppies should be vaccinated 12 and 16 weeks, and thereafter twice a year.

Lyme Disease

Lyme disease can affect both animals and humans, and is transmitted through a bite from an infected deer tick nymph or adult. Symptoms of Lyme disease include fever, joint and node swelling, and eventual kidney failure and death. Although there have been cases of Lyme disease in all 50 states, 85% of all diagnosed cases come from the New England and mid-Atlantic states. There is both a test and treatment available for dogs who have contracted Lyme disease. There is a vaccination against Lyme disease, although its efficacy is questionable. Consult your veterinarian for her recommendation, especially based on your location. Should vaccination be recommended, puppies may be vaccinated at 12 weeks of age, and receive a second dose 3 weeks later, with a yearly vaccination thereafter. Another method of controlling your dog's exposure to Lyme disease is to use tick prevention methods.

Parasite Control

Once you and your veterinarian have decided upon a vaccination schedule for your puppy, there is another topic to consider: parasite control and heartworm prevention. Parasites may be external or internal: fleas, ticks, or worms (including heartworms). Most likely your breeder began the process of deworming your puppy, and you will want to consult with your veterinarian about continuing this process.

Unless your Siberian was acquired for showing and potential breeding, you should plan to have your puppy altered.

Depending on your area, climate, and the time of year, your veterinarian may recommend testing and preventative treatment against worms and external parasites. Parasites can be harmful to your puppy— some invite more disease, while others could be fatal. The treatment of parasites will be discussed in greater detail in Chapter 8, but don't forget to discuss your puppy's parasite control with your veterinarian.

Puppy Health Problems

Siberian Huskies are generally very healthy animals, so there are no particular puppyhood diseases to which they are very susceptible. However, some hereditary problems may initially appear in young dogs. Although somewhat unusual, inherited cataracts have been known to appear at a young age (prior to 6 months). These can only be diagnosed by a canine ophthalmologist, and would be difficult for an owner to discern. However, if you suspect any eye problem, please consult with your veterinarian for possible referral to an ophthalmologist.

Spaying/Neutering

Unless your Siberian was acquired for showing and potential breeding, you should plan to have your puppy altered. Although there is some current controversy about the appropriate age to spay a female and neuter a male, it is generally accepted that the best time is between 5 and 8 months of age, and before the female has reached her first heat.

A large number of myths exist about spaying and neutering of animals, most significantly that altered animals become lazy and overweight. This is not true. The metabolism of a dog will not change after being altered. If, after altering, a dog becomes overweight it is either due to overfeeding or some other cause, which should be looked into.

By the Numbers

- 7 to 32% protein and 18 to 22% fat: these are good percentages for your puppy's food, to be assured that he's getting the nutrition necessary to grow.
- 3 years: After the puppy series of shots, the core vaccines are administered every 3 years.
- 5 to 8 months: Spaying or neutering are best done between 5 and 8 months of age (and should be done before the female's first heat).

To the contrary, spayed females and neutered males are often healthier than their intact counterparts. If a female has an ovariohysterectomy prior to her first heat, she has a significantly reduced chance of contracting mammary cancer. Additionally, her chances of developing reproductive tumors are significantly reduced or eliminated, as is the chance of uterine infection. She will not "spot" around your house, neighborhood dogs will not camp on your doorstep while she is in heat, and the occurrence of false pregnancies will be eliminated.

Likewise, a neutered male will be an easier-to-live-with pet, as he will have decreased aggression and roaming, and will be less inclined to "mark" his territory. He will have no chance for testicular tumors. He will have a significantly lower chance of developing hernias, perianal tumors, and prostate problems.

There is no time like that first veterinary visit to make plans for spaying or neutering your puppy. So, don't leave the office without scheduling that appointment.

CHAPTER 4

TRAINING YOUR SIBERIAN HUSKY PUPPY

Bringing a puppy into your home is always a bit chaotic, and a Siberian Husky puppy may be more like bringing a little Arctic blizzard into the house! Puppies have no manners, no limits, and no bladder control. They are wild little hooligans, and you may question your sanity for deciding on a puppy—especially a Siberian Husky! Before you pull your hair out from the roots, sit down and cry, or pack the little bundle into the car to return to his breeder, just remember this: Three things enable us to survive the antics of puppyhood: exhaustion, time, and training. Other owners have survived this phase, and you can, too. But to do it right, you need to form a proactive plan for peaceful coexistence and mutual love. It's time to get serious.

Early socialization, basic commands, and beginning training are all essential for puppies. The work you accomplish during these first few months, when your puppy is most susceptible to training, will become the framework for turning him into a loving pet and welcome member of the family. You can accomplish all of this by yourself, but you may find this process easier if you have an experienced trainer helping and supporting you. With a good support system, consistency, and your

time and commitment, you'll not only survive his puppyhood, but thrive and make positive steps toward turning your adorable Siberian puppy into your perfect companion.

CRATE TRAINING

If you've never used a crate, you may be wondering why crate training is important. It can be summed up in one word—safety. Your Siberian will be safe when he is in his crate, whether at home, in a car, or in an airplane. Your goal with crate training is to be able to crate your puppy for the night or for any other time that you need to control where he is, such as when you need to run to the store or when company arrives. Crates have other uses too. Crates are good places for your puppy to sleep. Plus, crate training is a great companion to housetraining, as dogs generally do not soil where they sleep.

As a general rule, Siberian Huskies love their crates. Siberians naturally like dens, and their crates quickly become their own private space. However, puppies must be trained to feel comfortable in a crate.

How to Crate Train
Your puppy will be happy in his crate if he's

becomes distressed. Slowly increase the time your puppy is in his crate with the door closed. Don't open the crate door when your puppy is fussing to get out. Rather, wait until he is quiet, and then open the door. These methods should help make him comfortable in his crate.

Put your puppy in his crate with some toys after he has relieved himself and is tired from extended play. When he falls asleep, keep the crate door closed until he awakens, then take him out to his potty area.

Never use the crate as punishment. It is important that you have a place where your dog is happy and where you *know* he is safe. In an emergency, while being shipped, during a car trip, when workers are coming in and out of your house—there are many situations in which you'll need your dog to be safe, secure, quiet, and *happy*. If your dog has been crated as punishment, he will not be content there.

Make sure that you do not turn his crate into the canine equivalent of "solitary confinement." If you must crate your puppy, make sure he has adequate water and he is given time out of his crate for exercise and potty breaks. Remember that a puppy cannot go very long without relieving himself. As he gets older, this time will increase, so let him be your guide. Figure out how long he usually sleeps after play. Start by crating him for that length of time and go from there. The eventual goal is that he's able to sleep through the night, but this will take some time and control to achieve.

exposed to it properly. Start crate training as soon as your Siberian puppy comes home. Keep the crate in an area where you will be spending time. You may find that your puppy is happiest if you move his crate with you from room to room as you do chores, and bring it into your bedroom at night. This way, your puppy will still be able to see and hear you when he is in his crate.

Make the crate a fun place for your puppy to spend time. At first, leave the crate door open. Feed your puppy in his crate; put toys in his crate; give him treats in his crate. A hollow rubber toy, like the ones Nylabone makes, filled with treats or peanut butter, provides a great reason for your puppy to spend some quality time in his crate. All of these activities will reinforce the idea that the crate is your puppy's special place.

Once he readily enters the crate on his own for treats, begin to close the crate door. Select a special time for your puppy, such as mealtime or a filled-treat time, to close the crate door. Keep the door closed for only a short time at first, and try to open it before your puppy

HOUSETRAINING

In concert with crate training, you will be working on housetraining your puppy. Although your puppy does not have perfect control of his bladder and bowels, you should begin housetraining as soon as you bring him home. Successful housetraining comes with repetition and attention.

How to Housetrain

Housetraining takes your undivided attention. You must constantly supervise your puppy. Initially, your puppy may not give you enough advance warning to take him outside to relieve himself. Find out if your breeder used a specific potty area, and how it was so designated. If, for example, your breeder trained the puppies to use newspaper or puppy pads in the potty area, you can replicate this in your home. Try to find a place, preferably near the outside door, to set up a temporary relief station. As your puppy gets the urge to relieve himself, he will run toward the paper. When you see this, quickly pick him up and take him outside to the preferred relief area. You'll be surprised by how quickly he will become housetrained using this process, but constant monitoring

and quick reactions are needed here. You will be supervising him at all times, even outside. A puppy on his own in a yard will be tempted to do other things than relieve himself. Make sure he is in the designated relief area, and praise him when he is successful.

If your breeder did not paper-train her puppies, you can still use the same basic principle to housetrain your puppy. Puppies need to relieve themselves after they wake up, and after play, running, or eating, so take your puppy to his potty area at these times. When you are inside the house, watch for signs of frantic behavior or circling, and take your puppy outside at these times, too. Exercise your puppy prior to bedtime, prior to leaving him in his crate for a time, and after he awakens from a nap. By exercising and

If your breeder paper-trained your Siberian puppy, use this training to help teach him to potty outside.

taking him out to relieve himself at specific times you accomplish two things. You react to his internal "clock" by taking him out when he'd have to relieve himself anyway. And, by creating and sticking to a plan, you are establishing consistency—a consistent process of when and where to relieve himself. You will find that, although there may be a few puddles and messes to clean, your puppy will be housetrained in short order if you are watchful and consistent.

When those few accidents do occur, clean them up immediately. A number of products are available that will help neutralize the scent of urine while also disinfecting the spot. Use one of these products, as nothing encourages a puppy to urinate in the house more than the scent of a previous accident. When you find a puddle, just clean it. Do not punish your puppy for the accident, because he will not be able to understand that the puddle and the punishment have anything to do with each

For the rare Siberian who is not food motivated, try rewarding with a favorite toy.

Training Tidbit

You will find that praise and reward are the keys to success when training a Siberian Husky puppy.

other. If, however, you catch your puppy in mid-puddling, pick him up and immediately take him outside to the preferred area. Praise him lavishly when he finishes outside.

POSITIVE TRAINING

Everyone reacts better to praise than to punishment, and your puppy is no different. Dogs, especially puppies, do not understand cause and effect the way humans do. So punishing your puppy for poor behavior won't have the desired effect. When training a puppy, you'll have more success by using a reward system rather than a punitive one. Rewarding your puppy for doing something you like is called *positive reinforcement*, or sometimes *positive training*. Whether your puppy likes tummy rubs, pats, toys, or treats, encouraging his good behavior with his favorite reward will lead to training success. Positive training does require more effort from you, because you need to be aware of what your puppy is doing so you can dissuade him from bad behavior and encourage him toward good behavior.

GETTING HELP WITH TRAINING

Whether this is your first dog or your tenth, whether you want to compete in formal obedience or just have a well-behaved dog, both you and your puppy may benefit from the help of a good trainer.

How to Find a Trainer

Finding a trainer does not mean leaving your puppy at a facility for a day, week, or month and then picking up your "perfectly trained" Siberian. While he may learn some manners after being sent away, your dog won't learn to respect you as an important member of his pack if someone else trains him. Sending a dog to boarding school may work with some breeds, but it's a waste of money with a Siberian Husky. Training your puppy takes a hands-on approach, ideally on the part of all family members.

Dog training classes are conducted by a variety of groups throughout the country, including local recreation departments, pet supply stores, national dog training businesses, kennels and doggy day-care centers, and kennel clubs and obedience training clubs. In most areas, you have the option of choosing between individual training in your own home or classes with other dogs and owners in a park or training facility.

How do you decide between individual in-home training and class training? Look at cost and convenience first. An in-home trainer will cost far more than going to an existing class, but may be more flexible about fitting into your busy schedule. In-home training also makes it easy for the whole family to participate in lessons. Then, ask yourself what type of results you want. If you are just looking to teach your dog some basic commands, in-home training might be fine. If, however, you are interested in socializing your Siberian with other dogs and people, a group class would be better.

Once you've decided on group or individual classes, an Internet search on "dog training," the clubs section of the American Kennel Club (AKC) website (www.akc.org), or the Association of Pet Dog Trainers (APDT) website

Finding a good, experienced trainer whose goals are the same as yours is critical to your success.

(www.apdt.com) will all give you a long list of options. From this group of possibilities, narrow your choice down to one. Consult with local people involved with dogs in your area: your breeder, your veterinarian, Siberian Husky fanciers in your area, neighbors, and friends. Often the best place to start is with a recommendation from a trusted advisor.

Regardless of the type of training you prefer, it is very important to meet potential trainers, watch them at work, and ask questions about their backgrounds, experience, approaches, and goals. Finding a knowledgeable, experienced trainer with whom you can establish a good rapport, one with whose approach

Puppies "learn to be dogs" by interacting with their littermates.

a Siberian succeeds with a creative trainer, one who makes the activity fun, and who finds a way to motivate the dog (often with treats). Your best choice for a trainer is one who has experience working with a number of breeds—from the "very trainable" to those with short attention spans, one who has run into a number of training challenges and overcome them, and one who has a lot of experience working with lots of dogs and their owners.

As in all things, let common sense be your guide. If your trainer does or wants you to do anything that makes you uncomfortable, stop the exercise. You may simply need more explanation to feel comfortable with the approach and activity, or you may discover the need for a new trainer. Your comfort, and that of your dog, is paramount to the success of any training program.

SOCIALIZATION

Two disciplines actually fall under the larger umbrella of "training"—what one traditionally thinks of day-to-day dog training (housetraining, obeying simple commands, etc.) and something called *socialization*. Socialization is getting dogs used to things they will encounter in their world, such as animals, people, loud noises, crowds, and the like. Both of these types of training are important for a growing puppy.

Early Socialization

According to canine behaviorists who have studied puppies and their socialization needs, there are a number of developmental stages in a dog's life when he is influenced by different stimuli. During these stages, a puppy needs to be exposed to certain things in order to develop his social skills. Believe it or not, your puppy's socialization began at birth.

you agree, and whose goals are the same as yours is critical to your success. Additionally, as you evaluate trainers, you will want to find one who understands and enjoys the antics of Siberian Huskies. In a rigid training environment, not all trainers appreciate Siberians. Although you do not want a trainer who allows misbehavior, likewise you do not want to select a trainer who does not recognize and enjoy the differences between various breeds, their temperaments, and their unique approaches to situations.

Siberians are not motivated to follow blindly. A strong hand and demanding voice will not allow a Siberian to thrive. Rather,

Developmental Stages

During the neonatal period (the first 2 weeks of life), a puppy cannot hear or see very well, but he can taste and feel. Therefore, he stays close to his mother and littermates for all his needs.

In the transitional period (the following 2 weeks), his eyes open, he begins to hear, his teeth probably start to appear, and he starts walking. During this time, he may show some interest in toys, and may use his voice for the first time. At this stage, a good breeder will provide some toys for play and spend more time holding all of the puppies in the litter, so they begin to have contact with humans. A breeder will also expose the puppies to some noises and new surfaces.

The period of time after the transitional period to 12 weeks of age, sometimes called the *awareness period* or *littermate period*, is one of the most important times in a puppy's life, as this is the main socialization period. The first half of this period is spent with his mother and his littermates at the breeder's home. This is the time when puppies "learn to be dogs" by interacting with their littermates. They play, learn to walk and even run a bit, bark (or, in the case of the Siberian Husky, probably howl). They learn to accept their mother's discipline. They practice biting, fighting, and showing dominance with littermates, and they begin to learn the hierarchy of a pack environment. This is the crucial time when puppies begin to learn Siberian Husky pack behaviors—ones that you

A puppy can't be enrolled in puppy kindergarten until he has had all of his shots, so it's essential to start the socialization process before then.

Use a positive and gentle approach to help your puppy through any frightening experiences.

been exposed to seven challenges, eaten from seven different containers, and eaten in seven different locations. While the actual number seven may not be all that important, the lesson is—introducing new experiences to a puppy by the time he is ready to go to his new home is critical. And a good breeder will take this rule to heart.

Socializing Your Siberian Puppy

Socialization does not end when your puppy comes home, because this is a very important time for bonding with people. Many canine behaviorists believe that during the 2- to 4-month period of a puppy's life, his basic character is formed—especially his attitude toward people. This is a time of rapid learning, when puppies are curious about their world and the people and things in it. They will test the boundaries of what is acceptable behavior, and you will have the opportunity to help them refine their social skills.

Noted canine behaviorist Dr. Ian Dunbar, PhD, believes that dogs should meet 100 new people by the time they are 12 weeks of age. So, this is the time to have friends over to meet your new puppy. By this time, your puppy should be adequately inoculated to receive company (but please consult your veterinarian for her advice). These people can be adults, teenagers, or children, but they should be well-behaved. The lesson your puppy should be learning is that people are nice—so, you do not want anyone whose noisy, erratic, or harmful behavior will destroy this lesson. However, you will want both men and women, and people of all sizes and ages. Provided that your puppy has received his last puppy vaccines, this is also the time to go to parks and shopping centers. Unless the area is confined and controlled, keep him on leash. Avoid areas with numbers of other dogs (such

will see throughout your puppy's life.

This is also the critical time for increased contact with people. A good breeder not only takes care of her puppy's physical needs, such as providing solid food after weaning and establishing a potty area, she also begins socialization. She exposes a puppy to more human contact, and she gets him used to being held and to the rudiments of grooming. She exposes her puppies to more noises, different surfaces, new people, and new experiences—all of which help build your puppy's social skills and make him more confident.

The "Rule of Sevens" is a theory among some canine behaviorists. Simply put, it says that by 7 weeks, a puppy should have walked on seven different surfaces, played with seven different objects, been in seven different locations, met seven new people, as a dog park), and be cautious any time you encounter other dogs. If he is ever unsure of himself, he will still be small enough to pick up in your arms.

This is also the time when your puppy may begin to experience fear. Occasionally, normal objects, noises, and experiences can frighten a puppy, and anything that frightens a puppy during this sensitive period could have a lasting effect. Therefore, it is very important to use a positive and gentle approach to help your puppy through any frightening experiences. Don't let him avoid what has frightened him, but never force him to face his fear. Rather, try a more fun and matter-of-fact approach to show him that there is nothing to fear. Try offering treats to entice him to face the frightening object. How you handle these situations is critical to your puppy's socialization. You do not want a grown dog who won't approach a fire hydrant because he was frightened by one as a puppy!

Puppy Kindergarten

Puppy kindergarten class can address both types of training. Local dog or obedience clubs, or professional dog training schools often hold these classes for puppies, usually weekly for 6 to 8 weeks. Puppy kindergarten classes usually have small numbers of puppies and their owners (six to ten). Occasionally, the puppies are split into classes based on their size, but not always. All puppies will be required to provide proof of complete inoculation for their safety and that of the other puppies in the class. Each class usually has two parts. First, you are taught how to give a basic command and how to get your puppy to respond. The second is puppy playtime. Do not think, however, that puppy playtime is not serious business. It will be monitored by the trainer and all the owners, and puppies will

be taught good puppy manners, such as not bullying others or showing aggression. The trainer will teach you how to address early problem behaviors. The class trainer will help you begin the work necessary for socialization and training, and will give you "homework" to do on your own time with your puppy. If this sounds like a significant commitment of your time and energy, it is! Training a puppy is a big responsibility, and the first months are very important.

Puppy kindergarten will help you and your puppy through the various stages of socialization, teach you what to do in each phase, and help you to lay the groundwork for some basic obedience training. Between 2 and 4 months, your puppy learns very quickly, and this time period usually coincides with most puppy kindergarten classes. However, because a puppy can't be enrolled in puppy kindergarten until he has had all of his shots, it's essential to start the socialization process before then, as soon as he arrives in your home.

The Terrible Teens

Nearing 4 months of age, as your puppy is cutting his teeth, he may attempt to challenge your leadership. If, all along, you have been consistent and vigilant in your socialization and training activities, this challenge should be a non-event. If not, prepare for some remedial training.

As your puppy reaches puberty (between 4 and 8 months of age), all of your training and socialization will be called into question. Similar to a teenager, your puppy may challenge you at every turn. (Coincidentally, this is a not-so-subtle reminder that it is about the time to have your puppy spayed or neutered.) For a while, you may not even recognize your darling puppy. Not only will he have grown, but he will be chewing on everything (provide him with safe Nylabones to chew, as his adult teeth will be coming in), he will not listen to you as much, and he will do bad things that he hasn't done since he was little. Your ability to recognize what is happening, be kind and consistent (but firm) in your approach, and above all, keep your sense of humor, will serve you well through this difficult time.

In addition to challenging authority, some dogs may become protective, territorial, and afraid from 6 months to a year. This is, again, tied to hormones and maturity. During this time, do not reinforce bad or fearful behavior. If possible, try to avoid confrontation. But the best solution is to build your puppy's confidence by setting him up for success. Dissuade him from being protective or territorial by reasserting and reaffirming your role as leader of his team, but do so benevolently. Help him get over frightening situations and instill his self-confidence. Additional training sessions using praise and rewards in areas that prompt poor behavior can refocus his attention and reinforce his feeling of safety in your presence, and his confidence in himself.

BASIC OBEDIENCE COMMANDS

Whether or not you ever want to compete in the obedience ring, all dogs should learn some basic commands. A puppy who's trained to walk nicely on a leash makes it pleasant to take him for a stroll. And you never know when a "come," "sit," or "down" might keep your puppy out of danger or even save his life. Of course, you can never forget that you are training a Siberian Husky. Occasionally, after learning to obey a simple command, he may find no reason to show you he knows it. But it's always a good idea to train any dog you have—even a Siberian.

Getting Started

Your training sessions will probably begin in puppy kindergarten class, but you can also train at home. At this point you are just starting your puppy's training, so stay positive and keep the following in mind:

- Keep the training activity fun.
- Offer lots of praise and treats, like pieces of puppy biscuits, kibble, or round oat cereal; make sure you have treats in your pocket before you begin the lesson.
- Be consistent when giving commands. Say your puppy's name first to get his attention. Then, after you have his attention, clearly give the command. For example, if you want your puppy, Ted, to come to you say, "Ted, come." If you want him to sit, say, "Ted, sit."
- Although repetition is the key to learning, your puppy does not have a very long attention span. Keep each lesson fairly short, but repeat the lesson a few times each day.
- Teach the first set of commands (*come, sit,* and *down*) in a fairly small, controlled area

with your puppy off leash
- Don't start off with too many distractions. As your puppy learns the command, slowly start to add distractions.
- Don't expect perfect responses.

Come

To begin, wait until you and your puppy are in the same general area (5- to 10-feet [2- to 3-m] away), he can see you, and he is engaged in another activity, such as wandering, lying down, or playing quietly with a toy. Don't begin this exercise if he is engrossed in his favorite activity or playing with his favorite toy. You want your Siberian puppy to be successful—you do not want him to have to decide between coming to see you or continuing to play with his favorite toy. Don't wake him from sleep to come when called. One other don't—don't ever call your dog for something unpleasant. If you want him to come when called, he will not do so consistently if there is a chance of unpleasantness when he gets there.

Teaching Come When Called

The command word for this activity is "Come." So, you will clearly say, "Ted, come." Since this command is asking your puppy to stop what he is doing and come to you, the best time to praise your puppy is when he takes that first step toward you—that is the time to show him the treat and praise him lavishly. Initially, he might be uncertain what you want him to do, so that first praise you give him as he takes his first step toward you is the most important—it lets him know what you want. If he doesn't make a move to come toward you, give the command again, encourage him, show him the treat, and praise for any step in your direction. If he becomes distracted on his way to you, repeat the command and encourage him—

remind him what you asked him to do.

If he makes no move to come to you, go to him and hold the treat in front of his nose. Give the command again, "Ted, come," and immediately back away from him. As he begins to move toward you (and the treat), lavishly praise him.

When your puppy gets to you, praise him and give him the treat. If your puppy tends to get excited with effusive praise, tone it down. Let him know that you are pleased that he obeyed your command to come, but don't let your praise get him too out of control. After the praise and reward, your puppy will eventually return to his previous activity or find something new to do. This is what you want. Wait a bit, give him the command once again, "Ted, come," and follow the same process.

Puppies don't have long attention spans, so keep training sessions short and fun.

Practice this command three to four times in a training session. Try the command in different locations, such as the backyard, puppy kindergarten—anywhere your puppy is safely enclosed. As your puppy learns the command and becomes reliable, try the command when he is more distracted, for example while he is playing with other dogs or people. Again, follow the same process: name, command, praise for first step, encouragement (and additional command, if necessary), and praise/reward upon completion.

Using praise and treat rewards with Siberian Huskies often means the difference between success and failure. However, your eventual goal is to have your dog reliably come when called without requiring a treat as reward. The reward method of training relies on you gradually and eventually eliminating the reward completely. However, puppy training should begin with rewards.

Due to the various stages of socialization, you will probably notice that your puppy's response to this and other commands will falter as he reaches some of his developmental stages. Those are the times to reinforce with treats.

Sit

The next command is asking your puppy to sit on command. Keep the sessions for the *sit* command short, and keep your puppy controlled in a fairly small area without too many distractions. However, unlike the *come* command, for *sit*, you will want your puppy close to you.

Practice the *come* command in an area where your puppy is safely enclosed.

Teaching the Sit

As you did for the *come* command, say your puppy's name (to get his attention), and with a treat in your hand give the command (*sit*). If your dog's name is Ted, say, "Ted, sit." Hold the treat in front of your puppy's nose, then move the treat slightly up (above his nose) and back (toward his forehead). Your puppy will follow the treat with his nose (and his mouth), and should automatically sit. Remember not to bring the treat straight up or hold it up too high, as this may cause your puppy to jump up rather than sit. Once your puppy is sitting, praise him and give him the treat.

Try the command again once your puppy is standing close to you. Practice the command three or four times at each session. Try the command in different locations, with different distractions.

When your puppy is very reliable both with the *come* and *sit* commands, try combining them. Call your puppy to you, and praise and reward him. Then give the command to sit, and again praise and reward him. Soon you will be able to use the same treat for obeying both commands.

Show Dogs and the Sit

If your dog is destined for the conformation ring, you may wish to modify the *sit* command, replace it with the *stand* command, or delay teaching the *sit* command altogether. Because conformation dogs do not sit in the show ring, this command could prove problematic for them. It's best to teach the command with treats (especially with a Siberian), and eventually your puppy will equate receiving treats with sitting. Show dogs do receive treats (called "bait") in the show ring, but not for sitting; they are given treats when they stand. While it is a good idea for all dogs to learn to sit on command (even show dogs), you do not

Multi-Dog Tip

Puppies can learn a lot from older dogs in your household. However, when starting puppy training, it is a good idea to remove distractions, such as other dogs, from the training session.

want to confuse your puppy about whether you want him to sit or stand.

If you want to teach your show dog to sit, do not use treats. Instead, offer him a Nylabone or filled rubber chew toy. Give the command and move the toy to his nose, then up and back. Once he sits, give him the toy. This may be a longer training process than using treats, but it will eventually be successful, too.

Down

There are several ways to train the *down* command. They all begin with having your puppy in a relatively small area without too much distraction. Again, you will use small treats as rewards. The process will be to say your puppy's name (to get his attention) and the command (*down*). You will use the treat to help show your puppy what to do (luring), and once he has done it, praise and reward him.

Teaching the Down

The first method is to put your puppy in a sit, then give the command, "Ted, down." Move the treat to your puppy's nose, then slowly bring the treat straight down to the ground by his forefeet, and move it away from him. When your puppy is lying down, praise him and give him the reward. You must first move the treat down and then forward—otherwise

You'll want your puppy close to you when teaching the *sit*.

the dog will stand and move forward to the treat. This method is usually more successful with puppies, as they are closer to the ground and more likely to lie down than to get up and follow the treat from a standing position.

If the first method doesn't work, try this: With your puppy in a sitting position, give the sit command. Gently pick up the puppy's forefeet and move them forward along the ground, which should cause him lie down. Once he has achieved the down position, praise him and give him the treat.

Finally, you can try the tunnel method. Start with you seated on the ground, and your puppy either sitting or standing. Sit with your right leg either straight in front of you or with your knee bent and completely on the ground (as in a half-cross-legged position). Bend your left knee and place your left foot flat on the ground, which forms a "tunnel" under your left knee. Begin with your puppy on your left

side. Show him the treat with your left hand, and give the command, "Ted, down." Move the treat from his nose to the ground and under your knee. Hand off the treat from your left to your right hand, and move the treat to your right along the ground. As your dog follows the treat, he will need to flatten himself to fit through the tunnel of your legs. If your tunnel is too high, reduce the height by moving your left foot forward. Soon, your puppy will be lying down under the tunnel. Praise him and give him the reward.

Using any of these methods to teach *down*, you will find that, with some practice, you can eliminate any physical help to get the puppy into the down position. The command, praise, and reward will be all that is needed.

Walk Nicely on a Leash

The three simple commands were probably relatively easy to train. You started with little distraction, and then added more as the puppy became more confident. And you hopefully experienced success even with some distractions. One reason for this success is that, although your puppy has a short attention span, demonstrating these commands takes a very short time, so your puppy can quickly return to what he was doing or find something new do. Basically, you didn't ask him to pay attention or keep him from doing what he wanted to do for very long. Although the commands you have trained are very important, they are rather like "tricks" that your puppy can demonstrate. The next activity, walking nicely on leash, asks for much more concentration and extended participation from your puppy. It is not so much "trick" as it is a pattern of behavior that requires him to pay attention to you, ignore whatever else he wants to do, and refrain from being distracted by things he encounters. This training calls for much more sophisticated learning.

Why Teach Walk Nicely?

An uncontrolled dog on a leash is danger to his owner, passers-by, and himself. As the owner of a Siberian Husky, please do not fall into the trap of believing that your Siberian must be allowed to pull you when he is on a leash, or worse yet, that he needs to wear a harness rather than a collar. It is true that Siberian Huskies (although not freighting dogs) do have a natural instinct to pull, and they are strong. They love getting into harness and pulling sleds. However, they can and should

Once your puppy is in the down position, praise him and give him a treat.

Benefits of the Three Basic Commands

The benefits of having your puppy trained to respond to the three simple commands (come, sit, down) are obvious. You will use these commands, and any others you teach him, throughout his life—sitting while his veterinarian examines his ears, lying down quietly in a crowd, or coming to you if he is approaching something dangerous. You should reinforce these commands over his lifetime—an easy task because you laid the groundwork while he was a puppy. Nice job!

be taught manners for all situations, including walking nicely on a leash. Learning to behave well in a variety of situations does not inhibit a Siberian's ability to work.

When to Start

Begin to train your Siberian puppy to walk nicely on a leash at around 3 months of age, and you should have established a good, strong learning basis by around 18 weeks of age, when your puppy's world is expanding and there will be far more distractions. It is probably a good idea to begin this activity after you have trained the simple commands of *come*, *sit*, and *down*. While you won't need these commands to begin training to walk on a leash, that training gives your puppy gets your puppy used to hearing commands from you and getting rewards for pleasing you. This prior knowledge will help reinforce the process of training your puppy to walk with you.

Teaching Walk Nicely

As strange as it may seem, controlled leash walking begins off leash. You will want to begin this training in a fairly large and secure area. You will not need a collar or leash, but you will need some small treats in your pocket. The keys to this activity are to keep moving, to encourage your puppy to keep up with you on your left-hand side (preferably with his head near your left leg), and to turn away from your puppy if he turns or moves

away from you, even a little bit. The idea is to have your puppy follow you, at your side, continually.

Although this activity may eventually lead to the more formal *heel* command, you will not be expecting your puppy to sit when you stop, so you may not wish to use the command *heel*. Rather, just say something like "Let's go." As always, set your Siberian up for success by keeping the training sessions short.

Begin walking by moving briskly away from your puppy. With your left hand, pat your left leg, call your puppy's name, and give the command, "Ted, let's go." As he joins you on your left, praise him, but keep walking briskly. You can, if desired, use your left hand to give him a small treat. If he stays with you, continue walking in that direction, or you may turn away from your dog, again patting your left leg, and saying, "Ted, let's go," to encourage him to turn with you. If your puppy gets distracted, lags, forges ahead, or turns from you, turn away from him, pat your

Multi-Dog Tip

Walking on a leash with an older, well-trained dog can help instill proper leash walking behavior in a puppy.

left leg, and give the command again. Don't forget to reward with an occasional treat.

The purpose of this exercise is to keep your puppy voluntarily staying beside you, or doing so with some encouragement and rewards. Every time your puppy deviates from you, remind him that you are there and you want him to be with you. Don't slow down or run to keep up with him or turn with him when he turns. Always make him come back to you—to follow you. And don't use the *come* command, because you've already taught that command and it has an entirely different meaning.

When your puppy consistently stays with you, find different, secure places to walk with him. Your biggest challenge is your Siberian Husky's strong instinct to run. While this instinct is not as overwhelming in a puppy, never put him in any danger, such as dashing into the street. You may feel comfortable practicing this brisk off-leash walking in a park when your puppy is quite young, but be cautious as he gets older and the world begins to distract him. Better yet, keep to your yard, a fenced park, or even a fenced tennis court. A fenced dog park will probably only work if it is not occupied by other dogs, as it would be too distracting.

The more time you spend walking with your puppy in this manner, the easier leash training will be. Try to spend time on this exercise every day. Although practicing anywhere is beneficial, because most of your future leash walking will probably be out of doors, try to practice outside.

Once your puppy is progressing nicely with this off-leash "following," and you'd like to start training in more public areas, add a light

Want to Know More?

What if the unthinkable happens and your Siberian slips his collar and gets away from you? Find out what to do in Chapter 10: Siberian Husky Problem Behaviors.

collar and leash to your walks. The leash and collar are not for controlling the puppy, but rather to act as a security line. Keep the leash in your hand or attach it to your belt. In fact, if you use a light enough lead (such as a thin cord), and you're very careful not to trip, you can just let it drag on the ground. This still provides you with a way to grab your puppy in an emergency. The security line allows you to continue the exercise without worry. Clip the security line to your puppy's collar, and give the command, "Ted, let's go." Then start moving, changing directions, giving the command, praising him, patting your leg, and rewarding.

Eventually, the patting of your leg, the command, and the treats will keep your puppy in the *heel* position as you begin more formal leash walking and further obedience training.

At this point, you may wonder if there is any magic time when dog training and socialization can end. The answer is, unfortunately, no. Set up a good training foundation for your puppy, but reinforcement and consistency are needed for the rest of his life. Luckily, as your Siberian grows and becomes more secure, if you continue fair and consistent training, he will be a cooperative and easy dog to have in your home.

PART II

ADULTHOOD

CHAPTER 5

FINDING YOUR SIBERIAN HUSKY ADULT

Puppyhood can seem a bit daunting. Bringing a puppy of any breed into one's home demands an enormous commitment of time and energy, and the particular nature of Siberians adds even more challenges. While many people find that the rewards of puppyhood far outweigh the pain, you may prefer to avoid some of those challenges and consider adding an adult Siberian to your family.

Re-homing adult dogs of certain breeds can be a somewhat difficult undertaking due to a breed's temperament and the individual dog's prior relationship with people. For example, dogs who develop great loyalty to a single person or to a family may find it difficult to transfer that loyalty to a new owner. Or, dogs who are protective of their territory may be confused when they find themselves in a new territory.

Siberian Huskies, due to their nature as pack and team animals, their friendliness toward all people, and their amazing adaptability, make excellent candidates for re-homing. Of course, Siberians feel deep affection for their owners and may be confused when leaving one home for another. However, an adoptive owner will find that, if she treats a Siberian well, feeds him, and plays with him, he'll be content to call his new location home.

WHAT AGE?

If you are considering bringing an adult Siberian into your family, first consider how old a dog you want. Look at the various life stages and explore the advantages of each age.

Older Puppies

If you're looking to avoid most of the major challenges of puppyhood, consider looking for an older puppy, one from 6 to 18 months of age. At that age, a puppy should come to you already spayed or neutered, and should have been exposed to the rudiments of training. An older puppy may still be accepting of other animals in your household, and he hasn't been alive long enough to pick up too many bad habits. Probably the biggest benefit of adopting an older puppy is that some of the most challenging aspects of puppyhood are behind him, but he is still young enough so that you'll have a long time together with your new companion.

Some of the drawbacks are that he'll still have enough energy to play like a puppy (this could be good or bad, depending on what you're

Sometimes older puppies are available for adoption, which allows you to avoid the major challenges of puppyhood.

looking for) and he'll still require training. In fact, the biggest challenge is that you may be getting the puppy just as he approaches his most difficult development stage, when he may challenge you and could be prone to fear.

The most successful adopter of an older puppy may well be someone who currently owns or has owned Siberians in the past, or at least someone who has experience in training dogs.

Young Adults

If you want to avoid the perils of puppyhood completely, you might be interested in a young adult Siberian, one between 18 months and 5 years of age. These dogs are still quite young and will be part of your family for a number of years. While they are still active dogs, you'll

be able to avoid some of the exuberance and behavioral challenges of puppyhood. At this age, his size and personality tendencies will be known. Before you bring your young adult home, you can find out if he is trustworthy in the house and yard, and if he gets along with other animals and children.

Want to Know More?

Siberian Huskies have an average lifespan of approximately 12 to 13 years. If you're considering adding a veteran to your family—dogs 9 years and older—you'll find more in-depth information on these dogs in Chapter 12: Finding Your Siberian Husky Senior.

Middle-Aged

Siberian Huskies may act like puppies for many years after puppyhood is over. So, if you are looking for a more mature, reserved adult, you'll most likely want a middle-aged Siberian, one between 5 and 9 years of age. The mature Siberian is usually reserved in his demeanor, and calmer and quieter than a puppy. If he has come from a good home atmosphere, he should easily adapt to yours. But, even if he has come from a less than ideal environment, a mature Siberian is still able to flourish in a new home.

The main drawbacks for adopting a middle-aged adult Siberian are that you might have to remediate some poor behaviors, he may not be as trustworthy in the house and yard, and most importantly, he may not be trustworthy with other animals and children.

ADULT ADOPTION IDEAS

If the idea of adding an adult Siberian to your family is appealing, you may wonder how to find them and why are they are available for adoption. With a bit of time and some creativity, you should be able to locate some adult Siberians available for placement. These dogs could come from a variety of situations.

Why Are Dogs Given Up?

Unfortunately, probably the most common reason for the availability of older puppies/young adult Siberian Huskies is the owner's inability to live with the dog. One of the most difficult times in a puppy's life (especially a male Siberian Husky) is between 6 and 14 months. It is during this time that a Siberian is reaching his full height; he has a dog's body with a puppy's brain. He's at the stage where he's testing his owner. This is also a time when a Siberian Husky is not as attractive as that adorable, furry puppy. He may appear gawky and gangly. He may be blowing his coat for the first time, and resemble a scrawny coyote. During this age, that darling Siberian isn't what his owner expected. Owners who were not carefully screened and prepared for this potentially difficult time may question their decision to get a Siberian Husky. While a good breeder can usually help an owner survive this time, occasionally these dogs will be looking for new homes.

Life changes can also put a Siberian in the sad place of needing a new home. He may be the unsuspecting victim of divorce.

Siberians are sometimes given up due to an owner's life changes.

If both parties of a divorce are forced to sell their home and move, it is often impossible for either of them to keep the dog. Military service people who are transferred are also occasionally unable to bring their dogs to a new posting. Changes in the economy may lead to abandoned dogs. And the seizure of puppy mill dogs or cases of mistreatment can a cause an influx of available dogs.

Siberians purchased from an ethical breeder who stands behind her dogs will be returned to the breeder. Otherwise, these dogs are surrendered to shelters and often wind up in breed rescues.

Shelters

One of the best reasons to adopt from a shelter is that you are most likely saving a dog's life. Although a great many local shelters try hard not to euthanize the animals surrendered to them, not every facility has the ability to keep every abandoned pet. Adopting from a shelter is one very positive way to make sure that at least that one dog is not destroyed. After all, a shelter dog deserves a "forever home" as much as any other dog.

Shelter dogs usually come at a nominal cost, which includes spaying/neutering, vaccinations, and microchipping. Depending on your area, this fee can be as high as a few hundred dollars.

Many shelters have Internet sites that are periodically updated with listings of all dogs available for placement—and you can even

Many shelters have Internet sites that are periodically updated with listings of all dogs available for placement.

By the Numbers

6 to 14 months: A dog's "teenage" time, between 6 and 14 months, is the age when many Siberian Huskies find their way to shelters and rescues.

see pictures. If you are looking for a Siberian Husky, it is a good idea periodically to check all of the shelter Internet sites in your area.

There are a couple of things to keep in mind when considering a shelter dog. Although shelter staff try their best to identify the breed of dogs up for adoption, they may not be well schooled in recognizing breed traits. Inadvertent errors can occur, such as calling any dog with erect ears and a slightly curled tail a "Husky." While these mixed-breed dogs make great pets, you may not be getting what you bargained for. A Siberian Husky–Great Dane cross may resemble Sgt. Preston's Yukon King when young, but when fully grown may look more like Marmaduke. Go see the dog in person before you make any decisions.

An additional consideration is that, frequently, the shelter may not know a particular dog's background. Although sometimes people relinquishing their dogs do provide background on the dog's past, it's more likely that the shelter won't have back stories on most of their dogs. Certainly, a dog's past shouldn't be held against him. However, knowing if the dog was previously mistreated, taunted by a child, or was an avid cat killer may affect your decision to bring that dog into a home with children or cats.

If you take care to properly introduce all family members to any adult dog you wish to bring into your household, you should avoid potential problems. And, if you find the shelter dog who completes your family, be proud that you have saved the life of a deserving dog!

Siberian Rescue

It may be difficult to find purebred dogs in local shelters. If your area has a significant group of purebred rescue organizations, most of the purebred dogs who are surrendered, even at local shelters, will find their way into their local breed rescue. Purebred dog fanciers make significant commitments of time, money, and emotions to help every adoptable dog of their particular breed find a "forever" home. These breed rescue groups usually have local, experienced owners who provide foster homes for the rescued animals. These foster parents house dogs in family or kennel settings, and have a good opportunity to assess the dog's adoptability. By fostering a dog, Siberian rescue groups can get an idea of a dog's response to different situations, such as interacting with children and other animals, loud noises, reactions to men or women, and a number of other things. The knowledge gained by fostering helps place the rescued dog in a suitable home.

Training Tidbit

Any older puppy or adult Siberian joining your family should be carefully watched for house and yard manners. Even though you are bringing an older dog into your house, training (and even re-training) will be required.

Rescue organizations may know the histories of their dogs, because often owners surrender pregnant females or dogs directly to these groups. There may be a higher percentage of successful placements from rescue groups due to their breed knowledge and access to the dogs' histories, as well as because of their assessment of the dogs.

Breed rescue organizations do not euthanize any adoptable dogs, and will even arrange for necessary surgeries or treatments to make the dogs healthy for adoption. For the most part, breed rescue organizations are nonprofit volunteer groups of committed dog lovers. For information about Siberian Husky rescue organizations, contact the American Kennel Club (www.akc.org), the Siberian Husky Club of America, Inc. (www.shca.org), and any Siberian Husky clubs in your area.

Breeder Placement

Reputable breeders are the last good source for adoptable adolescents and adults. Occasionally, experienced Siberian Husky breeders have a dog they have kept who, for some reason, did not achieve his potential, but has no flaws that would preclude him from being a wonderful pet. Breeders occasionally have a retired show dog who needs a good family to spoil him. Last, breeders may have dogs to re-home who were returned from their original owners because, for one reason or another, the puppy did not work out.

These dogs, unlike shelter dogs, are well

When introducing an adult into your home, monitor his interactions with other pets.

cared for by their breeder-owners, loved, and in no danger of being euthanized. A reputable breeder provides a home for her dogs as long as necessary, and she wants the very best placement for each of her dogs. And, although it might be difficult to let an old friend go to a new home, a responsible breeder sees a "retirement" home as the very best way to thank a dog for his hard work in the show ring or for producing puppies. Watching a retired show dog move into a home with his own family, children to play with, and an honored place on the couch, brings a tear to a breeder's eye and a smile to her face.

The benefit of getting an adult dog from a breeder is that the breeder knows the dog's entire history: family, temperament, health, idiosyncrasies. The breeder knows how the dog relates to children, and if he chases cats or other small animals. Plus, the breeder will have the dog's registration slip, and the dog could be signed over to you. This means that he could be easily shown in companion events (obedience, rally, agility) or handled in junior showmanship. It is amazing to see how retired show dogs thrive in a different type of competition with their new families.

A list of reputable Siberian Husky breeders

Multi-Dog Tip

If there are other animals in the house (especially cats and small dogs), make sure that any adult Siberian joining your family has a good history with small animals.

Just as it is important to monitor any introduction between a new puppy and existing dogs, it is equally important to do so when introducing an older Siberian to the other animals in your home.

by state is available through the Siberian Husky Club of America, Inc. Or, you may contact your local Siberian Husky club for recommendations.

Giving a home to an older dog is the perfect solution for many families. Siberian Huskies are a great breed for this plan, as they will bond easily with their new family and adapt to their new world quickly. Or, if the Siberian Husky has his way, he will train his new family to do his bidding in record time!

CHAPTER 6

SIBERIAN HUSKY GROOMING NEEDS

Your Siberian Husky requires grooming throughout his life. He will need bathing, brushing, dental care, ear care, and nail trimming on an ongoing basis, as well as significant grooming during the shedding season. Like all aspects of dog ownership, setting and keeping to a consistent schedule will make grooming activities easier both for you and your Siberian.

INTRODUCING AN ADULT TO GROOMING

If your Siberian joined your family as a puppy, and you have been consistent about grooming since he was a couple of months old, you should already have an established grooming regimen. As your puppy ages, the process does not really change, although it may become a bit more extensive—especially during shedding times. If, however, your Siberian came to you as an adult, he may not be used to the grooming process, and you might be in for some challenging sessions.

When introducing an adult dog to grooming, take small steps, as you would with a puppy. Let the adult Siberian get used to the tools slowly. Keep grooming sessions short and fun, and don't forget the treats. Be very aware of the dog's reaction to having his nails trimmed, or hearing a forced-air blower or nail grinder. If his reactions are strongly negative, continue with the sessions, but make them more frequent and shorter. Only by building his confidence will he begin to relax and accept the grooming that is necessary to keep him happy, healthy, and clean.

BENEFITS OF GROOMING

Although the purpose is to maintain the appearance of your dog, one of the most important side benefits of routine, periodic grooming is to get your hands on your dog. It is through this direct physical contact that you will be able to feel your dog's overall condition: Is he in good weight? Does he have good muscle tone? You will also be able to check for any abnormalities: Do you feel any growths or bumps? Are their signs of external parasites? You will be able to note any injuries: Does he seem to have any sensitive areas? Are there any scabs? Due to his somewhat stoic nature and well-furred appearance, a Siberian Husky may hide many problems and maladies. Therefore, each and every grooming session should include a complete body "massage," where you run your hands over the dog's entire

Grooming does more than keep your Siberian looking good—it's a chance to check him for injuries or other problems.

body, checking for any areas of concern.

Another benefit of routine grooming is keeping control over the amount of fur in your living space. Although Siberians tend to shed once or twice a year, depending on hormones, relative air temperature, and other factors, the shedding period can last from days to weeks. Even if you are lucky enough to have a dog who sheds his coat quickly, some errant fur will always dislodge at seemingly random times. You will find the best way to minimize the apparently never-ending shedding season is consistent, periodic grooming.

The recommended frequency for maintenance grooming varies from dog to dog, and also with coat condition. During significant shedding times, you may wish to groom your dog every couple of days, or even daily. However, there may be times

when monthly or bi-weekly grooming is sufficient. Your dog will help you decide on the frequency. Initially, especially if you are trying to train a dog to accept grooming, you may want to establish a weekly grooming schedule.

WHERE TO START?

What comes first, bathing or brushing? The answer is that it depends on the condition of the coat. You *never* bathe without brushing, but you might well brush without bathing. You can bathe before brushing, but you *always* brush after bathing. If you are now completely confused, here are some common situations:

- In many instances, especially if your dog is not particularly dirty, you might choose not to bathe him, but you will brush and comb him.
- When your Siberian is at the stage where

his coat is "tufting" (the fur is loose and you can easily pull out tufts with your bare hand), bathing and drying will be easier if you brush out as much of the loose coat as possible beforehand.

- Brushing is required after all baths.

You may wish to perform some of the other grooming tasks, such as brushing teeth, cleaning ears, and trimming nails, prior to bathing your dog.

BATHING

Successful bathing requires a way to restrain your Siberian, a source of water (preferably warm water—especially in cold climates and during cold weather), shampoo, a dog, and a bather (that's you!).

There are a couple of significant considerations regarding bathing, some directly relating to you (the bather) and others to the dog (the bathee).

Where to Bathe

First, you'll need to decide where to bathe your dog. You can bathe a Siberian Husky in a variety of places, indoors and out: your shower or bathtub, a large utility sink, a specially made dog bath, an outdoor bench or table, or a self-service commercial dog washing facility. The choice of bathing location should include your comfort as the dog washer.

Bathtub

If your knees can tolerate it, using a bathtub with a fiberglass or tempered enclosure or curtain works fine. You'll need a place to clip your dog's collar in order to free your hands while still keeping the dog in the bath. A simple eye screw from your local hardware store will work. Make sure to get a sturdy one and firmly secure it to a wall stud. During and after a bath, Siberians shake a great deal, so

you'll want to make sure they cannot flood your bathroom during a bath, or your house after the bath.

Shower

An enclosed shower provides similar advantages to a bathtub. However, you, the bather, will have to be inside the shower enclosure with your Siberian, and you will get as wet as the dog.

Utility Sink

A large utility sink is similar to a bathtub, but usually allows you to stand, not kneel, throughout the bathing process. You will need a method of restraining your dog if you use a large sink. Usually, there's no sink enclosure or shower curtain, so your utility room may get quite wet.

Free-Standing Bath

With a free-standing dog bath or an outdoor bench/table, you will need access to water

Gray Water Laws

Most relatively clean household waste water is considered "gray water." It gets its name from its cloudy appearance and is usually relatively free of hazardous components. However, some communities do not allow gray water to be freely added to the aquifer from ground absorption. Rather, they have laws requiring gray water be disposed of through the sewer system. You should research if your area has any "gray water" laws if you are considering a bath location, such as outside on the driveway, without drainage into a sewer system.

Cold Tail

Cold tail is a phenomenon most often associated with sporting breeds, but it is also seen occasionally in Siberian Huskies. When a dog's tail gets chilled, instead of being normally active, it is carried limply down, and can often be painful. One way to avoid cold tail is to bathe the dog in warm water and keep the wet tail from getting chilled.

(preferably warm water) through a hose. The dog bath usually comes with some method of restraining the dog, but if you use a bench or table you'll have to add your own.

The benefits of an outdoor facility are obvious: your house will not get doused in water, and you will not have to kneel to bathe your dog. However, there is usually no easy way to drain the bathwater to the sewer.

Self-Service Dog Wash

Finally, you may choose to use a commercial self-service dog wash. Such facilities are usually found in pet supply stores or in conjunction with full-service grooming shops. The dog wash usually places the dog at waist height, has a method of restraining him, provides warm water, and often provides supplies, such as shampoo, towels, and even forced air. The drawbacks are that there will be a fee charged,

Once your Siberian is used to his grooming routine, he may end up loving the attention!

and you may get drenched by your Siberian in public.

Supplies

To bathe your dog, you will need a few supplies. The first is a good dog shampoo. Dogs have a skin pH that is different from humans, so it is important to use a good-quality dog shampoo. A number of pet grooming products by various manufacturers and suppliers are available at pet supply stores, dog shows, or through catalogs and Internet shopping. Ask your breeder or other Siberian Husky fanciers for recommendations. You will probably want to find two shampoos, one exclusively for your dog's "whites" (his legs, belly, chest—wherever he has white fur), and a good conditioning shampoo for the overall coat.

The only other supplies you'll need are a waterproof tether, dry towels, and possibly a forced-air blower to help dry your dog's coat after the bath, as well as his comb, brush, and any post-bath conditioner and coat protector you wish to use.

How to Bathe Your Siberian

- As previously mentioned, it may be advisable to do some initial brushing (specifically to remove loose coat) prior to the bath.
- Make sure to remove all tags and collars from your dog, with the exception of a waterproof tether.
- You may wish to wear a water-resistant smock or apron, or clothes you do not mind getting wet and possibly covered in shampoo.
- Tether your dog to the bathing area.
- Regulate the temperature of the water. Use warm water to avoid what is commonly referred to as "cold tail."

- Wet the dog all over with a fine spray of water. This is a Siberian Husky, and his coat is somewhat water resistant, so you will probably be unable to get him truly wet with water alone. It will take your hands working the shampoo and water deep into the coat to create a lather that will get your dog wet down to his skin.
- If your dog's "whites" are particularly dirty, apply the whitening shampoo to the white areas, adding water as needed to wet the coat down to the skin and create a lather. If your shampoo has a whitening agent (such as bluing), you may find it beneficial to leave

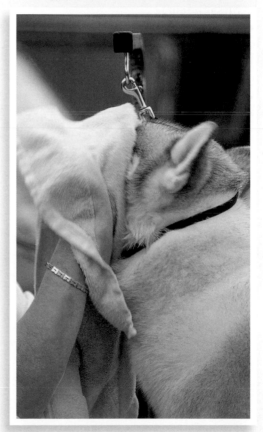

Use several towels to towel dry your dog's entire coat.

Grooming Tables

A grooming table is a rectangular table with foldable legs that measures approximately 2 feet (61 cm) wide, 3 to 4 feet (91 to 122 cm) long, and 2.5 to 3 feet (76 to 91 cm) high. The top is usually waterproof and non-slip. A metal bar—the grooming arm—attaches to the table and rises vertically with a crook or angle at the top to attach your dog's leash or tether. Grooming tables are available at pet supply stores, dog shows, catalogs, and Internet dog supply retailers.

the lather on his white fur for a few minutes. Rinse the white fur thoroughly.

- Apply the conditioning shampoo to the dog's entire body, adding water as needed. Work the shampoo into a lather over all parts of the dog. You may find that a grooming glove that fits over your hand and has small, rubber nubbins in the palm helps lather the dog and remove loose hair. Follow the shampoo instructions—it may direct you to leave the shampoo on the dog's coat for a certain length of time.

- With warm water, completely rinse the shampoo off the dog's entire body. You'll know when all of the shampoo has been rinsed away when the rinse water running off the dog is clear. Use your hands to make sure all shampoo is thoroughly rinsed. Be very careful to rinse all shampoo from your dog's coat. Suds and shampoo left in a coat can cause skin irritation and should be avoided.

- If your dog has not already done so, ask him to shake to remove some of the excess water in his coat. A good way to encourage shaking is to blow air gently into his ear.

- After a few good shakes from nose to tail, use several towels, one at a time, to towel dry the dog's entire coat. At this point, his coat is very roughly dried, but still fairly wet.

- If you do not have a forced-air blower:
  - Continue trying to dry the coat using a combination of brushing and towel drying.
  - Keep your Siberian in a warm place, such as in your house or outside in the warm summer sunshine.
  - Try to have him dry before bedtime.
  - *Please note: Do not ever use a heated hair dryer to dry your Siberian's coat. Burning of the coat and skin irritation can occur too easily with a heated dryer.*

- If you do have a forced-air blower:
  - Find a place to use the blower. If your Siberian is shedding, the use of a forced-air blower will cause the drying area to be covered in fur, so pick a place where this won't be a problem.
  - To use a forced-air blower effectively, you will need the use of both of your hands. Therefore, you will need a way to tether your dog. This can be done with the help of another person or by having a secure place to tie his tether. Most dog owners who use forced-air blowers use them in conjunction with a grooming table and a grooming arm.
  - With a sturdy grooming table and your Siberian tethered to the arm, use a brush or comb to bring the fur off the body while using the blower nozzle to concentrate the force of the air to dry the coat.
  - This process may take as long as two hours, depending on the power of the dryer, the thickness of the dog's coat, and the humidity of the air.
  - An additional benefit of a forced-

air blower is that it will help loosen and remove shedding fur from your Siberian's coat—that same fur that will turn your yard snowstorm white, and will soon line every bird's nest for miles around.

Once the dog's coat is nearly dry, has been thoroughly brushed, and all of the loose coat has been removed, you may wish to apply a good canine coat conditioner to keep your Siberian's coat as healthy as possible.

A bit more drying of the conditioner-dampened coat, and the bathing process is nearly done.

You may want to apply a canine sunscreen to protect the coat further. Allow that to dry, and your Siberian is now ready to begin the process of dirtying his newly cleaned coat!

BRUSHING

"Brushing" your Siberian is actually a catch-all term for brushing, combing, and raking—in short, keeping the coat healthy, open, and free of loose fur. This is a never-ending process for a Siberian Husky owner. Even if you will not be bathing your Siberian on a weekly basis, you should count on brushing him at least weekly. Brushing may be done in concert with bathing, but it's not required.

Supplies

You'll probably want to invest in three essential grooming tools: a combination brush with two lengths of natural and nylon bristles, a steel coat rake with at least 1-inch (3-cm) long tines (with or without non-stick coating), and a standard steel comb with two different spacings between the tines.

Have a spray bottle filled with water on hand if the coat is dry. To minimize coat damage, it is best not to use a metal grooming tool on a dry coat. If you want to use metal tools and the coat is dry, spritz the coat with water prior first.

You may also be interested in a flexible rubber curry brush or a grooming glove with rubber nubbins, which can be very helpful during the shedding season.

Tools to Avoid

It's best to avoid using slicker and pin brushes on your Siberian's coat. Slicker brushes are made of very fine angled wire pins and are beneficial for long coats. The pins in the pin brush are a bit thicker and are not angled, and are very useful for curly or long coats. The medium length, double coat of the Siberian is not appropriate for these tools. The tips of the wires can be very sharp and may even scratch a dog's skin if not used carefully.

Coat stripping and fur removal tools that you find advertised on television, in grocery stores, and in pet supply stores are also not advisable

Multi-Dog Tip

Want an easy way to get your Siberian to want to be groomed? Have him watch while another dog gets your attention (and some treats) during grooming. Pretty soon, they will be pushing each other out of the way to be first into the bathtub!

for a Siberian's coat. These tools actually cut the fur, which is not correct for a Siberian. Also, as these tools include sharp blades and cutting surfaces, they can be dangerous.

How to Brush Your Siberian

With tools in hand (including a spray bottle if the dog's coat is not at least a bit damp), follow this process for brushing and combing.

There are two levels of brushing: when your Siberian is "blowing" his coat and when he is not.

If your Siberian is blowing his coat or shedding:

- Use the rubber curry or grooming glove to loosen and remove the obvious tufts of coat.

You'll need to line comb your Siberian when he's shedding.

Run the rubber curry over the coat gently but firmly, allowing the rubber "tines" to bring out the loose and tufting hair.

- With the rake, begin the technique known as *line combing*. This is a long process, so be forewarned. This method requires that you comb (or, in this case, rake) one small section of coat at a time.

    - Make sure you begin with a damp coat and start near the dog's head.
    - Hold the coat you are not raking with your non-dominant hand, and rake the exposed coat completely to the skin, removing any loose coat. You usually rake in the direction the fur grows. However, if you have a shedding coat that is particularly stubborn, try raking a very small portion of the coat in the opposite direction of growth, or even at 90 degrees to the growth direction.
    - When the rake will go through that section of coat easily, move your hand to expose another section of coat and repeat.
    - Follow this process until you have raked through the entire coat.

If your Siberian is not shedding (or he's shedding and you've already line raked):

- Spritz the coat with water as needed.
- Follow the exact same line-combing process outlined above, but use the wide tines of a steel comb to move through the entire coat.
- Once you have line combed using the widely spaced tines, repeat the process with the narrowly spaced tines.
- When you have completed the line combing with the narrow-tined side of the steel comb, use the two-level, two-bristle brush for a final finish of the coat.
- Even if you have not bathed the dog, you may wish to add a canine coat conditioner, as well as a canine sunscreen to help protect

the coat from the sun. (As odd as it seems, some Siberian Huskies like to sunbathe, and these dogs can be in danger of damaging their coat from too much sun.)

EAR CARE

Unlike drop-eared dogs, the erect ears of the Siberian Husky are not usually prone to ear infections. However, routine grooming and external maintenance should include ear examination and care. Checking your dog's ears whenever you groom him is a good habit to adopt. Occasionally, an ear may get a yeast or bacterial infection, a foreign object like a seed pod or other plant material may get implanted, or the ear may become infested with parasites.

Supplies

For basic ear care, have available gauze or a thin, soft cloth, and possibly some ear cleaner. Canine ear-cleaning products are formulated with the specific pH of the canine ear, so it is important to use products designed for dogs. Ear cleaners are available from your veterinarian or from pet supply vendors.

Unlike drop-eared dogs, the erect ears of the Siberian Husky are not usually prone to ear infections.

How to Care for Your Siberian's Ears

The basic ear care process begins with your examination of your dog's ears:

- First, smell the inside of the ear. If there is a strong or pungent odor in one or both of your dog's ears, there could be a problem.
- Next, feel the inside of the ears with your finger. If one or both of the ears is particularly hot, this could also indicate a problem.
- Look inside the dog's ears. If one or both of the ears appears inflamed, this could indicate a problem.
- If you notice any wax in the ears, wrap a piece of gauze or a soft cloth around your finger and try to dislodge the wax.
- Another option is to use an ear cleaner to soften and dislodge any wax. If using a liquid ear cleaner, gently massage the ear before letting the dog shake his head. Then, wrap a soft cloth around your finger and clean out the interior of the ear. Remember that, unlike the human ear, the canine ear canal takes a significant bend, so you are in little or no danger of damaging your dog's ear drum by putting your finger in his ear.

After cleaning your dog's ears, be prepared for him to shake his head for some time—this is completely normal. However, if the head shaking does not stop, or if he shakes his head or scratches his ear when you haven't cleaned them, this could indicate an ear problem. If you observe any signs of possible ear problems, make an appointment for your dog to see his veterinarian.

EYE CARE

Siberian Huskies, although prone to some hereditary eye diseases, rarely contract the eye problems seen in other breeds. These disorders include distichiasis (a condition in which eyelashes grow inward toward the eye), ectropion (a condition in which the eyelid droops out), entropion (a condition in which the eyelid folds in), and eversion (a condition in which the third eyelid appears to be fold over on itself). Although these rarely occur in the Siberian Husky, it is possible for them to occur in any breed. If left untreated, these disorders could cause irritation that could lead to infection or damage to the eye. If you note any of these eye abnormalities in your Siberian, please seek advice from your veterinarian.

Although Siberians tend to have relatively healthy eyes, make a visual eye check part of his normal grooming regimen. It is always a good idea to check your dog's eyes for redness, haziness, discoloration, excessive tearing, or any other abnormal occurrence. Should you discover any of these abnormalities, consult your veterinarian.

Tear Stains

It is not uncommon, especially in dogs with light-colored hair around their eyes, to see reddish brown tear stains near the inside corners of the eyes. This is frequently also seen in small dogs and cats. The hair beneath the eye acts as a sponge or wick and pulls tears from the eye. The discoloration is due to the presence of bacteria in the warm, damp fur. In some breeds, this discoloration can indicate a blockage of the tear ducts, which can be addressed by surgery. With Siberians, this discoloration is more often an indicator of environmental or food allergies.

Products are available to help reduce the discoloration, but they often further inflame

Dogs with light-colored hair around their eyes may develop reddish brown tear stains near the inside corners of the eye.

Want to Know More?

To learn more about allergies that may possibly cause tear staining, go to Chapter 8: Siberian Husky Health and Wellness.

the eye. If you encounter tear stains on your Siberian, visit your veterinarian so he can help you eliminate some of the sources of the tearing. If the tearing appears to be caused by allergies or a pH imbalance, refer to the section on allergies in Chapter 8.

NAIL TRIMMING

Dogs rarely enjoy nail trimming (or dental care, which we'll discuss later in this chapter). Your Siberian might find it intrusive and maybe even painful. However, nail care is important to your dog's overall well-being. So, please make a serious effort not to ignore it just because it may be difficult.

Unfortunately, it is a fallacy that all dogs' nails are ground down during normal play and running. Nails will need to be trimmed, and it's important for your Siberian's health to do so. Long, untended nails are easier to get caught on things in the yard, which could cause them to tear. This usually produces a lot of blood and some pain for your dog. Additionally, nails allowed to grow too long may cause your dog's feet to flatten and his gait to become stilted and difficult. And a dog with long nails tends to scratch things and people much more easily—you do not want gouges in your hardwood floor, scratches on your leather chair, or nail marks on your arm. The only way to assure these things do not happen is to perform routine nail maintenance.

Supplies

You will need some tools to help you keep your Siberian's nails short. Most people use nail trimmers or nail grinders. Trimmers are less expensive and are silent, but they make it easier to cut through the nail's "quick" (the blood vessel that runs down the middle of the nail), which causes pain and bleeding. There are two basic styles of nail trimmers: the scissors type and the guillotine type. Either one is effective as long as the cutting blade(s) are sharp, so replace the blade or trimmer periodically. Because cutting may leave sharp edges on the nail, keep a metal nail file on hand to file down rough edges after trimming.

A grinder is an electronic or battery-operated rotating stone or sandpaper-like disk that grinds down the nails. It is noisy and causes some vibration, which dogs often dislike. However, grinders are less likely to cut to the quick.

Regardless of your tool of choice, you will also want to have styptic powder or a silver nitrate pencil on hand in case you cut the quick and cause bleeding.

Dew Claws

Siberian Huskies are usually not born with dew claws (thumbs) on their rear paws. If they

Most people use nail trimmers to keep their dog's nails short.

When attempting to get your dog to accept, and even enjoy, grooming, initially keep the sessions short. It may take you several weeks to get through a routine that will eventually only take a couple of hours.

are born with rear dew claws, it's likely their breeder will have removed them in the first few days of life. Therefore, you will usually only have four rear nails to trim on each foot. You should check for the rear dew claws just to verify that they have been removed. If they exist, you will find them on the back of the foot, between the toes and the hock joint. If your Siberian has rear dew claws, these will also require trimming.

Siberians are usually born with dew claws on their front legs. Many breeders will also have these removed after birth as they can easily become caught on things (like sledding lines) and torn. To check for front dew claws on your dog, run your hand up the back side of each front leg from paw to elbow. If your dog has front dew claws, do not forget them in your nail-trimming regimen. If left to grow too long, front dew claws can actually grow into the leg.

Nail Color

A Siberian's nails can be black or light colored. The color is based on the dog's pigmentation, and one paw can have both dark- and light-colored nails. White or light-colored nails are easier to trim for two reasons. First, white nails tend to be softer than black nails. Second, with light-colored nails, it's easier to avoid "quicking," or cutting through to the quick of the nail because you can see it. To avoid the bleeding and pain this causes, cut the nail about 1/16 to 1/8 inch (1.5 to 3 mm) from the quick.

With dark-colored nails, proceed carefully to avoid cutting the quick. Rather than cut off one large piece, take off several thin slices. If the same foot also has light-colored nails, you can use their length to judge how much to cut from the dark nails. As you work, check the end of the nail after each cut. When you see a gray and/or pinkish oval begin to appear where the nail was cut, you are approaching the quick and should stop cutting. (If you are using a grinder, these same guidelines apply.)

How to Trim Your Siberian's Nails

- You can trim/grind nails anywhere. A grooming table is a fine place to work on your dog's nails, but if you are more comfortable on the floor, that is fine, too. Avoid any place where possible blood stains would be difficult to remove.
- Inspect the length of the nails. You will probably find that the rear nails are shorter than the nails on the forelegs. If the nails are a good length and don't need trimming, just file off any rough edges.
- If the nails need trimming, hold the scissors-type trimmer at a right angle to the nail. Make sure it is sharp, then quickly position the trimmer and cut the nail.
- If you are using a guillotine-type trimmer, hold the trimmer with the blade side toward you and away from the dog. Quickly position the trimmer and cut with a smooth fast action. If you forget and use the guillotine with the blade toward the dog, you are in danger of taking too much off the nail and cutting into the quick.
- If any sharp edges remain, use a file or grinder to smooth them.

- Give both you and your dog a treat for a job well done!

If Your Siberian is New to Nail Trimming

If your Siberian has been with you since his puppyhood, and you have routinely trimmed his nails as part of his grooming regimen, he should be tolerant of this process. If, however, your Siberian came to you as an adult and is not used to regular grooming, nail trimming may be quite a struggle. If this is the case, enlist the help of a friend. Have lots of treats available! Your friend can help restrain your Siberian and keep him still (even bribe him with treats) while you trim his nails. You may find that your untrained dog will only tolerate one paw being trimmed at a time, or even one nail. That's okay. Wait until he is not fighting you, praise him for being good (even if you only trimmed one nail), reward him, and stop the trimming session.

DENTAL CARE

The last of your grooming activities is dental care. Dogs are prone to many of the same types of dental disease as people, including plaque and tartar buildup, gingivitis, periodontal disease, abscesses, and broken teeth, to name a few. These problems can lead to tooth loss and even the loss of skeletal bone. Although dental care does not have as much potential for inadvertent pain that can occur with nail trimming, dogs do not usually like having their teeth brushed. However, regular tooth brushing and dental care can reduce or eliminate the chance of canine dental problems, so you've got to teach your Siberian to accept it.

Supplies

You'll need canine toothpaste, a soft-bristled toothbrush (either specially designed for dogs, or one made for babies or children), and gauze. Find a canine toothpaste your Siberian thinks is tasty; they come in a variety of flavors: beef, poultry, mint, etc. It is a good idea to buy a small amount of each flavor and see which one your Siberian seems to prefer.

How to Brush Your Siberian's Teeth

If your Siberian Husky has not been part of your family since he was a puppy and has not experienced the process of tooth brushing, introduce him gradually to the activity. Take a few weeks to go through this entire process of desensitizing him.

- With his favorite flavor toothpaste, use your finger to put some on a couple of his teeth. He should enjoy this activity. Praise and reward him for being a good dog.
- At the next session, wrap your index finger with gauze, put some of his favorite toothpaste on the gauze, and stroke the toothpaste-covered gauze over one or two of the teeth near the front of his mouth. Again,

Use canine toothpaste and a soft-bristled toothbrush or finger brush.

praise and reward him.

- Continue using the toothpaste on the gauze over a few days until you have been able to stroke each of his teeth, including the molars.

- In the next few sessions, introduce the soft-bristle toothbrush. Using your finger, put a small amount of toothpaste in your Siberian's mouth. At the same time, touch the toothbrush to one of his teeth, and remove it quickly. Praise and reward him.

- Next, use the toothbrush to introduce a small amount of his favorite toothpaste into his mouth, and follow with praise and reward.

- As this process continues, keep the toothbrush in his mouth for a longer period of time, and touch many teeth, eventually rubbing them gently with the brush.

- By the end of this time, your Siberian should be used to having you brush his teeth. Now make it a part of his regular grooming.

Veterinarians encourage you to brush your dog's teeth every day, but not everyone will find this practical. However, the more frequently you brush, the healthier your dog's mouth will be. Begin with a weekly or twice-weekly brushing and closely monitor the buildup of plaque and tartar, which will tell you if you need to brush more frequently.

Other Dental Care Options

In addition to brushing your Siberian's teeth, have your veterinarian periodically scale and clean your dog's teeth. This usually requires some form of anesthetic, so it should be chosen as an infrequent option, only when tartar buildup is great. You may also have some success in trying to scale his teeth yourself. Ask your veterinarian for some pointers before attempting this.

Other dental care options include supplemental gels and food/water additives. Also, some foods and treats are formulated to inhibit the formation of tooth tartar, like the ones Nylabone makes. It may help to encourage your dog to chew on treated rawhide or rubber bones to help clear the teeth of tartar. There is even a new vaccination designed to combat periodontal problems. It is U.S. Food and Drug Administration (FDA) approved for safety, but its efficacy has not yet been proven.

Of all of the grooming activities, good dental care is one that can significantly help with your dog's quality of life, so please do not ignore it or allow your Siberian to dissuade you from making this a part of his regular grooming regimen. Dogs are prone to a great many, often painful dental diseases. If your dog's breath smells bad or you see cracked or broken teeth, or anything questionable in your dog's mouth, seek help from your veterinarian.

PROFESSIONAL GROOMING

If all of this grooming seems a bit daunting, never fear, as professionals are available to help you with any or all aspects of your Siberian's care. Many veterinarians' offices, boarding kennels, and pet supply stores offer grooming. And most communities have dog groomers—and some will even come to your house!

Finding a good groomer will take some time and effort. To become a groomer, most individuals have attended a professional training program, and many are members of a professional organization. When looking for a groomer, ask about their training and affiliations. As is always the case, it is very beneficial to ask your breeder or local Siberian fanciers for recommendations. Visit the shops of possible candidates, checking for cleanliness and happy clients (both human and canine). Ask them about their experience with Siberians. Ask how they restrain dogs while grooming. Discuss products used, and find out if they will use shampoo/conditioner you provide. Don't forget to ask for references, and follow up with them.

One conversation to have with anyone who might be grooming your dog is to make sure they've never trimmed or shaved a Siberian—regardless of how hot it might be. The Siberian's coat insulates him from heat as well as cold, and

By the Numbers

- **1 to 2 hours:** The time it may take for you to dry a Siberian Husky's coat with a forced-air dryer.
- **Once a week:** The frequency Siberian Huskies should be groomed when not shedding.
- **1 year:** The length of time a nail clipper's cutting blade should last before being replaced
- **Never:** How often a Siberian Husky's coat should be trimmed

you need to know that your groomer will not do anything to affect that balance.

Once you have found a groomer you want to try, make an appointment and drop off your dog. Discuss what you want done, and provide the products you want used, if desired. If you are concerned about anything, ask if you can stay and watch the grooming session. If not, when you come back to pick up your dog, see if he is overtly friendly toward the groomer. Check out the grooming job. If all is well, you may have found someone to help you keep your Siberian in great condition!

CHAPTER 7

SIBERIAN HUSKY NUTRITIONAL NEEDS

The good health of your Siberian comes from a combination of many things, including genetics, training, exercise, external care, veterinary care, and good nutrition. Nutrition for the Siberian Husky is always an interesting topic, especially when you look at the breed's origins. The area in Siberia where the Chukchis and their dogs originated is a particularly desolate environment. There are no trees, few bushes, mountains, bitterly cold temperatures, high winds, and permafrost tundra. The Chukchis trapped, hunted, and fished in that harsh environment. Although their dogs were important to their survival, it is assumed that there was not much food to go around. Most likely, those early Siberian Huskies existed on a diet of primarily protein and fat from fish and the animals their people hunted. Siberians had to develop a metabolism that would allow them to succeed in this environment and with this available diet.

The metabolism of the Siberian Husky is very efficient. Relatively speaking, he does not need a lot of food to survive. Recent studies have shown that, when called upon to work, sled dogs seem to have a metabolic adaptation that makes them capable of great endurance.

Of course, additional fuel is required for the metabolic change from rest to activity. But, even at work, the Siberian Husky is very efficient at turning food into energy. This efficient Siberian Husky engine, which allows him to be both a lazy family pet and a great sled dog, requires proper nutrition.

Feeding your Siberian properly requires an understanding of the basic building blocks of canine nutrition, including how much of each nutrient is necessary for a balanced diet, and how much of that balanced diet to feed your dog.

WHAT SHOULD DOGS EAT?

The diet of wild canids, such as wolves, is almost completely comprised of protein and fat. However, wolves probably do ingest a small amount of carbohydrates by eating some fruits and berries. But these carbohydrates form a very small percentage of their total food intake. By comparison, most commercial grocery store dry dog food is about 20% or less protein and 10% or less fat. Premium brands of dry food are between 25% and 30% protein and 15% to 20% fat. These percentages are still a far cry from the diet of the dog's wild ancestors and of the Chukchi native dogs.

The metabolism of the Siberian Husky is very efficient, due to his origins as a sled dog.

For dogs in general, and Siberian Huskies specifically, incorrect quantity, quality, and composition of food may become apparent in a number of ways. Often, one of the most obvious signs is weight loss or gain. Other signs may include an unhealthy coat (dry brittle, changed color), lower energy level (which may be difficult to discern), and the appearance of staining around the mouth (often seen as a pH imbalance or food allergy). These signs, however, may take some time to appear. But the one sign that is immediately apparent is diarrhea. If your dog develops diarrhea, it may be a sign that his food—or the amount you're feeding—doesn't agree with him.

BUILDING BLOCKS OF NUTRITION

Just as with humans, dogs have recommended nutritional building blocks. To achieve optimum performance (at whatever he does), your Siberian's diet must include these essential components. The three most important food groups found in dog food are proteins, fats, and carbohydrates. These, in addition to vitamins, minerals, and water, all work together to keep your Siberian as healthy as possible.

Proteins

Your Siberian Husky needs proteins for growth and development and for his immune system and to give him energy. Proteins, and their major components—amino acids—may be the most important building block of canine nutrition.

Although there are some amino acids that dogs create naturally, quite a number must be added to a dog's diet through the proteins he eats. On the surface, this may seem straightforward and easy enough to achieve. However, proteins from different sources are not always equal. Every protein is calculated for its biological value. The highest biological value indicates a protein with the most easily used amino acids. Eggs top this list, followed by fish, poultry, and beef; much further down the list are rice, wheat, soybeans, bone meal, and corn. So, the percentage of protein in your dog's food is important, but so is the source of that protein.

And, if this isn't confusing enough, there is another factor to consider—the overall quality of the food leads to its digestibility. Some foods are more easily and completely

digestible. It is generally believed that higher-quality foods are probably about 75% digestible, whereas lesser-quality foods are perhaps 60% digestible.

In short, what you are looking for is a good-quality, highly digestible food with an acceptable percentage of protein from good sources. The question is, how much protein is needed? As a rule, assume that the amounts of protein in high-quality, commercial dog food (at every stage of a dog's life) provide what is generally accepted as the protein requirement for the average dog. In an adult dog, this is usually between 15% and 25%. However, experience has shown us that Siberian Huskies seem to thrive on a higher protein-value and protein-quality food.

Siberian Huskies tend to need higher levels of protein and fat than do other breeds of dogs. If he's fed a good-quality adult dog food, in order for a Siberian to ingest the amount of nutrients (among which are proteins) required to fuel his body efficiently, he may need to be fed too large a volume of food (and thus consume an excess of carbohydrates). If this is the case, the immediate result will be loose stools. And if the quality of his food is lower (both in the percentage and quality of protein), the situation will be even worse.

To avoid this, feed your Siberian a high-quality food that contains about 30% protein from a good, easily digestible and usable

protein source (such as chicken). Or, find a food that may have a slightly lower percentage of protein but is sourced from a protein with an even higher biological value, such as a fish-based food.

Carbohydrates

Unlike proteins, the role that carbohydrates play in the canine diet is widely debated. As you know, the dog's wild canid ancestors ate very few carbohydrates, and they survived or even thrived on these low-carb diets. The addition of carbohydrates to dog food occurred with the advent of commercial dry dog food. Dry dog food needs a starchy substance to form the pellet-like kibble. Plus it's a cheap filler and helps give the protein source a longer shelf-life. Most commercial dog foods contain a large percentage of carbohydrates, perhaps as much as 70%. Dogs are capable of turning

Siberian Huskies tend to need higher levels of protein and fat than do other breeds of dogs.

Fats and fatty acids supply energy to your Siberian.

nutrition. Many of the carbohydrates found in commercial dog food contain both fiber and non-fiber components. Differing types of fiber can lead to constipation as well as diarrhea. Most commercially available dry dog foods contain approximately 5% fiber.

Siberians seem to be one of the breeds that may not tolerate carbohydrates well. Watch for signs of weight gain or loss, unhealthy coat, coat staining, low energy level, and diarrhea. These may indicate that your dog is getting too large a volume of food and/or excessive carbohydrates in his diet.

It is not unusual for Siberians to develop allergies to some carbohydrate sources, most commonly corn and wheat, and even to plant-based proteins, such as soy. Pay close attention to obvious signs of allergies, and modify the food sources as needed.

both proteins and carbohydrates into energy, so many people see the carbohydrates found in dry food as an energy source. However, some breeds have difficulty metabolizing these large amounts of carbohydrates.

There are two types of carbohydrates: fiber and non-fiber. Non-fiber carbohydrates include the starchy part of cereal grains, such as corn, rice, and wheat. They can lead to obesity and should be avoided, especially if your Siberian has diabetes. When a dog ingests too much non-fiber carbohydrate, it may cause gas and diarrhea, as well as bloat (although bloat is fairly rare in Siberian Huskies).

Although fiber-based carbohydrates, such as whole grains and bran, are viewed more favorably in human nutrition, they are just as debatable in the canine world as their non-fiber counterparts. There appears to be no need for fiber carbohydrates in canine

Fats

There is no debate about the need for fat in your Siberian Husky's diet. Fats and fatty acids supply energy (by weight, about double what protein and carbohydrates supply), make food taste good, and aid in the delivery of fat-soluble vitamins. Inadequate amounts of fat in a dog's diet can lead to reproductive problems, poor skin and coat, and slow wound healing.

How much fat should be in your dog's diet? High-quality, commercial adult dog foods generally contain between 10% and 20% fat. As long as your Siberian is not obese, he might do better with a higher-fat food. If you wish to add a supplement of fatty acids to your Siberian's diet, try a source high in omega-3, such as fish oil.

Vitamins

In addition to proteins, carbohydrates, and fats, dogs need vitamins. Most commercial dog foods supply the appropriate quantities of effects, including muscle weakness. However, a dog would need to be fed massive doses of vitamin A for perhaps one or more years to reach a toxic level. Toxicities to vitamin D are even rarer, but could include calcium deposits within muscles (including the heart) and other tissues. Toxicities to vitamins E and K are not even known. Unless your dog has a sensitivity to these vitamins or ingests massive quantities of them, he is probably not in danger of over-supplementation.

vitamins, and higher-quality dog foods often add supplements to achieve optimum nutrition.

Vitamins are divided into two groups: water-soluble and fat-soluble. Water-soluble vitamins are excreted by the body, and fat-soluble are stored in the body. It's hard to reach toxic levels of water-soluble vitamins, as any excess is eliminated from the body in the urine. It is particularly important that your dog receives these vitamins daily. Water-soluble vitamin C is found in fruits and vegetables, meat, and dairy products. Other water-soluble vitamins include the B complex vitamins, such as niacin, folic acid, and biotin, which are found in meat and grains. If your Siberian does not ingest adequate amounts of these vitamins, he may become anemic, suffer appetite loss, lose nerve control, experience poor growth, develop coat and skin problems, and suffer from other problems.

Fat-soluble vitamins include vitamins A, D, E, and K. Because these vitamins are stored in fat cells, there is a danger of over-supplementing. Fat-soluble vitamins are available from meat, vegetables, oils, and dairy products. Without them, a dog could develop reproductive issues, hemorrhaging, and other significant problems. Because these vitamins are stored in fat, it is not necessary to feed them every day.

Vitamin A is one of the vitamins which, if over-supplemented, could have negative

Minerals

Like vitamins, minerals are both synthesized from and supplemented in commercial dog food. Among the necessary minerals are calcium, phosphorous, magnesium, potassium, sodium, chloride, iron, copper, manganese, zinc, iodine, and selenium. These essential minerals are found in meat, fish, and poultry, bone meal, dairy products, oil, grains, and iodized salt. Either a deficiency or overabundance of these minerals can cause stunted growth, brittle bones, hip dysplasia, kidney disease, anemia, dehydration, diarrhea, reproductive problems, hypothyroidism, hyperthyroidism, and skin and coat problems, among other symptoms and diseases.

For the most part, these minerals are needed in fairly low quantities or proportions, which are often based on the size of the dog or the amount of food he eats daily. The minerals must be present in specific combinations or exclusions in order to be as effective as possible. A number of dogs have a breed-specific tendency to some of the mineral-deficient diseases. Siberian Huskies and other Arctic breeds may be prone to a zinc deficiency known as zinc-responsive dermatosis.

Water

The last building block of nutrition for

your Siberian Husky is water—lots of water. Having plenty of clean, fresh water available is absolutely essential for your dog's health. Under normal conditions, your dog's water needs range from between two and three times the amount of dry food he eats each day. Other influences, such as temperature, humidity, stress, and activity will significantly raise that amount. These quantities are just your reference—*do not limit your dog's consumption of water*. Keep clean, fresh water available at all times, so your Siberian can drink whenever necessary.

Use similar guidelines for your dog's water quality as you would for your own. If you do not drink your well or tap water, don't give it to your dog. Make sure his water bowl is clean to eliminate the growth and exposure of bacteria, algae, and viruses.

Don't forget to have plenty of fresh water available for your Siberian.

Be aware of the amount of water your dog normally consumes. Drinking too much water can often be a sign of a health issue, such as kidney failure or diabetes. Not drinking enough water might indicate illness and can lead to dehydration if untreated.

WHAT TO FEED

With an idea of what your Siberian's food should contain in terms of nutrients, the big question is: What to feed him?

Commercial Food

The most common diet for dogs is based on commercial dog food. It has many benefits, including easy availability, the ingredients and guaranteed composition are standardized and displayed on the package, and it generally contains the nutrients (including vitamins and minerals) that your Siberian needs.

Three basic types of commercially produced dog food are available: dry food, semi-moist food, and canned food. Each type of food has its own specific characteristics.

Canned

Canned dog food is frequently comprised of recognizable ingredients, such as meat and vegetables. However, canned food contains significantly more water than does dry food (75% or more), so you are paying for, carrying, and storing water. Therefore, canned food is often a more expensive and cumbersome option.

Semi-Moist

Semi-moist food is generally lightweight and convenient. However, it often contains a significant amount of sugar, salt, and artificial color, which is not good for teeth. You'll probably want to avoid this type of diet.

Dry/Kibble

A high-quality dry food is probably the most cost-effective choice. It is easy to store and doesn't require refrigeration after opening. However, you need to check that any dry food you choose provides your Siberian with all the nutrition in the correct amounts he needs to remain healthy.

Cooked and Raw Commercial Foods

Recently, commercially prepared "home-cooked" and raw dog foods have become available, but usually on a limited basis through specialty pet food stores. These foods usually contain recognizable meat and other contents, and are available in tubes or frozen packages. Because these foods rely on refrigeration or freezing to keep them fresh, they are often made with organic ingredients, usually undergo less processing, and contain fewer chemicals in their list of ingredients. As with all types of dog food, read the labels carefully to make sure that they meet your Siberian's needs and that they do not contain unneeded sugars, salts, and other ingredients. Look carefully at the label's guaranteed analysis chart to determine the protein, carbohydrate, and fat minimum percentages, and check the ingredient list to determine the sources of those food building blocks. Finally, consider the price: These foods tend to be more expensive than many others.

Non-Commercial Options: Home-Cooked and Raw

Just as people are becoming more interested in organic and natural foods for themselves and their human families, the pet food market is also turning in that direction. Whether in response to a current fad, as an attempt to combat or avoid illness, as part of the holistic pet movement, or because of a desire

Want to Know More?

For information about zinc-responsive dermatosis, see Chapter 8: Siberian Husky Health and Wellness.

to promote optimum pet health, a growing group of dog owners are cooking special diets for their pets. There are even those who aren't cooking at all, but rather feeding their Siberians a raw diet.

These owners wish to eliminate preservatives, artificial colors, and poly-syllabic ingredients from their dogs' diets. Many also believe that dogs are carnivores, and that canine nutrition is not adequately addressed by the significant presence of carbohydrate grains in most commercial foods.

Cookbooks (or ingredient books) are available to help you prepare home-cooked and raw diets. The ingredients vary, but generally include fish, poultry, and/or meat, including raw bones and organ meat; vegetables and/or fruit; some grains; oils; and some supplements. Some people opt to cook meals for their dogs, while others think there is value in feeding their dogs a raw diet, which is closer to what wild canids eat.

Advocates believe that these natural diets improve skin and coat condition and digestive health, help avoid cancer, promote dental health, combat premature aging, improve joint health and help avoid arthritis, and combat canine allergies.

The drawbacks to these non-commercial diets include the amount of time and trouble required to create the food (although, as mentioned, this has been addressed by the commercially available diets now available on a small scale). You also must make sure that these homemade diets have all the nutritional components required for the overall health of your dog. Plus, throughout his life, a dog's nutritional needs change. Therefore, makers of homemade diets need to take this into consideration when feeding a dog over the course of his lifetime. There are many concerns regarding the ingestion of bacteria, viruses, and parasites when a dog is fed a raw diet. And, as always, one must take care when handling any type of raw meats, as improper handling and cleaning can also be dangerous for humans.

Taking these concerns into account, a dedicated owner who studies all available information about canine nutrition should still be able to create a balanced, nutritionally complete homemade food regimen for her dog.

Special Diets

There may be times when the health needs of your dog require a special diet. Whether he has skin problems, kidney disease, arthritis and joint problems, or digestive issues, or if he is aging, obese, or is going through chemotherapy, specially formulated foods are available for these problems. Most of the premium pet food manufacturers have done extensive research into canine health and corresponding nutritional needs. A number of special foods, or veterinary "prescription" foods, are the result.

These special foods provide your dog with a certain type of nutrition and supplements to help boost his immune system, recover from illness, combat degenerative conditions, or minimize effects of long-term diseases. Due to the special nature of these foods and the seriousness of the health conditions they are made to address, your veterinarian may prescribe—and may be able to supply—one of these special diets for your dog. Special

You might want to consider a home-cooked diet for your Siberian.

diets make caring for an aging or ill dog much easier, since he'll be receiving the optimum nutrition for his condition. When discussing the plan of action for combating any canine disease, remember to ask your veterinarian if a special diet might help your dog.

Supplements

You might consider giving a number of supplements to your dog, especially if you have opted for home-cooked or non-commercial food, which may require a vitamin and mineral boost. For the most part, if you have selected a premium dog food, it should provide complete nutrition for your Siberian. But even with a high-quality diet, there may be a need for additional supplements. Your Siberian may need additional protein and/or fat. Canine protein supplements or omega-3 fatty acids can be added to your dog's food. Dogs who are stressed by running on a sled team or campaigning in the show ring, for example, will have additional nutritional and caloric needs. Certain health conditions may also prompt the need for a supplement.

When selecting a supplement, follow these rules:

- Consult with your veterinarian about the need for the supplement.
- Buy only canine supplements from reputable manufacturers.
- Ask your breeder or other Siberian Husky fanciers for recommendations. They may have run into a similar problem and have some experience with existing products.
- Review the product contents and quantities and evaluate them in conjunction with your dog's existing food.
- Monitor any reactions/results of the supplement. If anything unusual occurs, stop using the supplement and contact your veterinarian.
- Realize that some supplements will require prolonged usage before showing results.

Treats

You should give just as much thought to dog

Your Siberian may benefit from supplements, but speak to your veterinarian before adding anything to your dog's diet.

To keep the calories down, break biscuits into smaller pieces to use as training treats, or even use kibble from a dog's daily food ration to fill interactive hollow toys.

treats, biscuits, and bones as you do to your dog's food. Dogs should be fed their own treats rather than table scraps, which may include some items that are dangerous for a dog to eat, including bones that easily splinter and could damage your dog's digestive tract. Often table scraps are mostly comprised of meat fat, which could lead to painful pancreatitis. And, of course, feeding your Siberian table scraps will turn him into a beggar, and he'll be bothering you whenever he sees you sit down for a meal. So, refrain from rewarding your dog with table scraps—buy him his own treats.

A vast number of canine treats are available for your Siberian's pleasure. Before selecting treats, do your homework and read the labels. You'll find that some of the treats contain significant sugar and salt, and perhaps artificial colors and flavors. Just as you would avoid semi-moist food because of these unnecessary ingredients, you will probably want to avoid such treats. On the other hand, treats such as freeze-dried liver and biscuits are not only quite palatable from your Siberian's perspective, they are well balanced and good for your dog.

If you give your Siberian treats frequently, they must be considered as part of the dog's overall food intake. Dog biscuits range from 20 kilocalories (kcals; for a small biscuit) to over 100 kilocalories for a large biscuit. If you feed by measuring cup, figure out how many biscuits you could fit in your food scoop and multiply that number by the calories. This will help you equate the calories in biscuits to your dog's food. All too often, owners cannot figure out why their dog is gaining weight when they only feed him one cup of food a day. Once questioned, they remember that they feed him the equivalent of two cups of treats! Be aware of everything your dog ingests, so you are prepared to make changes should he need to gain or lose weight.

Chews

Dogs love to chew. Chewing is good for their teeth and gums. If you do not provide your dog with something to chew, he will find something of his own choosing—maybe your favorite shoes, a table leg, or any number of other unacceptable options. Therefore, it is imperative you provide him with some safe alternatives.

Many options are available for dogs, including chew toys, rawhides, rubber/plastic bones, real bones, and even formed dental chews. As with anything that goes in a dog's mouth, some chew toys stir up canine controversy, because of concerns over choking, splintering, perforation, and intestinal obstruction. So, what canine chewing options are safe? The answer, of course, is that it depends on whom you ask.

Most people agree that chicken necks and small chicken bones are choking hazards and should be avoided. Likewise, bones from cooked steaks, such as T-bones, tend to

Feeding once or twice a day is fine for the typical adult Siberian.

splinter, which could cause perforations or intestinal obstructions.

Not everyone agrees on the safety of rawhide chews, but some experts believe that premium rawhides made in the USA without chemical treatment are safe for your dog. However, as with any item, your dog should be monitored when chewing, and you should remove any small pieces that could become choking hazards.

Some people advocate raw femur or knuckle bones, as they are initially large enough to not present a choking hazard, are soft enough not to splinter or cause broken teeth, and are completely consumable. However, others discourage this practice. Smoked or cooked, sterilized femurs and knuckle bones are also used as dog chews, but the concern with these is the possibility of splintering or of breaking teeth.

The best answer is to ask your veterinarian

for her recommendations, and if you agree, follow them. And, to keep him safe, always keep a close watch on your Siberian when he is chewing anything.

HOW MUCH TO FEED

Now that you know what to feed your Siberian, the next question is how much to feed? First and foremost—especially when it comes to Siberian Huskies—*do not feed the amount recommended on the food bag*. Never lose sight of the fact that Siberians require less food than one would imagine. This is a case where your dog breeder's recommendation is going to be your best source for how much to feed.

Most high-quality commercial dry dog foods will recommend between 2.5 and 5 cups (20 and 40 oz) of dry kibble each day for dogs the size and weight of an adult Siberian. This can translate into a range of between 650 and 2500 kcals each day! That's quite a large range, and potentially a huge volume of food. You will probably find that a Siberian who is not working, showing, extremely active, or stressed will remain at a good weight when eating approximately half that recommended amount.

If your Siberian adult has been with you since puppyhood, you will know how much to feed him as an adult. If your Siberian has joined your family as an adult, question his breeder, previous owner, or foster family about his food quantity. If you have no one to ask about his feeding history, and he is in good weight, start feeding him two cups (16 oz) a day. Watch his stools and monitor his weight to determine if you need to modify the food quantity. If he is underweight, it is probably a good idea to begin feeding two cups (16 oz) a day, and as he can tolerate more, slowly increase the amount you feed him.

HOW OFTEN TO FEED AN ADULT

Adult Siberians are often fed once a day. They can easily tolerate one meal a day, and most owners find this convenient for them, too. However, there are reasons for feeding twice a day. If your Siberian is a slow or picky eater, you may find that by splitting his food into two meals, he might clean his dog dish. Two meals might also minimize intestinal distress caused by eating one large meal. And, although it is not all that prevalent in Siberians, many believe that two smaller meals in place of one larger meal may reduce the chance of torsion or bloat. Either one or two meals a day will be fine for an adult Siberian.

The time to feed may depend upon your

By the Numbers

- **30/20:** The percentage of protein and fat that many Siberian Husky owners like to feed their dogs.
- **20 to 100:** The number of kilocalories in dog biscuits. Don't forget to count biscuits and other treats when you are determining how much food your dog is eating.
- **75%:** The amount of moisture found in most canned dog foods.
- **2 to 3 times the amount of food:** The minimum amount of water required by a dog each day. This significantly increases with temperature, humidity, stress, and increased activity.

Height at the Withers	Weight (Male)	Weight (Female)
20 in (51 cm)	n/a	35 lbs (16 kg)
20.5 in (52 cm)	n/a	38.75 lbs (18 kg)
21 in (53 cm)	45 lbs (20 kg)	42.5 lbs (19 kg)
21.5 in (55 cm)	48 lbs (22 kg)	46.25 lbs (21 kg)
22 in (56 cm)	51 lbs (23 kg)	50 lbs (23 kg)
22.5 in (57 cm)	54 lbs (24 kg)	n/a
23 in (58 cm)	57 lbs (26 kg)	n/a
23.5 in (60 cm)	60 lbs (27 kg)	n/a

schedule. It may be more convenient for you to feed in the morning or the evening. Or, feeding time may be influenced by temperature and other external forces. For example, those living in a hot climate with an abundance of flies may find it preferable to feed in the evening rather than in the morning. Or, because dogs often eliminate based on when they are fed, an evening meal often causes elimination during the night. The poop can be scooped before the warmth of the day, which reduces flies in your yard. The inverse—feeding dogs in the morning—might cause a Siberian to eliminate during the day, which should reduce the chance of nighttime accidents in the house.

Whatever schedule you select, try to follow it every day. A steady routine is always best for your Siberian.

CORRECT WEIGHT

The driving forces behind how and when to feed are your Siberian's weight and condition. Your dog's weight will affect the amount and quantity of food, and possibly even the frequency of his meals.

There are several ways to determine if your dog is overweight, underweight, or just right. The first is by weighing him. The Siberian Husky standard tells us that the breed's weight is in proportion to height. Therefore, if you know your dog's height at the withers and his weight, you can determine if they are in proportion. Here is an interpolation of those corresponding measurements:

This chart is meant as a guide to help determine the correct weight for your dog. It is not absolute. Some Siberians who have lighter bones may appear in good weight based on this chart, while actually being a bit overweight. So, you need to perform some additional checks to determine if your Siberian is in good weight.

Physical Check

First, look at your Siberian from the side and from the top. The underline of the Siberian Husky's body should slightly rise from the deepest part of his chest toward the back of the dog. This is referred to as a slight tuck-up. If your Siberian has a lot of coat, it may not be as easy to see this tuck-up as it is to feel it. When viewed from the top, your Siberian should have a noticeable "waist," and his hips should be slightly narrower than his body at the chest. Again, you may need to feel these areas through his thick coat. If you are not finding a

Do a physical check of your Siberian to determine if he's at his proper weight.

waistline or tuck-up, your Siberian is probably a bit heavier than he should be. Likewise, if his waistline or tuck-up seem extreme, especially when checked against the weight and height chart, your Siberian might need to gain a bit of weight or muscle to be in optimum condition.

Feel for the bones on your Siberian's body. You should be able to feel each rib separately. If you cannot, he is too heavy; if they protrude, he is too thin. You should also be able to feel his spine and hip bones through his coat and skin, but they should not feel sharp or be visible through his coat. If you can't feel them, your Siberian may be overweight.

This physical check should tell you if your dog is in good weight, underweight, or overweight. If you believe your dog is not at his optimal weight, consult with your veterinarian.

Sometimes weight issues are symptomatic of medical problems.

Underweight Dogs

If your veterinarian agrees that your dog is underweight and can find no medical reason, slowly increase his food consumption. The worst thing to do to an underweight dog is to overfeed him, which causes diarrhea and possible dehydration. Rather than just increasing his dry food, add an extra protein and fat source, such as meat or oil. But remember not to add too much, and closely monitor your dog for any sign of intolerance to the supplementation.

Overweight Dogs

Obesity in dogs can cause a number of health

problems. As with people, obesity can prompt the development of diabetes; damage bones, joints, and connective tissue; cause cardio-pulmonary problems; increase the risk of cancer; and decrease the expected life span. Therefore, it is important to address this problem and eliminate it.

Depending on the extent of your dog's condition, you may have to reduce his caloric intake. This can be done by reducing the quantity of food (don't forget the treats), by reducing the amount of fat and carbohydrates by eliminating supplements, or by changing to a lower-calorie food. It seems to take much longer to lose weight than it does to gain it, so adhere to a sensible food plan and be patient. Just as with humans, increasing exercise can also help with weight loss. However, be careful to do so slowly, building to longer walks or runs, for your sake and your dog's.

WHAT NOT TO FEED

No discussion of feeding a Siberian Husky is complete without mentioning what *not* to feed him. A number of human foods are quite dangerous to dogs. As a general rule, it is a good idea not to feed your dog any table scraps or anything not on his normal canine diet.

Here is a list of some common items toxic to dogs. This list is not complete, but it should make you aware of some of the important foods to keep from your Siberian.

- Anything with caffeine, including chocolate. (The theobromine in chocolate can be toxic to dogs, affecting the heart and nervous system.)
- Grapes and raisins contain a toxin that can damage kidneys.
- Macadamia nuts contain a toxin that can affect the nervous system.
- Milk and dairy products contain lactose, which may cause diarrhea.
- Mushrooms contain toxins that could result in death.
- Onions and garlic (in any form) contain sulfides that can cause anemia.
- Pits from stone fruit (such as peaches, plums, and apricots) can cause intestinal obstructions.
- Raw eggs may contain salmonella.
- Tobacco contains nicotine, which can cause rapid heartbeat and death.
- The artificial sweetener Xylitol can cause liver failure.
- Acetaminophen, the non-aspirin pain reliever in Tylenol, can cause liver failure and stop a dog's blood from carrying oxygen, which can lead to death.

CHAPTER 8

SIBERIAN HUSKY HEALTH AND WELLNESS

Throughout his life, you are responsible for your Siberian Husky's health and well-being. Therefore, you need to be aware of anything that might pose a danger to your Siberian's health. Although Siberian Huskies are generally a very healthy breed of dog—one free from many debilitating genetic predispositions—certain conditions can affect any breed. You should be aware of these issues—what to watch for, how to treat them, and, if possible, how to prevent them.

ANNUAL VETERINARY EXAMINATION

Preventative health care begins with good nutrition, training, exercise, and veterinary care. After puppyhood, a time when your Siberian has many opportunities to visit his veterinarian, a normal, healthy dog probably will only see his vet once a year at his annual veterinary exam.

At the annual exam, your veterinarian will check your dog's weight and give him a complete physical exam, including taking his temperature and pulse; listening to his heart and lungs; checking his eyes, ears, and mouth; and checking his body for parasites, tumors, and sore areas. Your vet will verify the status of your Siberian's vaccinations. She will ask questions about parasite control and your dog's overall health and behavior.

Depending on the results of the examination, your responses to health questions, and your Siberian's vaccination status, your veterinarian may suggest additional tests, vaccination boosters, additional parasite control measures, some treatment, or even a change in diet. Listen carefully to your veterinarian's recommendations, and ask questions to make sure you understand the recommendations completely. Remember that a good partnership between yourself and your dog's veterinarian is essential for your dog's well-being. When your Siberian leaves his annual veterinary examination with a clean bill of health (or a plan to get there), you will have the peace of mind that your dog is leading a healthy life.

PARASITES

A parasite is an organism that lives in or on another organism, and receives its nourishment from its host. There are internal (living within the body of the host) and external (living on the exterior of the host's body) parasites. Parasites can cause damage and discomfort, and introduce bacteria and

A number of daily and monthly heartworm preventatives are available to prevent an initial infection.

disease. For the most part, common canine parasites can be treated or prevented.

Internal Parasites

Worms are the most common canine internal parasites, and these can usually be treated and fairly easily prevented. Dogs can be infected with worms in a variety of ways, including through insect bites, by coming into contact with infected rodent feces, or by ingesting eggs or larvae, or they may have been born with them.

The prevalence of worms often correlates to the local temperature, humidity, and potential for ground freezes. To keep your Siberian as healthy as possible, please follow the advice of your veterinarian, who will be familiar with local specifics about prevention and treatment.

Heartworms

Heartworms (*Dirofilaria immitis*) are among the most dangerous internal parasites, and they have been found in all 50 states. Heartworms slightly resemble roundworms in appearance, but are far more dangerous, as they affect the heart and its blood vessels.

When an animal infected by heartworms is bitten by a mosquito, the tiny heartworm larvae in the infected dog's blood are transferred to the mosquito. Within a few weeks, the larvae grow and move into the mosquito's mouth. When that mosquito bites a non-infected dog, the larvae are transferred to the dog through his skin. Within a few months, the larvae reach the heart, where they grow to their adult size, a length of 14 inches (36 cm). As adults, the heartworms mate and produce more tiny larvae, which can then be transmitted to new hosts (most likely via mosquitoes) to become heartworms in other dogs. This entire process takes about 6 months.

If infected, a dog can host several hundred adult heartworms that can live for five years in the dog's body. These worms can cause significant obstructions in the blood vessels near the heart and lungs, as well as within the heart itself. Heartworm, if left untreated, can cause death in dogs.

Most dogs infected with heartworms do not show outward signs of infection. They may cough, lose some weight, or be a bit lethargic, but these symptoms might not be noticeable. Heartworm is diagnosed by a blood test in combination with an x-ray or ultrasound. Should these tests show the presence of adult heartworms, the course of treatment is based on the severity of the infestation.

The treatment to kill heartworms consists of a series of injections given over a period of weeks or months. The treatments are not without their side effects, including blockage of blood vessels by the dead worms, and even death. In some severe cases, adult heartworms may be removed surgically.

The good news is that heartworms can be prevented. A number of daily and monthly heartworm preventatives are available to prevent an initial infection by the tiny larvae. These medications do not kill adult heartworms, so it is important that dogs are tested before being put on these heartworm larvae preventatives. Many of these medications also prevent other worm infections, such as roundworms, hookworms, and whipworms. An environmental treatment option also is available. It is a good idea to control the local mosquito population to help reduce immediate heartworm hosts and infectors.

Hookworms

Hookworms (*Ancylostoma* and *Uncinaria*) are among the most common canine parasites, especially in puppies. Hookworms attach themselves to the wall of the intestines and feed off their host's blood. Adult hookworms lay eggs in the host's intestines, which are eliminated through the host's feces. In a matter of days, the eggs hatch, and the larvae await a new host animal.

These larvae may enter the host dog in a number of ways. Some enter through the skin, where they move through the bloodstream and into the lungs, eventually to be coughed up and swallowed. Larvae may also be found in water and food; when ingested by a dog, they make their way to the intestine. Some larvae remain dormant in muscle and eventually migrate to a female's uterus where they infect

Want to Know More?

For information about finding the right veterinarian for your Siberian Husky, see Chapter 3: Care of Your Siberian Husky Puppy.

unborn puppies, or they travel to mammary glands and are transferred to the puppies through nursing.

Left untreated, hookworms can cause anemia. An infected dog will become weak, and may vomit and have diarrhea. His stools may be black. He may appear listless, pale, and even contract pneumonia. In severe cases, death can occur. Depending on the type of hookworm, other animals may serve as hosts.

A worming medication designed for hookworms or roundworms is the most common treatment—most medications combat both types of worms. Because these treatments only kill the adults, it may take multiple treatments to eradicate the worms completely. Puppies, the group most often affected, should be treated a few times, at 2-week intervals, beginning at 2 weeks of age.

The use of a year-round heartworm preventative product that also attacks hookworms is the best prevention. Your veterinarian may also recommend a periodic fecal exam. If you have an infestation of hookworms, consider treating your environment: frequently scoop poop and clean kennel areas with a product that kills worms.

Roundworms

Roundworms or ascarids (*Toxascaris leonina*, *Toxascaris canis*) are very commonly found in the digestive tract of dogs. In fact, most puppies are born with roundworms. Roundworms can infect your dog in a number of ways. The simplest method of infection in dogs occurs when a dog eats something contaminated by roundworm eggs. The eggs hatch and the larvae live in your dog's intestines. Females lay eggs that pass out of the dog in his feces, where they can be eaten by another host and the cycle begins again. Similarly, a dog may eat a small animal (such as a rodent) that is host to eggs and thus become infected.

Within the dog's body, some of the larvae may move out of the intestines to other parts of the body, including entering body muscles or tissues, where they can remain dormant for a dog's entire lifetime. A pregnant female with such dormant roundworms in her body can pass them along to her unborn puppies, or they can enter the mammary glands and she can infect her puppies during feeding. That's why so many puppies have worms at birth. These puppies can also reinfect their mothers as she's cleaning them.

Roundworms are a threat both to dogs and humans. A dog with a slight infestation of roundworms may show no symptoms. However, a dog with a severe roundworm infestation may have diarrhea and vomiting and may become anemic. In some cases, roundworms can enter the lungs and cause pneumonia in both dogs and people.

It's standard to assume that all puppies have roundworms, so an early treatment (starting at 2 to 3 weeks of age) is recommended, as are follow-up treatments every 2 weeks. In adults, your veterinarian can do a fecal check for roundworms, and she may recommend doing this regularly. However, this test will not be able to determine if your dog has dormant roundworms in his body. Many heartworm preventative medications also prevent roundworms, but these medications will not kill dormant roundworms within your dog's body.

If roundworms are present on your property, scoop poop frequently and clean the area weekly with a product that will help kill the hearty roundworm eggs.

Tapeworms

The flea is the most frequent host of tapeworms, and it's most likely through the flea that your dog will become infected. A number of species of tapeworms can infect your dog, including some that can also infect humans.

Most tapeworms have a similar appearance and lifecycle. Tapeworms are comprised of a head, neck, and a series of segments. These segments are formed at the neck, and the older segments at the end eventually detach, usually full of eggs. Tapeworms can get very long (some may get as long as 20 feet [6 m]), and they rely on an intermediate host during their lifecycle.

The common tapeworm found in dogs uses fleas, ticks, or lice as its intermediate host. The flea will eat the eggs from the dog's feces and become infected. In the intermediate host, an immature worm is formed. Then, when the dog eats the insect, the worm grows and attaches itself to the dog's intestines to being the process again.

The symptoms depend on the species of tapeworm, and range from discomfort, diarrhea, and itching, to weight loss. Humans can contract some species of tapeworm by coming in contact with the eggs. Human symptoms also vary by species of tapeworm, but may include anemia and anaphylactic shock.

An infection is usually spotted visually by seeing segments in a dog's feces. Your veterinarian can do a fecal test for tapeworms. The best way to combat tapeworms is to eliminate intermediate hosts. Eradicate

Frequently scoop poop in your backyard to prevent a worm infestation.

rodents, fleas, and lice. Many of the heartworm preventative medications also help control tapeworms. But, due to the number of species of tapeworms, please consult your veterinarian for the correct treatment and preventative.

Whipworms

Whipworms (*Trichuris vulpis*, *Trichuris campanula*, and *Trichuris serrata*) are very commonly found in dogs. They are whip-shaped, running from thick to thin from end to end. They live in the large intestine or at the meeting of the small and large intestine.

Whipworms are transmitted to dogs much like other worms, by ingesting whipworm eggs. The larvae then mature into adults and attach themselves to the intestinal wall, where they lay eggs. The eggs pass out of the dog through his feces, and the cycle begins again.

If infected with whipworms, your dog may lose weight and become anemic. Severe cases can lead to hemorrhaging within the intestines. Your veterinarian can check for whipworms by performing a fecal exam. However, due to the egg-producing cycle of the worms, eggs may not appear daily in the feces. Therefore, a fecal exam may need to be done repeatedly. If whipworms are discovered, your veterinarian will treat them with any number of products. Some heartworm preventative products also are effective in preventing whipworms.

To hinder the spread of whipworms, areas where you house your Siberian should be cleaned thoroughly. Unfortunately, whipworm eggs can live in the soil for years, and are even resistant to freezing weather, so they are extremely difficult to completely eradicate from soil—only soil replacement will do the job.

External Parasites

External parasites include fleas, ticks, and mites, plus the fungal infection called ringworm.

Fleas

By far, the flea is one of the most prevalent and previously difficult-to-manage parasites. There are over 2,000 different species of fleas. Fleas feed on the blood of their hosts (which can include humans), and although each species has its preferred host, fleas will feed on whatever animal is available. Fleas are tiny, very agile, and can jump very long distances for their size. They sense heat and vibration to help locate hosts. The design of their legs enables them to attach themselves to your dog or to the fibers of your clothing. The most common fleas you might find on your Siberian are the domestic cat flea (*Ctenocephalides felis*), which actually prefers a dog as its host, and the domestic dog flea (*Ctenocephalides canis*).

The main problem with fleas is that once they enter your environment—either your home or your yard—they are very difficult to eradicate. A female flea reaches maturity in 30 days, lives an average of 60 to 90 days (although under perfect conditions of heat and humidity, she can live longer than this), can lay 50 eggs a day. During her lifetime, she can lay a startling 1,000 eggs! These eggs are often laid on your dog and fall off into your home and yard.

You may be able to see fleas on your Siberian, especially on his face or belly, where his coat is the shortest or thinnest. You may also find "flea dirt" on your dog, which is actually flea excrement. It looks like little dark specks, but when it's wet, flea dirt turns dark red because it is essentially dried blood. You also may see your Siberian scratching himself, or you may find welts where he has been bitten. Flea saliva often contains allergens, so people or dogs with allergies may develop lesions and skin ulcers. In addition to the discomfort, fleas can be intermediate hosts for a number of parasites and diseases, such as tapeworm, bubonic plague, and typhus.

Should your dog, yourself, your home, or your yard become infested with fleas, there are several steps you must go through to eliminate fleas from your life. First, contact your veterinarian and put your Siberian on a flea control product. A number of products are available in the form of shampoos, sprays, dips, topical applications, collars, and injectable and oral products. Your vet may recommend a combination of products, but please seek her advice, as some products should not be used together. Realize that you still may see some fleas on your Siberian until his environment has been treated long enough to eliminate all of these pesky critters.

Now start the program to eliminate fleas in your home. Due to the probability that there may be hundreds or thousands of fleas and eggs in your home, you *must* treat your home for fleas. Vacuum your home completely, including furniture, your dog's bed, and any area where your dog has been in your home. Empty your vacuum into a plastic bag, seal it, and discard it. Treat your home with a flea product that kills both adult fleas and stops eggs and larvae from developing. These products come in the form of sprays, powders,

Multi-Dog Tip

Internal and external parasites may infest all animals in your household. Be sure to treat them all, not just the one showing symptoms.

Medications for Parasites

Although internal and external parasites are very unpleasant, current preventative medications are inexpensive, simple to administer, and very effective at controlling these unwanted pests. Working in close contact with your veterinarian to get your Siberian on a preventative schedule will pay off.

and foggers. Consult your veterinarian for recommended products. You can also contract with a professional exterminator. Wash your Siberian's bedding and sleeping area (including his crate) with the chosen product. Treat any other area where your dog has been, including other rooms in the house and the car.

Next, treat the outdoor area where your dog spends time. Clear away any leaves, fabric, etc., from warm and humid areas, including his dog house, favorite lawn furniture, or outdoor bed. Wash any fabric and seal anything that needs to go in the garbage. Ask your veterinarian about recommended products for outdoors. As rodents also host fleas, try to eliminate them from your yard. (Again, you may wish to contract with a professional exterminator.)

Once you have followed this process, keep a watchful eye out for signs of more fleas. Although current products should be able to eliminate a flea infestation with one-time usage, additional follow-up may be necessary. When the fleas are gone, keep your Siberian on his flea prevention products so fleas will not return.

Mites

Mites are closely related to ticks, and there are various types. The most common mites to infect dogs are ear mites and nasal mites. Ear mites are nearly microscopic arachnids, while nose mites are tiny, but visible to the naked eye.

The most common ear mite (*Otodectes cynotis*) is very contagious, and can easily be spread among dogs and other household pets. However, ear mites cannot be passed along to humans. Although they are referred to as ear mites, these tiny creatures can live anywhere on a dog and may cause significant ear scratching or head shaking. If your dog has these symptoms, look in his ear for an accumulation of dried blood that will look like dark grains.

If you suspect your Siberian might have contracted ear mites, take him to his veterinarian. The vet will prescribe any number of treatments, including ear flushing with products containing insecticides to kill the

Mites can cause a dog to scratch at his ears or shake his head.

mites. Such treatments should be continued 2 to 4 weeks for complete eradication. You may also wish to treat the dog's bedding, but usually your house will not require treatment. Some worm and flea preventative medications may also be prescribed. Ear mites, if left untreated, could damage your Siberian's ear and even lead to hearing loss.

Nasal mites (*Pneumonyssoides caninum*) are not as well known, but quite common in canids. They are rarely treated because most infected dogs do not show many symptoms. Symptoms, although rare, could include sneezing, nosebleeds, or significant nasal discharge. Infected dogs could pass nasal mites to other dogs, but not to other species. Your veterinarian can swab your dog's nose and use a microscope to locate the mites. Treatment may include a number of oral worm and/or external parasite preventative medications prescribed by your veterinarian.

Ringworm

Although its name includes the word "worm," ringworm is not actually a worm. Rather, it is a fungus that infects dogs and people alike. Ringworm is most often found in hot and humid climates, most frequently in fall and winter. You can catch ringworm directly from contact with an infected animal or by contact with ringworm spores.

Ringworm lesions appear on the skin and cause hair loss, usually on the head, legs, feet, or tail. Lesions start small and grow, but may not itch. These lesions may be similar in appearance to demodectic mange, or

Ticks can transmit Rocky Mountain spotted fever, Lyme disease, and a number of other diseases.

in Siberian Huskies may appear similar in appearance to zinc-responsive dermatosis.

Ringworm can be diagnosed by your veterinarian in a number of ways, including the use of a Wood's lamp, which shows this fluorescent fungal species. But the preferred method of diagnosis is to culture the infected skin. If diagnosed, your veterinarian will treat the infection topically with antifungal medication or prescribe a special shampoo or dip.

Ringworm is easily transmitted by touch, so it is very important to always wear gloves and wash up when treating affected dogs. Unfortunately, there is no vaccine or other medication to prevent your dog from contracting ringworm. The only available prevention is cleanliness.

Ticks

Ticks are related to spiders and mites, and are generally found in long grasses and weeds. Due to a unique sensory organ, ticks can sense odor and other characteristics of a potential host approaching, and then climb onto their new host. Ticks are not killed by frost, and often thrive in the autumn. This is the optimum time to contract Lyme disease, which is transmitted from deer ticks. Ticks can also transmit Rocky Mountain spotted fever and a number of other diseases.

Ticks have four stages: egg, larvae, nymph, and adult. Except for the egg stage, ticks are capable of latching on to a host with their mouths. Once attached, they eat blood. At the larval stage, ticks are very small, nearly microscopic, but they will eventually grow in size to a couple of centimeters.

The most common tick affecting dogs is the brown dog tick (*Rhipicephalus sanguineus*), and it is found in all 50 states. To reduce the chance of your dog picking up a tick, first eliminate

the tick's preferred environment. Mow tall grasses and brush around your house and yard. Rodents can transport ticks, so control them in your area. You may also want to contact your veterinarian for a recommendation for outdoor tick control products.

If you find a tick on your dog, use fine tweezers to grab the tick by its mouth parts, which are embedded in your dog's skin, and firmly pull the tick straight out from your dog. Drop the tick into a jar of alcohol to kill it, then flush it down the toilet. Clean your dog's wound. Since you found a tick on your dog, you should assume that there will be eggs somewhere. So, follow the same process you would for indoor and outdoor flea eradication.

Contact your veterinarian for products that will repel and kill ticks. Ticks may still appear on your dog even if you are using these products, but they will be killed within a day. A Lyme disease vaccination is available if you live in an area that warrants such treatment.

BREED-SPECIFIC HEALTH ISSUES

Siberian Huskies are relatively healthy dogs, with a fairly short list of breed-specific health issues. The most common Siberian Husky health issues are related to the eye.

Siberian Huskies have a number of familial eye problems.

Eye Problems

Siberian Huskies have a number of familial eye problems: hereditary cataracts (sometimes referred to as juvenile cataracts), crystalline corneal opacities (CCO, often called corneal dystrophy), progressive retinal atrophy (PRA), and to a lesser extent, goniodysgenesis (often a precursor to glaucoma) and pannus.

Cataracts

Hereditary cataracts are perhaps the most common and problematic eye abnormality in this breed. They should not be confused with cataracts that develop due to aging, and they are sometimes called juvenile cataracts as a way to distinguish the two. These cataracts are bilateral in nature, but may first appear in one eye before appearing in the second. They manifest as an opacity of the lens and may appear as early as 3 months of age, but typically appear between 6 and 24 months of age. Traditionally, juvenile cataracts develop in the posterior of the eye, along the "Y" suture in the lens, and allow less light to enter the eye. However, other cataract patterns are not unknown. These opacities traditionally impair eyesight but do not lead to blindness, except in some severe cases. It is believed that these cataracts are inherited as a recessive gene (although they could involve more than one gene). Currently, the only way to test for this type of cataract is to have a canine ophthalmologist perform a yearly eye examination. A dog without the outward signs of cataracts may still be a genetic carrier of the disease. Some research is being done on a genetic test for this eye disease.

Corneal Crystalline Opacity

Oddly enough, it was while studying corneal crystalline opacity (CCO, often referred to as corneal dystrophy) that Siberian Husky cataracts were actually discovered. It was originally believed that CCO was the significant eye disorder in Siberians, but this was soon eclipsed by the prevalence of cataracts. CCO in Siberian Huskies does not usually appear in puppies or young dogs, as is the case with cataracts. Rather, CCO generally appears in older adult dogs, often after a Siberian has been bred or used at stud.

CCO is a deposit on the cornea, often in a doughnut shape, that causes some opacity, but usually does not lead to blindness. It is believed that the mode of inheritance for this disorder is perhaps a recessive gene with a mutation. Like cataracts, the only way to be assured that your Siberian is free of CCO is to have his eyes examined each year by a canine ophthalmologist. Again, this exam will show if a Siberian has the eye abnormality, not if he is a genetic carrier of it.

Progressive Retinal Atrophy

The progressive retinal atrophy (PRA) found in Siberian Huskies is different from the incidences of PRA in other breeds, but similar to PRA in humans. Siberian PRA is sex-linked. That is to say, the eye disorder is carried on one of the "X" chromosomes of a female (who has "XX" chromosomes), and it is passed to her male offspring (who has "XY" chromosomes). So, a male with an affected "X" chromosome passed on from his mother will have the eye disorder. Females with only one affected "X" chromosome will show little evidence of the disease, but are carriers.

PRA will cause an affected dog initially to lose night vision, then day vision, and eventually to go blind as early as 5 months of age. Again, the only way to determine if a dog has PRA is to have him examined by a canine ophthalmologist. Work is currently being done to develop a genetic test for Siberian PRA.

Other Eye Problems

There are two additional eye problems that, although not as prevalent as cataracts, CCO, and PRA, have been seen in certain Siberian Husky bloodlines. They are included here for your information.

The first is goniodysgenesis, a problem in which the drainage angles from the eye have been compromised, making it difficult for fluid to drain from the eye. This condition may lead to glaucoma. A canine ophthalmologist can test for this condition by performing a gonioscopy, which is different test than that given for cataracts, CCO, and PRA. A number of treatments are available for goniodysgenesis and glaucoma, including medications and surgery.

Pannus is a progressive disease of the cornea and conjunctiva that is not usually painful, but causes a change to the cornea. On occasion, dry eye is also present. As the disease advances, pannus can cause blindness. It seems to be inherited, but it is also made worse by sunlight and often has autoimmune factors. Treatments and medications can be prescribed by a canine ophthalmologist.

Eye Tests

All reputable breeders have their breeding stock tested by a canine ophthalmologist within one year of any breeding. This helps assure that the sire and dam are free from any of these hereditary eye problems.

Siberians occasionally have problems related to hair follicles, although not as commonly as other Arctic breeds.

Follicular Problems

Siberians occasionally have problems related to hair follicles, although not as commonly as other Arctic breeds.

Canine Follicular Dystrophy

Canine follicular dystrophy (CFD) is somewhat common in many Arctic or spitz breeds, such as Alaskan Malamutes and Pomeranians. However, this condition is less common in Siberian Huskies. It appears as severely dry and brittle coat, hair loss (which often appears

as a "rat tail"), and blackening of the skin in affected areas. Although not common in Siberians, should you see any such symptoms, contact your veterinarian for diagnosis and treatment.

Hair Follicle Dystrophy

While CFD may be less common in Siberians, another condition, anecdotally referred to as hair follicle dystrophy (HFD), has been seen in the breed. In this condition, rather than losing fur, a Siberian's coat fails to shed properly. The coat becomes dry, brittle, and discolored, similar to a significant sunburn. Should your Siberian fail to shed his coat and begin to display these symptoms, please consult your veterinarian.

Skeletal Disorders

Another grouping of breed disorders occurs in the skeletal system, which includes bones and connective tissue.

Hip Dysplasia

Canine hip dysplasia (CHD) is a condition that occurs when the ball joint of the hip does not seat very well in the socket. This is either due to a poorly formed ball joint, a shallow socket, or both. Dogs affected with this condition may have a limp in their rear legs, show some pain or discomfort in this area, or show a stilted or somewhat stiff rear gait. CHD is diagnosed with an x-ray, which will provide your veterinarian with a clear picture of your dog's bones and joints.

All canines who will be used in a breeding program should be routinely tested for CHD after they are two years of age. Whether due to healthy genetics or swift action and monitoring on the part of Siberian Husky breeders, the incidence of CHD in Siberian Huskies is quite low: 2% of those Siberians checked by the

Orthopedic Foundation for Animals (OFA) are affected, as compared to the 11+% of Alaskan Malamutes and Samoyeds and 13% of Akitas.

Other Skeletal Disorders

Unfortunately, there seems to be incidences of other skeletal issues in the breed, which include patellar and elbow luxation, elbow dysplasia, osteochondritis dissecans (OCD). These problems affect joints such as the shoulder or the hock, and can cause popping, slipping, and double hocks. These skeletal issues generally involve cartilage, tendons, or bones moving out of place or even being malformed. Many of these problems lead to limping and even complete lameness. The treatment can include immobility and even surgery. It is believed that skeletal problems may be familial, but they can certainly be worsened by too much weight and by environmental factors. If your Siberian limps or seems to favor a leg or joint, consult your veterinarian. Some supplements may help these conditions, and in severe cases, surgery might be warranted.

Zinc-Responsive Dermatosis

A certain mineral deficiency, called zinc-responsive dermatosis, is prevalent in the Arctic breeds, including Siberian Huskies. Zinc is needed to help protect against infection. Although most commercially available dog food contains adequate zinc, some dogs are incapable of absorbing enough zinc from their food. It is believed that this reduced zinc absorption is a result of other minerals (such as calcium) blocking its absorption, or due to an excess of cereal grains in the food. Whatever the trigger, some Siberians cannot absorb adequate zinc. This tendency seems to be familial.

Zinc-responsive dermatosis often appears around puberty and is seen as lesions around the eye, mouth, and genitals. The lesions will appear itchy, crusty, red, and occasionally weepy. The dog's hair will fall out in these areas, and there may be some secondary infections in the lesions. It is difficult to determine low zinc levels by blood tests. Your veterinarian will take a punch biopsy of the affected area to make a final diagnosis. In severe cases, veterinarians can supplement zinc intravenously, although, for the most part, adding zinc orally is sufficient. The dosage is important, as is the source of the zinc, which should be zinc sulfate, zinc methionine, or zinc gluconate. Siberians under veterinary care and receiving zinc orally should show improvement in time. This condition may also improve or change with age.

Pigment Issues

Siberian Huskies are generally not prone to the pigment-related issues seen in other blue-eyed dogs, such as the pigment-related deafness seen in Dalmatians and Australian Shepherds. The issue (although often present in blue-eyed dogs of the affected breeds) is not the eye color, but the lack of pigment in the inner ear, which causes the deafness. Piebald or white Siberian Huskies, regardless of eye color, are usually black-and-white or red-and-white dogs with their color suppressed. So, a piebald or white Siberian will most likely have good pigment levels, and is therefore not susceptible to the problem.

GENERAL CANINE HEALTH ISSUES

In addition to those health issues specific to Siberian Huskies, this breed (as with all breeds) may be susceptible to other health issues.

Allergies

Allergies can be a response to environmental situations, such as fleas and airborne allergens, or to foods.

Atopy

Generally, the symptoms of canine atopy, or inhaled allergies, are similar to those in people. Your Siberian may have a runny nose or eyes, and he may sneeze or itch. Usually, inhaled allergies are of short duration—most often, only while certain allergen-producing plants are blooming. Your veterinarian can perform tests on your dog to determine the actual allergens, which can help you eliminate them from his environment. However, it may be impossible to eliminate all plant and tree culprits. If this is the case, your veterinarian may choose to treat your Siberian with an injection or oral antihistamine or steroids for a few critical weeks every year.

Flea Allergies

Flea allergies are fairly easy to discover. If your dog is scratching a lot, carefully examine him for signs of fleas (bite locations and flea debris). If you discover a flea infestation, please consult your veterinarian for her recommendations regarding flea treatment and prevention. Once the flea problem is gone, your dog should return to normal.

Food Allergies

Food allergies may be a bit more problematic than other allergies. Siberian Huskies are occasionally susceptible to allergies from soy, wheat, or corn—most of which are found in commercially available dog foods. The symptoms of food allergies are somewhat similar to those of atopy: scratching, runny eyes, chewing or biting at the feet. Although the symptoms are similar to atopy, they will not necessarily appear at the same time each year, last for a short duration, and end with the season. And, you may find additional symptoms. Due to the duration of food allergies, you may see pink staining of the white fur at the inside corner of your Siberian's eyes, around his mouth, and near his genitals. Your dog's coat may be dull, dry, and brittle. And, you may find he develops diarrhea, or the frequency of his bowel movements increases.

Allergies can be a response to environmental situations, such airborne allergens.

You can significantly reduce or eliminate your dog's chance of developing mammary and uterine or testicular cancer by having your Siberian Husky spayed or neutered at the appropriate time.

Your veterinarian may choose to treat these symptoms, but they will probably not respond to steroids. The preferred treatment for food allergies is to eliminate the allergen. To do this, change your dog's current food to one that has a different protein or carbohydrate source. It is not uncommon for a Siberian Husky to develop allergies to grains, so if you think the protein source is a good one, consider changing the carbohydrate source of his food, while trying to maintain similar protein and fat percentages in his new food. Also, remember to check the carbohydrate and protein source in his treats, and change them accordingly.

Make the food change gradually, over at least 2 weeks, and pay attention to your Siberian's stools during the process and when the change is complete. The new food may have a slightly different proportion of protein to fat, which may require a slight change in the amount of food you offer him. If he is getting excessive carbohydrates, his stools will soften. If this is the case, cut back on the amount of food, and consider supplementing the food with additional protein or fat. Realize that it will take at least from 4 to 6 months to see a marked improvement in your dog's condition after eliminating the probable food allergen. If your dog continues to suffer during these transitional months, your veterinarian may wish to prescribe an antihistamine or steroids. But, with some patience and perseverance, your Siberian will soon be free of his allergic reaction.

Cancer

Cancer, unfortunately, seems to strike every species, and dogs are no exception. As you have learned, however, you can significantly reduce or eliminate your dog's chance of developing mammary and uterine or testicular cancer by having your Siberian Husky spayed or neutered at the appropriate time. Also, routine physical examination of your dog should keep you aware of any growths or tumors, especially in the mammary glands and testicles, scrotum, and abdominal area. Should you encounter swelling or growths in these areas, contact your veterinarian immediately. These types of cancers, when discovered early, have a high chance for successful surgical removal.

Common Types

Some other common cancers are occasionally seen in the Siberian: hemangiosarcoma, osteosarcoma, and mast cell tumors. Mast cell tumors are growths that can develop at any time. Many skin tumors are mast cell tumors, and you should note these while performing your routine physical examination of your Siberian Husky. Your veterinarian can determine if a growth is a mast cell tumor by performing a biopsy or needle biopsy on the tumor and examining it. Not all mast cell tumors are malignant, and the malignant ones are graded and staged by their severity and development. Mast cell tumors may be removed, or treated by radiation or chemotherapy.

Osteosarcoma, or bone cancer, is most common in giant or large-breed dogs, although not unknown in the Siberian Husky. Unfortunately, by the time a dog shows signs of limping or stiffness caused by osteosarcoma, the cancer has often already metastasized (spread) to the lungs. Osteosarcoma is a very aggressive cancer that often requires amputation, as well as chemotherapy, which may not result in too long a life expectancy.

Hemangiosarcoma is a particularly aggressive cancer, and it may occur anywhere in the dog. It begins in the blood vessels. Again, as the cancer is usually internal, it takes a while to discover, at which time it may very well have metastasized elsewhere. Symptoms may include weakness or blood loss, and a biopsy is required to prove a diagnosis. The treatment is surgery and chemotherapy, and due to the aggressiveness of the cancer and its metastatic nature, the prognosis for a long life is not usually good.

Treatment

Cancer treatment for dogs is similar to that for humans. Generally, surgery is indicated in an attempt to remove the cancer. If the tumor is localized and not metastasized, radiation therapy is often recommended. Radiation therapy requires a significant commitment of time and money by the dog's owner, as the process may be long and costly. Dogs undergoing radiation therapy will be anesthetized so they do not move during treatment. Side effects do occur, and these should be discussed with your veterinarian. However, dogs do not seem to develop some of the same side effects as humans, such as appetite loss and nausea.

Chemotherapy may also be recommended for a dog with cancer. This therapy is often used in concert with surgery in cases where the cancer has metastasized, as chemo increases the survival rate. However, this also requires a commitment of time and money by the dog's owner.

The main consideration with canine cancers is the same as with human cancers: pain control. Cancers and cancer treatments may be long and painful times, and the job of the veterinarian and owner is to try to minimize the pain and discomfort for the dog. A good pain prevention program is recommended, as is good nutrition. This often becomes the time in a dog's life when his owner can thank her Siberian for years of love and companionship by helping to make him as comfortable as possible.

Eye Infections

A few problems might affect your Siberian's eyes. Just as in people, dogs can contract both dry eye and red eye. Dry eye, if left untreated, can become a painful chronic condition that could cause permanent damage to the eye. It could also be a symptom of pannus, an eye problem occasionally seen in Siberian Huskies. Treatments are available, so consult your veterinarian or veterinary ophthalmologist.

Conjunctivitis, or red eye, is an inflammation of the tissue, or conjunctiva, around the eyelids. Red eye, if left untreated, could spread and affect other areas of the eye and impair vision. And, as is the case with people, conjunctivitis can be transmitted to other dogs living in close proximity to an affected dog. Conjunctivitis can also be a symptom of a more serious disease, so it should not be ignored. Your veterinarian can prescribe a number of medications to help with the inflammation and infection. As is the case with all eye problems, do not diagnose and treat them yourself. Different eye ailments require very different treatments, and if treated incorrectly, additional damage can be done.

Hypothyroidism

Another health issue found in many dog breeds is hypothyroidism, or low thyroid hormone level production and secretion. In many dogs, hypothyroidism is not even noticed or treated, although some data indicate

Ear Infections

Siberian Huskies are not usually prone to ear infections. However, there are some ear specifics that you will want to address. You should be checking your Siberian's ears during routine grooming. If they are significantly warm or red, if they have an odor, or if he is scratching at his ears or shaking his head, this indicates that an ear infection, ear mites, allergies, a foreign body, or some other ear condition may be present. Contact your veterinarian.

that Siberian Huskies have a tendency toward low thyroid hormone levels. Some symptoms include obesity, lethargy, a dry and brittle coat, anemia, and infertility.

Diagnosis of hypothyroidism is done by means of a few blood tests. Each of the "T" tests has a range of results considered normal. Usually, if your dog's results fall within the normal range, all is fine. However, should your Siberian have some outward sign and score in the low part of the normal range, discuss possible treatment with your veterinarian. The treatment consists of adding a daily dose of a low-cost synthetic thyroid hormone, either thyroxine or Soloxine.

Seizure Disorder

Approximately 4% of all canines, wild and domestic, have epileptiform seizures, and Siberian Huskies are no exception. Seizures may be caused by many triggers, including brain tumors, chemical imbalances, toxins, or epilepsy. The problem with seizures is that it is often difficult to determine their cause. Veterinarians will take a variety of tests to rule out certain causes, but there is actually no test to prove epilepsy.

There does seem to be a familial tendency toward seizures. All dogs have a seizure threshold—the level at which a dog seizes. No one knows what prompts seizures, although some dogs' seizure threshold is lower than others. Dogs may seize during exciting events, such as heavy play, on an outing, or when guests arrive.

There are different types of seizures. Seizures can be partial, which involve only a small part of the body, or they may be generalized and affect the entire body. These are the most common, and fall into two categories: *grand mal* (the more common) and *petit mal*. In a grand mal seizure, the dog will have some type of uncontrolled muscle movement, like a convulsion. In petit mal seizures, there are usually no convulsions; rather it looks as if the dog has collapsed or fainted. The worst and least common seizure is *status epilepticus*, where the dog goes from one seizure into another without stopping.

Seizures have three phases. The pre-seizure begins minutes before the seizure, during which time the dog may be restless, clingy, or whiny. Next is the *ictus*, or the seizure itself, which usually lasts less than five minutes. Last is the *postictal* stage, in which the dog is recovering from the seizure and may appear disoriented. The postictal phase may last minutes to days.

If your dog has a seizure, remain calm. Unless he is in danger of falling, hitting his head, or being attacked by another animal, he is not in real danger. If other animals are present in the area, remove them. If he is in danger of falling or hitting his head, move him if possible, or protect him from the imminent danger. Keep your fingers away from his mouth; he is not in danger of swallowing his tongue, but you could get bitten. Watch the seizure closely, so you can provide your veterinarian with details of the event.

If the seizure lasts more than 3 or 4 minutes, contact your veterinarian or the emergency veterinarian immediately. If it is short in duration, call your veterinarian to report the event and get her advice.

Your veterinarian may wish to do some tests or just wait to see if more seizures occur. If she deems it necessary, she may prescribe antiseizure medication. However, this is usually not done after the first seizure. If your

Good breeders strive to ensure their Siberians are genetically sound, in order to avoid many heritable diseases.

Torsion and Bloat

Although not all that common in Siberian Huskies, gastric torsion or canine bloat is a life-threatening condition. Initially, the stomach fills up with air (bloat) and presses on other organs, making it hard for the dog to breathe and reducing blood flow to the heart. The bloated stomach may then twist (torsion), and the blood supply is completely cut off, causing the stomach to die, and putting the dog in serious danger.

There is a genetic predisposition toward bloat, and it also seems that some breeds' conformation tends toward bloat. Bloat is more likely to occur in older males and in dogs who are fed one meal a day and eat very quickly.

The first sign is a swollen belly. An affected dog will retch without vomiting, salivate, have shallow breathing, and show signs of abdominal pain. If you see any of these signs in your dog, seek immediate veterinary care. Immediate surgery is usually indicated to resolve the problem. Fast action on your part may save your dog's life.

dog begins to have regular seizures, realize that with good veterinary care and correct medication, they can often be controlled.

ALTERNATIVE THERAPIES

Alternative therapies for pets use ancient methods, coupled with new technology and the desire for less-invasive solutions and fewer chemicals, to provide other methods of treatment for dogs.

Acupuncture

Leading the way in alternative therapies is acupuncture, practiced by the Chinese for 3,500 years. The ancient theory is that opposing forces within a body (*yin* and *yang*) must be balanced to allow the life force (*ch'i*) to flow properly. The Chinese have identified 360 acupuncture points on the body, associated with organs and bodily functions, which can be stimulated to balance these forces. By inserting needles into these points, one can help balance the life force, reduce pain, and heal.

Veterinary acupuncturists use these ideas to perform the same functions on dogs. Acupuncture is used to reduce pain and treat epilepsy, and for many other purposes. Although there have been some studies in humans to help understand the process and how it might work, no significant research has been undertaken into understanding how acupuncture works with animals. In some states, veterinary acupuncturists must also be licensed veterinarians. Some organizations for veterinary acupuncturists, such as the American Academy of Veterinary Acupuncture (AAVA), can provide more information and referrals.

Chiropractic

Canine chiropractors can make adjustments to help vertebrae, bones, joints, nerves, and connective tissue become aligned. Chiropractic practitioners believe that correct alignment of these body parts aids in blood flow, alleviates pain, aids in range of motion, and relieves pressure. Canine chiropractic uses hands as well as an instrument that allows multiple adjustments to be performed easily. There are organizations for canine chiropractors, such as the American Veterinary Chiropractic Association (AVCA), from which you can seek more information and referrals.

Herbal

Chinese herbal healers have been around as long as acupuncturists, and these two disciplines are often practiced together. Seen as a natural alternative to medications, herbal cures have become very popular. Many current medications have their beginnings in the active ingredients of herbs, so it is no surprise that herbal medicine is being practiced on dogs as well as humans. Although herbal remedies are well known, they do not fall under the regulations of the US government's Food and Drug Administration (FDA), so some caution should be used. If you wish to investigate herbal treatments, please do so with your veterinarian's knowledge. Although herbs can be quite beneficial, like any other compound, they may have side effects, toxicities, and/or interfere with other substances.

Physical Therapy

Massage is often used with dogs in a number of ways. First, it can be used to help soothe tired muscles and joints and to enhance blood flow. It can be used as a type of physical therapy to help regain mobility and range of motion after surgery or an injury. Massage techniques can also be combined with acupuncture points to become *acupressure*, a massage version of acupuncture. A specific form of massage, called T-Touch therapy, uses massage to help calm excitable dogs and create a bond between owner and dog. T-Touch also aids in enhanced blood flow and recuperation. Just as massage relaxes, heals, and rehabilitates people, it provides the same benefits to dogs.

FIRST AID

The more time you spend with your dog, and the more traveling or activities you pursue, the more apparent it will become that you need to know basic canine first aid.

First-Aid Kit

The first thing to do is put together a first aid kit for your pet. You should assemble the kit in a plastic container and bring it with you when you travel with your dog. Here are some recommended items to include in the kit:

- Information about each of your pets: name, photograph, microchip number, current vaccinations, health problems, list of medications.
- Information about your veterinarian: name, location, phone, office hours, closest emergency vet.
- Supplies:
    - Ace bandages
    - Antibacterial wipes
    - Antibiotic ointment/cream
    - Cold/hot pack
    - Collar and leash
    - Diphenhydramine (Benadryl)
    - Flashlight
    - Forceps (if available)
    - Gauze pads
    - Gauze rolls
    - Hydrocortisone ointment/cream
    - Hydrogen peroxide
    - Muzzle
    - Nail clippers
    - Oral syringe
    - Povidone-iodine (Betadine)
    - Rubber gloves
    - Rubbing alcohol
    - Scissors
    - Sports drink
    - Tape
    - Thermometer

What's an Emergency?

In the following pages, you will learn how to administer some doggy first aid. But it is equally important to know the signs of actual emergencies. Seek immediate veterinary help if your dog:

- Has no pulse or heartbeat, is having problems breathing, or has stopped breathing
- Has been exposed to poisons or bitten by a snake, scorpion, or other poisonous creature; or has been bitten by a wild animal
- Is bleeding heavily and the bleeding cannot be stopped
- Has been hit by a car, fallen a far distance, or suffered head trauma
- Has a broken bone, compound fracture, puncture wound, incision, or skin-gaping wound
- Has significant swelling or hives
- Received an electrical shock, is burned, or has inhaled smoke
- Has a high fever, heat stroke, or frostbite
- Shows signs of bloat, is choking, or swallowed a foreign body
- Is vomiting blood, passing blood in his stools or urine, or is bleeding from the vulva, rectum, or penis
- Has collapsed, is seizing, is unable to walk, or is in severe pain

- Towels
- Tweezers
- Vet wrap

Common Emergencies

Following are some common first-aid situations.

Bites and Stings

If your Siberian is stung or bitten by insects, such as bees and hornets, such bites will usually occur in the areas where he has the shortest or thinnest hair. This means his mouth, face, ears, belly, and sometimes his feet. Within a few minutes of the sting, the area will swell, and your dog will scratch or paw at the area. Try to determine if the insect's stinger is still in your dog. As long as the stinger is attached, it may still be secreting venom. If the stinger is still attached, try to scrape it from your dog's skin, using a fingernail or the edge of a credit card.

In most instances, a cold compress can help reduce the swelling and relieve the pain. Topical cortisone will also help, as will an oral antihistamine; contact your veterinarian for dosage and recommendation. If, however, your dog is suffering a severe reaction due to repeated stings or sensitivity, contact your veterinarian immediately.

If your dog is bitten by a snake, try to determine what type of snake it was. Signs of snake bites are usually one or more puncture wounds, bleeding, and painful swelling. If your dog has been bitten by a snake, do *not* do the things you might think to do to a person—do not cut the bite, apply a tourniquet, or apply ice to the area. Seek immediate veterinary care.

Bleeding

If your dog is bleeding, he might also be in great pain. Consider putting a muzzle on him so that there is no danger that he might bite

Knowing basic canine first aid can help save your Siberian's life.

additional injury. If your dog has been hit by a car and he must be moved, gently immobilize him by putting him on a board or other hard surface. If the break is in a limb, create a splint from a stick and gauze or strips of cloth. Regardless of the type of fracture or location, do not let the dog walk, and keep him as quiet and immobile as possible. Seek immediate veterinary care.

Choking

If your dog is choking, perform a Heimlich maneuver for dogs. First, check his mouth for the choking hazard, and clear his mouth and throat. Be careful whenever you put your hands in a dog's mouth. To perform the Heimlich, lift the dog with his back against your chest. Place your hands together in a fist below his last rib. Push up and in with your fist. Check his mouth again for the object, and remove it. If the item is not freed, try to suspend your dog upside down, then check for the object. If your dog is not breathing or the object is not dislodged, seek immediate veterinary care.

Fly Bites

If you live in an area with livestock or wild creatures such as deer, you may well have a large population of flies. Some dogs are particularly susceptible to flies and will receive many bites along the ear rim. These bites, if left unchecked, can be very painful for your dog, and can lead to ear tissue loss and even to the appearance of maggots in the wounds.

If you notice many flies in your yard, try to eliminate them by keeping your yard clean and scooped, and by using fly traps or other means to control them. There are also products to apply topically to a dog's ears to heal the bites and to deter flies from biting. Some of the topical once-a-month flea and tick

you. Use clean gauze or a folded towel to cover the wound, and apply firm pressure to the wound until the bleeding stops. If the bleeding is profuse, keep the pressure on the wound for 10–15 minutes, periodically checking to see if the bleeding has stopped. Try to avoid applying a tourniquet, but if necessary, do so with the advice of a veterinarian. Seek immediate veterinary care.

Broken Bones

If your dog has broken a bone, he may be in great pain, so put a muzzle on him. Broken bones should be immobilized to avoid preventatives may also work at dissuading flies from biting your dog's ears.

Frostbite

Although frostbite is not usually an issue for Siberian Huskies, should your dog suffer frostbite, gently warm the affected area with warm, *not hot*, water. Do not rub the affected area. Once warm, keep the area warm, and seek immediate veterinary care.

Heatstroke

Frostbite may not be a common occurrence for Siberians, but heatstroke is more prevalent. If you see signs of heatstroke, which include weakness, dizziness, panting, thick saliva, and distress, remove the dog immediately from the heat. Lower his body temperature by wetting him with cool, *not cold*, water. Give him water or sports drink or some rehydrating solution, and seek immediate veterinary care.

Poisoning

If your dog is poisoned, it is important to determine what type of poison he ingested, as different poisons require different treatments. If he has ingested antifreeze, within several hours he will show impaired coordination, seizures, excessive thirst or urination, convulsions, or vomiting. If you suspect antifreeze poisoning, seek immediate veterinary care. Your veterinarian will use a test kit to verify the poisoning. If positive, your veterinarian will give your dog the antidote and possibly use dialysis to remove the ethylene glycol from his blood.

Heatstroke is more prevalent in Siberians than frostbite.

If your dog is poisoned by ingesting rodent poison, he will have difficulty breathing, show lethargy, have blood in his stool, vomit, urine, or nose. Seek immediate veterinary care. Your veterinarian will induce vomiting and treat your dog with vitamin K_1 within 24 hours of the poisoning.

You can call or visit the ASPCA's Poison Control center at: www.aspca.org or (888) 426-4435.

Seed Pods

Depending on where you live and what grasses and weeds are in your area, your dog's ears might be susceptible to seed pods, which are also known as foxtails. These seed pods are somewhat pointed and smooth when moving in one direction, such as into a dog's ear, nose, eye, skin. But the pods have bristles that keep them from moving in the opposite direction, like out of your dog. If one of these pods enters your dog's ear, he may paw at his ear, shake his head, or hold his ear or head at an angle. He will not be able to dislodge the seed pod.

Depending on where the seeds are lodged, they can burrow into the skin and even internal organs, where they can develop into very serious abscesses. They are to be taken very seriously. The best way to combat this potential hazard is to remove any such plants from your yard, and not allow your dog to play in areas with these types of seed pods. If your dog does come in contact with these pods, check his body carefully and remove all pods you find. Should you suspect a pod has lodged itself in your dog's ear, or anywhere else, seek veterinary help. The removal of these pods may require anesthesia and surgery.

Life-Saving Procedures

Knowing how to perform artificial respiration and cardiopulmonary resuscitation (CPR) can save a dog's life.

Artificial Respiration

Even if your dog stops breathing, his heart may continue beating for a few minutes. If this is the case, you can perform artificial respiration on your dog. With your dog lying on his side on a flat surface, check his airway for any foreign object, and remove it. Lift his chin to extend his head and throat. Hold his mouth closed with one hand. Put your mouth over his nose and blow gently—just enough for his chest to expand. Allow the air to be expelled from his lungs, and breathe into his nose again, at the speed of one breath every three seconds. Seek immediate veterinary care.

Cardiopulmonary Resuscitation

If your dog's heart stops beating, begin CPR immediately. If two people are available, have one perform artificial respiration while the other performs CPR. If, however, you are alone, one person can do both. With two people, the speed is one breath for three compressions. For one person, work at the pace of one breath for every five compressions. Again, make sure your dog is on his side on a flat surface. Place one hand over the other on the widest portion of the ribcage (not directly over the heart). Keep arms straight and push down on the rib cage. Compress 1/4 of the chest's width at a pace of about four compressions in three seconds.

Training Tidbit

A crate-trained Siberian will be safe and content in his crate during a disaster.

Continue until there is a steady heartbeat, and seek immediate veterinary care.

DISASTER PREPAREDNESS

Depending on where you live, you may be faced with a natural disaster at some time. Fire, flood, tornado, hurricane, earthquake, tidal wave—some come with warning, but many are unexpected. They all require immediate action for you, your family, and your Siberian Husky. Just as you develop an emergency plan for your family, complete with supplies of food, water, medication, and other survival necessities, such a plan is needed for your dog, too.

Advance planning can reduce the stress of a difficult time. First of all, make sure that your dog is microchipped and registered with a recovery service, such as the American Kennel Club's Companion Animal Recovery (AKC-CAR) service. Have both your contact information on file, as well as someone else's information, such as your Siberian's breeder, or a friend or relative. Keep up-to-date tags on your dog's collar, with current contact information, and have him wear his microchip recovery tag, too.

Make sure you have copies of his vaccination records and current pictures of your Siberian. Keep these with you in case you have to prove the dog is yours. Have contact information for your veterinarian, the emergency veterinarian, boarding kennels, and motels that accept dogs in your immediate area, as well as a bit farther from home.

When creating your emergency kit (food, water, and medications) for your family, include those for your dog, too, and add an emergency leash and collar. Keep your human

> ## Multi-Dog Tip
>
> In case of an emergency, keep other dogs away from the injured party. That way, it will be easier to treat the injured dog.

first-aid kit with your canine first-aid kit. Make certain you have a crate available, that your dog is comfortable in it, and that you have room for it in your car. Remember that some emergency shelters will not take animals, so your dog might have to stay in his crate in the car. Conduct emergency drills to practice packing your family, dog, and emergency gear into the car. Be as prepared as you can.

Should a disaster occur, bring your dog into the house or secure him in his crate. Disasters often include chaos, loud noises, storms, and other occurrences that may be frightening to your dog. Keep him calm and close to you to minimize any chance of losing him in the chaos. Also, remember that in the case of a disaster, *do not leave your dog at home*. You cannot know how long you may be away from home, and you do not want him to have to survive on his own.

If you are not at home when disaster strikes, have stickers on your doors to notify rescuers that a pet lives on your property. Ask a neighbor, with whom your pet is comfortable, to evacuate your dog in the event of a disaster. With a little advance planning, you can make sure that your pet will be safe in a disaster.

CHAPTER 9

SIBERIAN HUSKY TRAINING

As you have discovered, Siberian Huskies are intelligent and independent creatures. They are the best in the world at doing their job as endurance sled dogs, and Siberian owners appreciate them for all of their great qualities. Living with them can be a joy, but it can also be a challenge. Your adorable puppy has grown into a beautiful adult, or a new adult companion has joined your life. You now have a full-grown, independent-thinking Siberian in your family. He may know some basic manners, but now that he is an adult, his education must continue.

Whether your ultimate goal is to have your Siberian ready to compete in rally or obedience events, or to walk pleasantly on a leash and respond to some safety commands, it is time build on the basic manners you (or others) have taught him and continue his training.

TRY A CLASS

Consider enrolling him in a basic obedience course. If your Siberian joined your family as a puppy and attended a puppy kindergarten, contact those trainers and ask about an obedience class. If you need to find a trainer, try local kennel clubs and obedience training clubs for classes. You can find a list of clubs in your area on the American Kennel Club website (www.akc.org), or you can find trainers in your area from the Association of Pet Dog Trainers (www.apdt.com).

A class with a good trainer helps focus your time and attention on the basic skills that need reinforcing. Most classes meet weekly for an hour, usually in the evening or on weekends. Just keep in mind that an hour a week in class is not sufficient to train your Siberian. You need to be consistent and practice throughout the week. Your job is to continue training and reinforcing good behavior at home.

CAN I HAVE YOUR ATTENTION?

The key to training your Siberian Husky is to get and hold his attention. You are well aware that Siberians are curious and very gregarious by nature. If you take your dog out for a walk, his natural curiosity and desire to run may be far stronger lures than just wanting to be with you. Therefore, you must do something to get and keep his focus on you, which you can do by using any of three basic techniques.

WIIFM?

The first technique is showing your Siberian

"WIIFM"—what's in it for me? Figure out what motivates your dog. Some dogs have a favorite toy, some react to praise and petting, while others are motivated by food. Most Siberians are among the last group. You know your dog and what he likes. So, make sure that you have small pieces of his favorite treats or his favorite toy available before you begin your training session.

Be Unpredictable

The second technique is to be somewhat unpredictable. If you are walking in one direction and his attention strays, suddenly change directions. If you normally turn around to the right, turn to the left. If you always walk at a slow pace, speed up. By frequently changing what you do, your Siberian will not be bored and you will keep his focus.

Use the Right Equipment

The final technique is getting the right equipment and using it correctly. The recommended equipment is simple. You will need a sturdy leather or web leash that is at least 6 feet (2 m) long, with a strong snap. This lead should be wide enough so that it does not cut into your skin when in use. You will also need a properly fitted collar.

A number of dog-walking tools also are available: head halters, leaders, no-jump harnesses, and walking harnesses. The first two are comprised of straps that go around your dog's muzzle and head to give you control when walking. Head halters are designed to help you direct the dog's muzzle in the direction you want him to go, similar to a horse's halter. The leader enables you to control your dog by applying downward pressure on the dog's muzzle. The walking harness straps around your dog's chest and ribcage, taking leash pressure off of his neck. And the jump-inhibiting harness is strapped around your dog's neck and chest, body, and legs.

Although all of these tools have their uses, none is without a potential for harm. Often dogs are very unhappy with muzzle-like straps fitting around their mouths and noses. The head halter and leader must be carefully fitted and used. If incorrectly utilized, these halters can interfere with a dog's eyes, and can exert significant pressure on his head and neck, which could cause strain. A walking harness, in addition to not affording much control, is not padded, and could cause rubbing or bruising with prolonged use. The no-jump harnesses are

Training Tidbit

Some people think Siberian Huskies are difficult to train. But do not ever lose sight of their original job as long-distance, endurance sled dogs, and that they are the very best at that job. Other things you may want them to do are not as instinctive, so you must be a creative trainer.

comprised of a complex group of straps, and if put on incorrectly, can cause pain and injury to your dog.

All of these apparatuses have their uses, but none of these options should be a substitute for training your dog. Occasionally, the benefits of these walking halters and harnesses are lost because a strong dog will just pull until he gets his way. Or, a dog will behave well while wearing the halter or harness, but revert to poor behavior when on a collar and leash. For these reasons, it much better to spend the time training your dog on how to walk properly while wearing a simple collar and leash.

OBEDIENCE TRAINING

Training sessions should be in a large, secure area (such as your backyard or a park) without many distractions. Try to find a quiet area in the park, away from children at play or other pets. With small treats in your pocket and your eager dog attached to a sturdy leash, you are ready to begin your formal training.

Heel

The first lesson is having your dog walk nicely at your left side. The official obedience command for this is *Heel*. Although you may never compete in the obedience ring, you may still think of this activity as "heeling," and use the command, "Ted, heel." Heeling means your dog remains at your left side and walks nicely with you at whatever speed you choose, in whatever direction you go, and when you stop, he sits politely at your left side.

If you have practiced with your dog since his puppyhood to walk nicely with you, this more formal heeling should provide little challenge for your Siberian. If, however, he came to you as an adult, you may find the first heeling session a bit of an adventure. Remember to keep your training sessions short initially.

Use "What's In It For Me?" method for training your Siberian—find out what motivates him and use that to reward him.

Encourage good behavior by providing lots of encouragement, treats, and praise. Use redirection if your dog seems to get bored or distracted.

Teaching the Heel

To begin, you will probably find it easier to have the excess length of lead folded up in your right hand. That will allow you to encourage, pet, and reward your dog with your left hand. If your Siberian knows the command to sit, begin the training session with him seated at your left side. (If he doesn't yet know how

If your dog seems to be more enthusiastic than you would like him to be, you may want to tone down your praise and the frequency of treats. If your dog is reticent to join you, more encouragement and treats might be in order, at least initially. If your dog gets distracted, offer more praise and treats to recapture his attention, or change direction immediately (make a right about turn or turn one direction or the other) or change speed (begin a short jog or take very small steps).

to sit, begin with your Siberian standing at your left side.) You will say your dog's name, followed by the command you want him to obey. If his name is Ted, say, "Ted, heel," and walk briskly forward. Encourage your dog to join you by patting your left leg, gently petting his head, talking to him, or by giving him a small treat.

If your dog is paying you no attention at all, try to evaluate why this is the case. Are there too many distractions where you are training? Has he just eaten, so he is not interested in the treats you are offering? Is he too hot? Is he getting ill? If there is some legitimate reason why his interest is waning, it might be time to curtail the lesson.

Having your dog stay with you at your left side, at *Heel,* is used in obedience competitions and in the show ring.

Although Siberian Huskies are highly intelligent and usually very motivated by praise and reward, you may find it difficult to get your dog's attention at times. This could be due to a variety of things, from a good scent in the air, to a testing phase, to a distraction he cannot ignore. Siberian Huskies are very independent dogs—they have to be, to do their jobs as sled dogs. When those inherent character traits of independence and apparent stubbornness appear, you will find that continuing his training is a challenge.

If and when this occurs, do not become frustrated or angry with your Siberian. Curtail the training session or change what you were doing. This is the time to seek professional help. If you have not already done so, find a good trainer and training class and enroll yourself and your dog. Good dog trainers will offer suggestions and add other tools to your training regimen that can help you get and keep your Siberian's attention and continue your training success.

Teaching the Sit With Heeling

Once he seems to be walking well with you, it is time to refresh the *sit* command. With a treat in your left hand, put the treat directly in front of your Siberian's nose. Begin to slow yourself down in preparation for stopping. As you slow, say your dog's name and the command ("Ted, sit") as you bring your fingers with the treat up and back over your dog's head, while you stop. Bringing the treat up and backward will cause your dog's rump to drop to the ground. When he is sitting, praise and reward him.

From that point on, begin the heel command only when your dog is nicely sitting on your left side. Give the command, "Ted, heel." Continue encouraging, praising, and rewarding him when he is good. Change speed and direction to keep him interested. Ask him to sit when you stop walking.

Release Words

Over the course of training, your Siberian learns a number of command words that ask him to perform specific behaviors, such as *sit*, *stay*, and *come*. But there is one other word you should teach your dog—a release word that lets him know he is no longer in "training" mode, and he can act silly, like a dog, once again. "Okay" or "done" make good release words, but any word will do. Try to pick one that doesn't sound like a training command, and one that you and your entire family will be able to remember and use with your Siberian.

Daily practice will reinforce these new skills. Soon, you will find that you can use the command to *heel* in any situation, and your dog will walk nicely at your side. Although it is never encouraged to take any dog off leash out in the community, the Siberian's desire to run makes it even more challenging to teach off-leash heeling. However, if a securely fenced area is available to you (your yard, a fenced tennis court, etc.), heeling off-leash can further reinforce these commands. You may also wish to utilize a long, strong, and lightweight cord (such as parachute cord) as a security line when training a Siberian "off leash." The lightweight cord can easily be grabbed if needed to keep your Siberian from leaving.

Stay

The *stay* command is used to tell a dog to stay where he is. Teaching this command is important to his safety—use it to keep your dog from running into the street, from approaching a snake, from walking through wet paint. The command to stay can be given to your dog when he is in any position—lying down, sitting, or standing. From the time your dog is familiar with and somewhat consistent in responding to the position commands (such as *sit*), you can begin teaching *stay*, and slowly increase the two variables of duration and distance important to the command.

Teaching the Sit/Stay

Ask your dog to sit. Once he is sitting, calmly praise him, but do not give him a treat. Immediately give the next command, "Ted, stay." Wait a few seconds, praise him for his good stay, and give him a reward. By delaying the reward, you are training the idea of "stay." Slowly increase the time between the command and the reward. If your Siberian does not remain in the position (e.g., sitting) or does not hold his stay, repeat the commands and make sure he follows them before praise and reward.

To increase the length of the stay command and to prepare yourself to put more distance between yourself and the dog, after giving the sit and stay commands, step in front of your dog and face him. Keep eye contact, and repeat, "Ted, stay. Good stay" the entire time you are in front of him.

Another way to increase the duration of the stay command is to have your dog sit and stay before feeding him each day. Give the commands and have him sit and stay while you put his food bowl on the floor, making sure he waits until you are ready for him to eat. Start with short-duration stay commands, then release

Want to Know More?

For a refresher on how to teach the down command, go to Chapter 4: Training Your Siberian Husky Puppy.

him from the stay by using a release word, such as "okay," and watch him dive for his bowl!

Eventually, you will want to add some distance between yourself and your dog during the *stay* command. It's easy to do this when you are in front of your dog as he sits and stays. Continue making eye contact and repeating, "Ted, stay. Good stay" while taking a step backward, away from your dog. Over time, increase the number of steps, until you are at the end of the 6-foot (2-m) lead.

You can practice the *stay* command any time at home, such as when you are going from one room to another and you do not want your Siberian to join you, or when you want him to stay inside when someone leaves the house.

Down/Stay

If you trained the *down* command to your Siberian as a puppy, he should already be proficient at it. If your Siberian joined your family as an adult, he may be learning this position for the first time. As your dog becomes proficient with the *down* command, add the command to *stay*, just as you did with the Sit/Stay (above), ever increasing the duration and distance from you.

Stand

There are a number of times when you will want your dog to stand still, such as during a veterinary exam, or when you are cleaning mud from or drying his feet. Although often forgotten as a dog training command, *stand* is certainly one of the more important ones. Since you've already trained your dog to sit, training the command to stand is fairly easy. With your dog sitting at heel, give the command, "Ted, stand." Put a treat in front of your Siberian's nose and move it straight ahead of his nose. This will pull his head forward and cause his hindquarters to rise. Praise him

The entire family can participate in teaching your Siberian commands like the **down–stay**.

do. Select a time and place, such as in the yard during play. Just remember first to say his name to get his attention, and then be clear with the command. If he does not obey the command, be prepared to repeat the command and make sure that he accomplishes the task, and follow with praise and reward.

The better trained your dog is, the more challenges you can add to his training. Don't forget that Siberian Huskies get bored easily. Just as you used change of speed and direction to keep his attention while learning to walk with you, try adding some other training distractions as he gets more confident with his training. The more reliable your dog is at staying when there are distractions, the more solid his training, and the more confidence you will have in him.

The time you spend training your Siberian firmly cements the bond between you and your dog. Remember that you are not asking him to do things he cannot do. You want him to walk nicely with you. You want him to know how to sit, stand, and lie down when necessary. And you want him to stay in one place if needed. All of these simple tasks will help make your dog a more civilized member of your family, and could help keep him safe in potentially dangerous situations.

and give him his reward as soon as he is in a standing position. If he should sit again, repeat the command, process, and treat. If your dog has a natural tendency to sit, when he raises his hindquarters, position your left foot under his loin, thus making it difficult for him to sit.

Once you have taught your dog to stand on command, walk him into a stand or bring him into a stand from any other position, and vice-versa. You can also train him to *stay* from the stand position, as you did with the sit and down. Over time, increase the time and distance you are away from your dog.

ADDING DISTRACTIONS

When your dog knows his commands, test this knowledge by adding distractions. Train somewhere outside of your normal training setting or at a different time than you normally

Multi-Dog Tip

When starting your dog's training, make sure there are special training times when you are alone with just one dog. This special one-to-one time is not only great time for training, but a great time to build your relationship with your dog.

CHAPTER 10

SIBERIAN HUSKY PROBLEM BEHAVIORS

Siberian Huskies are usually easy dogs with which to live. However, from time to time as they grow up, or perhaps when you bring a new dog into your home, you may find the need to address some behavior problems. Most of these problems should be minor—ones you can resolve with good training advice and consistency. However, if the problem is serious, the best advice is to check with your veterinarian and find a good canine behaviorist who can help you resolve the issue completely.

BEHAVIOR CHANGES AND HEALTH

Puppy behavior problems should be expected, to some extent. You should be able to train a puppy not to misbehave. However, when an adult dog displays a behavior problem, such as aggression; excessive chewing, digging, barking, or howling; or biting, nipping, or other unacceptable behavior, you should take this seriously—especially if it's a big change in behavior. Behavior changes, especially vocalizing, biting, or showing aggression, can be symptoms of health problems. Therefore, the first step to take when encountering a significant change in your dog's behavior is to visit your veterinarian. Explain the change in behavior, and when it occurs. Your veterinarian will examine your dog, and may decide to do some lab work to check for a medical reason for the behavior change.

If your dog is given a clean bill of health, it is time to address the behavior issue. The severity of the problem will determine your next course of action. Some of these bad behaviors are annoying, but not dangerous. Therefore, you can attempt to resolve them through focused dog training. However, dangerous behavior, such as aggression or biting, *must be addressed immediately*, and it may be time to consult a canine behaviorist.

FINDING A CANINE BEHAVIORIST

There is a significant difference between a dog trainer and a canine behaviorist. Although dog trainers can be very skilled and professional individuals, they generally work on the fairly basic functions of dog ownership. Although some may be highly educated in their field and even be members of local or national dog trainers associations, others do not have much formal education in dog training. Successful dog training does require

Changes in behavior may indicate a medical problem, so see your veterinarian.

a modest understanding of dog behavior and motivation, but not the depth of knowledge and education required of a canine behaviorist.

A canine behaviorist usually has a college or graduate degree and certification in behavioral science and canine behavior. A good canine behaviorist understands motivation, conditioning, and desensitization techniques. Behaviorists usually work one-on-one to evaluate the dog's behavior, his environment, and his interaction with his owner. Canine behaviorists are also certified and are members of professional animal behaviorist associations.

If the situation with your Siberian Husky

indicates the need for a canine behaviorist, follow these guidelines to find the right one for you. First, ask for recommendations among your veterinarian, your dog's breeder, and other friends and Siberian fanciers in your area. Check the certifications of those recommended. To increase the list of potential behaviorists, visit the websites of national animal behaviorist organizations, which you can easily find by searching the Internet for animal behavior societies.

With a list of certified local canine behaviorists, ask for and check references. Animal behaviorists should have a list of clients with whom you can speak. If possible, meet with the behaviorists on your short list. It is great if you can meet each one before you make your final selection. If this is not feasible and you select one of the names from your short list, treat that first appointment as an "interview." If you do not feel comfortable or have a good connection with the selected behaviorist, try another name on your list. Likewise, if you feel uncomfortable with the behaviorist's approach at any time during your working sessions, do not feel shy about stopping the work to discuss it, or ending the relationship completely.

Use common sense in your selection and partnership with a canine behaviorist, and you will work successfully together to resolve whatever behavior issue your dog exhibits.

An overarching consideration when dealing with canine behavior problems is whether or not the dog was raised by you or if he came into your life as an adult. If your Siberian joined your family as an adult, you may not know what his puppyhood was like and what sort of temperament of his parents had. Behavior problems are often caused by two factors: heredity and environment. The one drawback to adopting an older dog is that you do not know his history, and you may be dealing with someone else's mistakes. For this reason, you may wish to err on the side of caution and seek help from a canine behaviorist early in the process.

AGGRESSION

Because there are different types of aggression, the first step is to identify what kind the dog is manifesting: Is he is trying to establish dominance in the family? Is it aggression toward other animals? Is it aggression toward people?

Challenges from a Young Adult

You may recall during the puppy socialization discussion in Chapter 4 that, between 18 and 24 months, your young adult dog may challenge you. He may protect his food or favorite toys, he may no longer like to be groomed, or he may test some of your rules, such as by jumping on the furniture. In addition to having your veterinarian eliminate any medical reason for his behavior, make sure that your pet Siberian has been spayed or neutered. An intact animal may test his dominance more so than would a dog who has been altered.

Examine your reaction to your dog's behavior. Often, one's reaction is to overdiscipline young adult dogs when they challenge authority. This is generally not the best solution, as it may escalate aggressive behavior. Frequently, you will notice that his testing coincides with your becoming a bit lax

in enforcing the rules. So, make sure you are consistent and fair in your approach to your dog. Remember to praise and reward him for good behavior.

Pay close attention that his behavior does not escalate. In dealing with any form of aggressive behavior, the most important consideration is safety—the safety of people, animals, and your pet. If his behavior becomes a more significant problem, or if he does not respond to the consistent application of your rules, it might be time to consult a canine behaviorist for some advice.

Toward Other Animals

A young adult's attempt at challenging you should not be ignored, but is often just part of growing up. The other types of aggression are potentially more serious. If your Siberian is showing aggression to other animals, you'll need to assess the behavior carefully.

Siberian Huskies have a strong prey drive and will chase—and if fast enough, catch—small animals, occasionally harming them in the process. If your Siberian is chasing squirrels in the yard or your neighbor's cat who jumped the fence, this is not aggression toward other animals—this is instinct. The best option in this instance might be to speak with your neighbor about keeping his cat indoors, or to cover your dog run.

By the Numbers

Zero: The tolerance for a dog displaying aggressive behavior. See a canine behaviorist immediately.

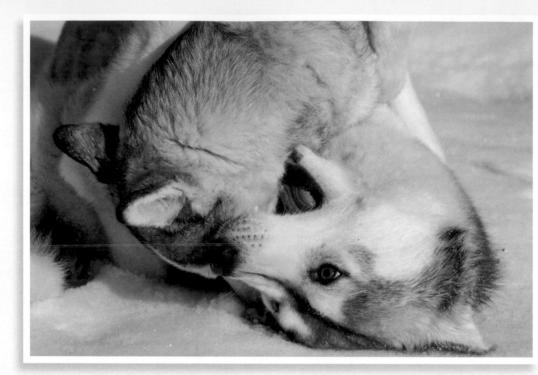

Siberians are known for what may seem to be ferocious play with each other.

Toward Other Dogs

When it comes to aggression among the dogs in your home, understand that Siberians are known for what may seem to be ferocious play. If you have a second dog (especially if it is another Siberian), learn the difference between rough play and aggression. Growling, mouthing, and even biting each other's well-furred hides are not uncommon during Siberian play. However, be aware of any escalation of that rough play.

Having multiple dogs in one home may prompt arguments over food, treats, or toys. If your dogs are squabbling over a favorite toy, or being protective of their food dishes, your intervention is needed. Feed them in different places, such as in their crates, or feed one in the kitchen and one in the family room. Give them chew toys only in their crates. If a favorite toy

is causing conflict, remove it. In short, remove the cause of the problem.

Never lose sight of this breed's inherent traits. These are pack and team dogs. Teams and packs are very structured groupings, with each member having his own role. The dogs in the pack work through their hierarchical issues with each member, and the biggest problems in a pack are frequently among animals of the same sex and age. You may well find the same problems if you have two dogs who are of the same sex and relatively the same age. In such instances, reinforcing that you are the leader of your "pack" will help establish some order. But sometimes dogs just need to work out their roles within the team. If this is possible to do without a truly violent fight, it just might be worth letting the dogs resolve their differences, with you keeping a watchful eye.

On Leash

Most dog-to-dog aggression appears while your dog is walking on leash outside of your home. Sometimes a dog spends his life in a home with his family, and he may become either wary of or excited by other dogs. Both of these reactions are normal for a dog who is not often in the company of other dogs. However, these over-reactions can cause problems and can be avoided. Good socialization with other dogs while on walks, starting from puppyhood and continuing as your dog ages, will make him comfortable with other dogs.

Learn to recognize and understand your dog's body language. An anxious, fearful dog can be just as dangerous as an openly aggressive dog. A fearful dog, when challenged, will often react aggressively. So, learn to recognize both behaviors. A fearful and anxious dog will be very stiff and tense, possibly low to the ground. His ears may be either partially or completely back. His tail will be carried low and may be tucked between his legs. He may whine or growl. A fearful dog can become aggressive very quickly.

An openly aggressive dog will hold his stance strongly. His ears will be back, and he will make eye contact. He may growl, or bark and bear his teeth. His tail will probably not be

Too Close

Sometimes two dogs of the same sex who are near the same age, including siblings, won't ever get along well.

wagging, but neither will it be tucked between his legs. The hair along his spine will be standing on edge.

If you observe in your dog either of these combinations of body signs, above all be safe. Remove your dog from the threatening situation. Because of the basic training you have done with your dog, say his name, and give the command to heel ("Ted, heel"). Move briskly away from the other dog. If necessary, give a second command, and offer a treat as a lure to walk with you. When your dog comes with you, praise him and give him a reward. Continue giving your dog commands to heel, while you move away from the other dog, and command your dog's attention. Reinforce that you are in charge, your dog should pay attention to you, and that you will keep him safe.

If you have an instance in which your dog does show extreme fear or aggression toward other dogs while on a leash, even if you

If you notice your dog taking an aggressive stance, such as around the food bowl, get professional help right away.

successfully resolved that particular issue, understand that there may be a problem growing. To remain safe, you will want to seek the help of a canine behaviorist. In the interim, if you need to take your Siberian near other dogs, consider using a head halter, which will additionally serve as a muzzle. The safety of people and other animals should never be taken lightly.

Toward People

Even more frightening is a dog who shows excessive fear or aggression toward people. The same body language cues will be apparent if your dog is fearful or aggressive around people. Should your dog demonstrate these behaviors, do not punish him, as it may make the situation worse. Again, say his name and give the command to heel ("Ted, heel!"). Encourage, praise, and reward him for responding to your command. Do not think this is an isolated instance. *Seek professional help immediately*.

A professional canine behaviorist will most likely treat this problem by desensitizing the dog through a series of non-threatening exposure to other dogs or people. By controlling the parameters of such meetings, the behaviorist can make the desensitization

sessions successful. However, it will probably be a long process to achieve the desired results.

CHEWING

All dogs chew. Chewing is actually good for dogs, as it helps keep tartar and plaque from forming on their teeth. The problem, however, comes when your Siberian chews your dining table leg or your new pair of shoes. So, the key is to direct his chewing away from your things on to more appropriate items. There are a few ways to do this.

The first rule is to not leave your Siberian Husky unsupervised with things you do not want him to chew. When you leave him at home alone, restrict his movement and access to things. At the same time, provide him

Give your Siberian appropriate items to chew on.

with items that he is allowed to chew, such as rawhides, chew toys, filled and frozen treat balls, Nylabones, etc. Don't just give him these chew toys when you are not around; also have them available when he is with you. Let him know that these are owner-approved chewing options by playing games with him using the toys. Play tug-of-war or hide-the-toy. Encourage him to chew by offering praise and a treat when he is chewing appropriately.

If you discover that your dog has been chewing things he shouldn't, bad-tasting products can be applied to the item to dissuade your dog from chewing it. If, however, you discover that your dog is chewing *himself*, this could be a sign of allergies, arthritis, or another medical condition. If this is the case, please seek veterinary advice.

DIGGING

Just as they love to chew, dogs like to dig. Dirt is dirt, and your Siberian will not be able to tell the difference between your favorite flower bed and an old dirt patch. Your job is to discourage him from digging where it is inappropriate, but allow him to dig where it is acceptable. There are three ways to help accomplish this.

First, locate a good place for him to dig and "seed" it with something appealing, such as a large bone or some other large treat that will bury well and be acceptably unearthed. Just imagine his surprise when his digging yields such a prize! You can periodically fill back his hole and bury another treat to keep his interest.

Next, put up some temporary fencing (even chicken wire, or short decorative fence) around those areas where you do not want him to dig. This will not actually keep him from digging, but it might dissuade him and give you time to redirect him.

Finally, if he does dig in an unacceptable place, bury some of his feces in the hole he dug

Siberian Huskies are exuberant and inquisitive, so jumping up is a natural behavior for them.

and fill it with dirt. Dogs usually do not like to dig up poop.

Digging is often a symptom of boredom, so consider more exercise for your dog. Or, if you are leaving him in the yard alone for a little while, leave some toys or filled chews that will provide him with challenges and entertainment.

Keep Safety in Mind

Make sure your Siberian is not digging near your fence line. An industrious digger could possibly dig his way out of your yard. If this is happening, consider burying large rocks or sink chicken wire below the fence to dissuade your Houdini.

Also, pay attention to the safety issues of

holes. Stepping in unseen holes can be very dangerous for children, adults, and even dogs. Make sure the excavation is done away from areas of human and animal traffic. Additionally, if holes become tunnels, there is the danger of collapse. Periodically refill the holes to avoid this.

JUMPING UP

Siberians are naturally inquisitive and friendly. It is not unusual that your dog will want to investigate the kitchen counters or welcome guests with a kiss on the lips. Siberian Huskies are medium-sized dogs, but when they stand on their hind legs, they are the perfect height for counter surfing or placing their paws on people's shoulders. Dissuading Siberians from jumping up is an ongoing challenge.

Counter tops can be dangerous places for dog paws and noses. You'll want to train your Siberian not to jump up by using the command "Off!" Do not use the command "Down!" for this purpose, as that is the command you use when you want him to lie down. When you see him trying to jump on your counter, stop him, and use the command, "Ted, off," followed by praise and reward. This takes vigilance on your part.

If you have a dog who is slow to learn this command (which usually happens after a dog has stolen something tasty from the counter), try another technique. Place light but noisy items along the edge of the counter—clean aluminum cans or plastic bottles work well. Then, when your dog jumps on the counter,

Want to Know More?

For a refresher on the *heel* command, see Chapter 9: Siberian Husky Training.

Multi-Dog Tip

Siberian Huskies are gregarious dogs who often get bored when left alone. Sometimes the best solution to a problem behavior is getting your Siberian a dog of his own.

his forepaws or nose will hit the cans/bottles, and make a loud noise. This noise will surprise him and reinforce your command, "Off!"

If your dog is jumping on you, use the same command, "Ted, off!" As you give the command, turn to the side to prevent him from jumping on you. When he stays on the ground, praise and reward him. If you are too late to turn and deflect him, and his paws are on your body or shoulders, give the command again, "Ted, off!" while you turn around and take a step away from him so he drops to the ground.

Teaching a dog not to jump is actually fairly easy, but requires consistency.

LEASH PULLING

Training your dog not to pull on his leash is just an extension of the heeling lessons from Chapter 9. If he is pulling, make him stop by changing direction while you give him the command to *heel*, and offer a lure/treat. You can also give him the command to *sit*, and offer him a treat.

The key is to do something to get your dog's attention, either through your voice, praise and reward, use of a squeaky toy, or misdirection. But you need to get his attention. If he is pulling a lot on his leash, he might be in need of a refresher period of intensive training to reinforce his commands. Plan your training sessions for on leash in the park or shopping center, as well as for off-leash sessions in a confined area.

NIPPING

Next to aggression, the canine behavior problem that causes most concern is nipping. Whether it is called mouthing, nipping, or biting, it should be taken seriously. This behavior generally begins as puppy's mouthing, and that is the time to stop it. However, during the life of your dog, it may reappear. And when it does, it must be stopped. No dog should ever initiate biting. The fate of a dog who bites is often left to the law, and the outcome is usually not good.

If your dog does start mouthing or nipping, immediately say "OW!" or "NO!" If he stops, praise him. If he does not stop, or nips again, say "OWWWWWWW!" or "NOOOOOOOOO!", stop whatever interaction you were having with the dog, and leave the room for a short time. When you return, if your dog has calmed down, praise and reward him.

If this behavior continues for any length of time, or if your dog seems to nip at children, seek the advice of a canine behaviorist immediately. Remember at all times that safety is paramount.

RUNNING AWAY

The most dreaded and scary time for a Siberian owner occurs when your dog gets away from you in the open. You know that this breed has a strong tendency to run, and should your Siberian ever slip his collar or dart out of your front door, the strong training you've provided can help with your response.

First, do not panic; remain as calm as you can. Get your dog's attention by calling his name and giving the *come* command. If you have a treat, show it to him. Better yet, if you have a dog dish with biscuits or kibble, rattle the loose food in the dish--the sound is unmistakable.

Above all, *do not chase your Siberian*! If you chase him, he will think you are playing a game, and he could dash into the street. If he does not come to you for his treat, try the command you use to get him walking with you, "Ted, let's go!" Pat your leg, and encourage him to join you for a walk. If he does not join you (although it will be difficult for you), give the command again, turn and walk quickly or even jog away from him, encouraging him to join you. Once he gets close, do not lunge for him. Rather, offer the treat, pet him, praise him, and then get hold of him.

VOCALIZING

Barking, per se, is usually not a problem among Siberian Huskies, because that is not their normal voice. However, Siberians do have a number of other ways of vocalizing that can be as annoying as barking. These include

Siberians usually vocalize by howling, grumbling, growling, whining, shrieking, and "talking."

howling, grumbling, growling, whining, shrieking, and "talking." And, of course, they are also capable of barking.

Happily, canine vocalization is not dangerous, but it can be very annoying to you and to your neighbors. Dogs vocalize for any number of reasons; they may speak in warning, in excitement, when anxious or bored, in accompaniment, or to seek attention. It also seems as if, especially with Siberians, canine vocalization has a familial component. Noisy dogs seem to beget noisy dogs. There are a number of ways you can dissuade your dog from vocalizing.

The first thing to consider is when and why your dog vocalizes. Is he noisy when you leave him alone? Is he noisy before meals? Is he noisy when someone comes to the door? If

he's noisy when you are not home, attempt to redirect your dog's attention.

Find a long-lasting, interactive treat that your dog particularly likes. This could be a bone or a hollow toy that you fill with peanut butter or soft cheese and freeze, or a "dog puzzle" that you stuff with biscuits and let your dog figure out how to extract them. When you leave the house, give your dog one or two of these toys so he can occupy his time. If he likes the treats well enough, he will concentrate on them and forget to make noise when you leave.

If your dog makes noise in your presence, you will need a way of letting him know you want him to stop. There are two ways you can work on this problem, and both of them require a command to be quiet. Try not to use the word "no" as the command word because it has too many meanings. Use a word like "Hush," "Shhhh," "Quiet," or "Enough" and have everyone in your family use the same word.

Before you can utilize this command, you need to first train your dog to vocalize on command. When you want your dog to talk, use a word like, "Woof," "Howl," "Speak," or even the sound of howling, "Arrrrooo." Once your dog is talking, give your command to be quiet, and put a treat at his nose. He will be far more interested in the treat than in what he's saying, so he will stop talking. Praise him and give him the reward. Encouraging him to vocalize will make it easier to teach him when to be quiet. The command to stop talking can then be used whenever your Siberian decides to speak on his own. Once you give the command to be quiet and your Siberian becomes quiet, wait a bit before giving him his reward.

Even if you have not trained your dog to vocalize on command, you can utilize the same process for getting him to quiet. The only difference is that you have less control over the training opportunities. However, if you are having a problem with an extremely talkative dog, you can probably make some educated guesses as to when he might be noisy. Have yourself prepared for those times with treats in your pocket. When your dog vocalizes, give the command to quiet, put a treat in front of

Engage Your Dog

Siberian Huskies can get bored easily. Hyperactivity, separation anxiety, or just plain boredom can all be symptoms of this situation. Siberians need companionship, exercise, and entertainment to avoid behavior problems. Make sure your dog is getting ample exercise—a tired Siberian Husky usually does not get into much trouble. Give him toys to play with. Pay attention to him when you are home. He is part of your family, so make sure he is included as such. The bigger part he plays in your family and the more engaged your Siberian is, the better a pet and companion he will be.

his nose, and when he is quiet, praise him and offer him the reward.

Whatever you do, do never, ever reward him for making noise. And physical punishment for making noise does not work. If you have a particularly noisy and stubborn dog, you might wish to consult an animal behaviorist or your veterinarian for some help. In some jurisdictions, nuisance barking can be cause for ticketing and animal confiscation. So, it should be treated very seriously.

CHAPTER 11

SIBERIAN HUSKY SPORTS AND ACTIVITIES

One of the reasons to have a dog in your life is for the companionship—not just at home, but when participating in some of your favorite activities. And Siberian Huskies are just the dogs to join you in any number of fun activities. Siberians are an obvious choice for walkers, joggers, hikers, and bicyclers. However, this is a very versatile breed that enjoys human companionship and can thrive in many other venues, such as therapy work or tracking—and their ability to pull a sled over vast distances is legendary. These are truly dogs for all seasons and all reasons.

The more activities you do with your Siberian Husky, the stronger your bond will grow, your training will pay off, and he will succeed at whatever you ask of him. Be creative and adaptable in finding a way for your dog to participate in your favorite activities. If you are an avid walker, hiker, jogger, bicyclist, or camper, you will find that your Siberian will make a great companion in all of those endeavors.

Before you include your dog in any of these activities, however, take a few precautionary steps. First, make sure your dog is in good health and at his proper weight. Although exercise is a good way for a dog to get fit and lose weight, go slowly. Regular gentle exercise and walks, coupled with careful calorie control, are the best ways to get your dog in shape for more strenuous sports and activities. Additionally, make sure he is current on his vaccinations and parasite control medications. Finally, be certain that he has no health issues. A trip to your veterinarian will help you accomplish all of these pre-exercise clearances. When your vet pronounces your dog ready for a new adventure, you are good to go.

ACTIVITIES

When including your Siberian in a physical activity, such as walking or jogging, keep a few things in mind:

- All dogs, especially Siberian Huskies, should be kept on leash at all times—including while walking, hiking, jogging, etc.
- Don't begin walking or jogging with your dog until he is a fairly well trained heeler and responds to your commands consistently.
- Don't take your dog out with you if he displays any aggression or biting problems.
- Pay attention to the weather, amount of sun, and the temperature of the ground surface

Before you start any new activity with your Siberian, take him to his veterinarian to make sure he's in good health.

on which your dog will be walking, to make sure that he will not get overheated or burn the pads of his feet.

- Make sure that the area you are going to is free of hazards, such as dry grass seeds, broken glass, unleashed dogs, etc.
- Make sure that both you and your dog are visible to traffic and other people, especially at night. Consider a reflective vest for yourself and a reflective collar and leash for your dog.
- Make sure you have all of the equipment and supplies required for each activity. However, there are a couple of things required for *all* activities: identification on your dog's collar and poop bags.

With all of these pre-planning items checked off your list, you are ready to begin.

Walking

People are always looking for easy and fun ways to exercise, and nothing is easier than taking your dog out for a walk. Whether you walk through your neighborhood, in a park, or on a walking trail, your Siberian is the perfect companion.

If this is will be a short walk and the weather is not hot, you probably won't need to bring along any water for your dog. Otherwise, carry water and a cup or dish from which your dog can drink. Start walks with your dog slowly and initially keep the distance and duration fairly short. Build up to longer, faster walks as you both get into better condition.

While exercising with your dog, watch for signs of distress. If your dog stops on his own, it is probably a good idea to curtail the activity.

If he starts to limp, stop the activity. If he seems to be panting excessively, stop, give him some water, and find some shade. If any other unusual symptom occurs, such as weakness, diarrhea, vomiting, excessive salivation, or anything out of the ordinary, stop, take your dog home, and consider contacting your veterinarian.

After your outing, give your dog plenty of fresh water and examine him for any parasites, seed pods, or other foreign substances. Check the pads of his feet for wear or injury. Feel his feet, legs, and joints for any inflammation or pain. If you encounter anything out of the ordinary, contact your veterinarian for advice. Most likely, both you and your dog will have enjoyed your time together in your new activity.

Jogging

The next logical step up from walking with your Siberian is jogging with him. All of the cautions for walking are equally true for jogging. And, regardless of the length of your jog, carry water both for yourself and your dog. Your choice of collar depends on the area in which you will be jogging and the level of your dog's training. Some joggers prefer a hands-free leash—one that connects to a waistband. Whatever you choose, just make sure that you have control of your dog at all times.

When starting out, jog for a short distance and moderate speed, and slowly build to longer distances and faster speeds. All running (for both of you) should begin and end with a warm-up. For a dog, the warm-up and cool-down are several minutes of walking before and after jogging. All of the cautions about temperature and symptoms to watch for are even more important while jogging, as is the post-exercise check. Pay particular attention to the pads of your dog's feet, which can become scuffed and sore. However, you should find that with time, his pads will become quite tough and withstand the exercise well.

These common-sense steps, coupled with your Siberian Husky's natural tendency to run, will find both of you looking forward to your jogs. Soon you'll realize that he can keep going—even when you can't.

Bicycling

Some Siberian Husky owners discover that they cannot keep up with their dogs or have as much endurance as they need. These

Whether you walk through your neighborhood, in a park, or on a walking trail, your Siberian can be the perfect companion.

Siberians can make excellent jogging partners.

to the bicycle, while keeping him away from the dangerous wheels and gears.

Once you have selected the bicycle-and-dog connection method, you are ready to get your dog used to running beside the bicycle. If your dog shows any concern over the bicycle, do not force him to be near the bike. Keep the bike in the house and let him get used to it. Ride the bike around the back yard, if possible, to show him that it is nothing to fear. Have a friend go out with you and your dog and the bike. One of you rides the bike, and the other walks the dog next to the bike. Reward and praise for progress. You should soon see that your dog is no longer apprehensive around the bike.

When both you and your dog are ready to try biking, attach him to the connection apparatus, and walk the bike with the dog attached. Next, get on the bike and pedal as slowly as you can. With your dog walking next to you, slowly pick up the pace, until the dog is gaiting at a comfortable speed. Try to keep fairly consistent at that optimum speed.

Keep the first session quite short, and pay close attention to any distress. Provide rest stops as needed, and lots of cool water. When you have finished, walk your dog around a bit to cool down. Perform your post-activity check, paying close attention to his feet.

For the first time, you may actually have tired your Siberian out a bit—what a great feeling!

Hiking

You may wish to add speed to your outings with your Siberian, or you may wish to add distance and elevation. If you are not a jogger, you may want to hike and even camp with your dog. Siberians who are properly conditioned are good hikers over any terrain. If you plan on hiking with your Siberian, take many of the same precautions as you would prior to beginning to walk, jog, or bicycle with your

owners often turn to bicycling with their dogs. Bicycling is great exercise for your Siberian, as it allows him to do what he does best— run at a moderate speed over great distances.

There are several additional safety considerations when biking with a dog. Do not even consider bicycling with your dog unless you are a good cyclist. If you are unsteady on a bicycle, adding a dog is a recipe for disaster. The main concern, of course, is making sure the leash and the dog do not get caught in the bicycle wheels, chain, or handle bars. There are a few commercially available tools that help alleviate this concern. These items, like the Springer, the Biker Dog, the Walky Dog, and the K9 Cruiser, are metal bicycle attachments that provide a way to connect your dog directly

dog. Make sure your dog is healthy and current on his inoculations and parasite control. Build up his stamina and feet gradually, until he is ready for a long hike. And remember, before beginning your hike, to make sure that the park or trail allows dogs.

Hiking, backpacking, and camping with your dog have some additional safety needs. If there is a ranger station or trail head, leave word when and where you are going. Prepare for your hike with some necessary emergency and survival items:

- Compass, GPS, cell phone
- Dog boots for him and extra socks for you
- Extra leash
- First-aid kit (for both you and your dog)
- Flashlight
- Foldable space blanket
- Insect repellant
- Multiblade knife or combination tool
- Plastic bags
- Snacks (for both you and your dog)
- Sunscreen
- Water bowl
- Water (for both you and your dog)
- Waterproof matches
- Waterproof poncho or extra jacket

If you are hiking with your dog, fit him with a dog pack and have him carry some of the gear. Many outdoor sports stores or pet supply vendors offer dog packs for sale. If you want your dog to carry a pack, gradually build up his ability to carry a load over time. When he is used to carrying weight in a pack, it should be equally distributed between the two sides of the pack, and he should never carry more than 25% of his body weight in his pack.

While you hike, pay close attention to your dog for any signs of distress. Provide him with rest and water breaks on a regular basis. And pay attention to dangers in the terrain or from other animals you may encounter. Also, always clean up after your dog. You should bag and remove any waste, or bury it off of the trail.

Examine your dog carefully after the hike (and during, if warranted) for injury, parasites, or foreign bodies. Keeping him safe and healthy will make hiking with your Siberian Husky a pleasant experience for both of you. If you enjoy hiking with your Siberian, you may wish to visit the website for the Siberian Husky Club of America, Inc. (SHCA) at www.shca.org. SHCA has a Working Pack Dog title program, and you might be interested in pursuing these titles with your dog.

Camping

The logical extension of hiking is camping with your Siberian. The amount of food and gear you take is obviously increased, but the process is similar. The one concern about camping with your dog is to keep him leashed at camp. Do not forget that Siberian Huskies have a very strong instinct to run, and you will want him under control in camp. A lightweight stake-out cable should serve this purpose well. With your dog helping to carry part of his gear and food, having him join you on your camping trip should be great fun. Make sure to examine him every day to make sure he is free of pests and injury.

CANINE GOOD CITIZEN

If your level of activity does not lend itself to jogging or hiking, there are myriad activities in which you and your dog can participate. A

Want to Know More?

There are ways you can use your bicycle to begin training your dog for sledding. See the section on "Sledding" later in this chapter.

great way to solidify your basic training and to affirm your responsible dog ownership is to participate in the American Kennel Club's (AKC) Canine Good Citizen Program (CGC). Currently, veterinarians, as well as state and local governments, are encouraging responsible dog ownership. You can prove your dog is a good citizen through your participation in this program.

The CGC program (and its pre-CGC program, called the STAR Puppy Program) is a great ways to validate that the training you have done with your dog has helped make him a good canine citizen. The program has two parts. First, it asks for a basic commitment to responsible dog ownership by asking each owner to sign a Responsible Dog Owners' Pledge. The pledge states that the owner takes responsibility for his dog's health, safety, and quality of life, while not letting his dog infringe on the rights of others.

The second part of CGC is a certification program to show that your dog is a good citizen. There are ten basic tests to successfully complete in order for your dog to receive his CGC certification:

- Accepting a friendly stranger: stranger approaches both you and your dog, and he does not act shy or resentful, and he stays with you.
- Sitting politely for petting: a friendly stranger approaches both you and your dog, and he allows the stranger to pet him.
- Appearance and grooming: your dog is presented in clean condition, and allows a stranger softly to comb or brush him, examine his ears, and pick up each front foot.
- Out for a walk (on a loose leash): loose leash walking nicely at your side.
- Walking through a crowd: you and your dog walk past at least three people. Your dog

may show interest in the people, but should continue to walk nicely at your side.

- Sit and down on command and stay in place: you ask your dog to sit and to lie down. Then, in one of those positions, you tell your dog to stay and walk away from him while he is on a long leash, and then you return.
- Coming when called: you walk 10 feet (3 m) from your dog, turn, and call him to you.
- Reaction to another dog: you are with your dog when another handler and dog approach. You and the other handler shake hands and talk, while each dog remains with his handler.
- Reaction to distraction: your dog is faced with two distractions, which may include a dropped chair, a passing jogger, dropping a crutch, opening an umbrella, etc. Your dog may react to the distraction and be curious, but should not appear afraid or aggressive.
- Supervised separation: you hand over your dog's leash to another person, walk away, and remain out of sight for three minutes. Your dog should not show significant distress at your departure.

All of these tests are done on leash, and you can encourage your dog verbally during the tests. Between tests, you may pet your dog, but

Training Tidbit

Much of the basic manners training you have done with your puppy and adult dog will pay off when you begin any other activity, such as obedience, agility, therapy, and even sledding.

you cannot use treats or toys.

These are the very same training exercises you have been doing with your Siberian Husky since he entered your life, so it should be fairly easy for him to pass these tests and show that he is a good citizen. Tests are administered all over the country by kennel clubs, obedience clubs, and other certified testers. For more information about CGC, please visit the website for the AKC at www.akc.org.

SPORTS

If you enjoy working as a team with your Siberian Husky, there are a vast number of organized canine activities in which you may participate. Do not worry if your dog came to you from shelter or rescue and is not registered, or if he came with an AKC "limited registration"—he may still be eligible to compete in companion and performance venues. AKC limited-registration Siberian Huskies are eligible to participate in all AKC and SHCA companion and performance events. The only venue in which they may not compete is the conformation ring. If you have a Siberian who came from a shelter or rescue without his registration information, you may apply for his AKC Purebred Alternative Listing (PAL) number. This will allow him to participate and compete in AKC's companion and performance events. For more information about the PAL program, visit the AKC website at www.akc.org.

Agility

Agility is by far one of the most popular human–canine partnership sports. In short, agility is an obstacle course for your dog. He runs, jumps, weaves, and goes through a tunnel; he's in the air, on the ground, and teetering in between. Agility competitions may look like chaos, but they are not. A number of

Agility is a timed obstacle course for your dog.

obstacles are laid out in a sequential course. Handlers direct their dogs through the course, striving to complete the course as quickly as possible with no errors or faults. The dog with the fastest time and fewest deductions wins the competition. However, dogs who finish within a specified time with fewer that the allowable number of deductions earn a qualifying time and score that leads to completing titles.

Due to the varied nature of the obstacles, learning each apparatus, perfecting each obstacle, responding to a handler's direction, and putting it all together takes some time. As exhausting as the activity may be for the handler, the dogs love the energy and vitality

- **15 points with two major wins:** The number of points a dog must amass in order to achieve his AKC Championship.
- **25 points with three major wins:** The number of points an AKC champion must amass in order to complete his Grand Championship.
- **3:** The number of qualifying scores a dog must receive in order to complete a rally, obedience, or agility title.

of training and competition. If you are at all interested in this fast-growing sport, a number of national organizations offer agility titles, and classes and events are held across the country each weekend. For more information about agility, contact the AKC (www.akc.org), or the United States Dog Agility Association (www.usdaa.com). Then, catch your breath and go for it!

Canine Freestyle

If obstacle courses are not your thing, how about dancing? The sport of canine freestyle consists of choreographed movements between you and your dog, performed to music. This sport blends traditional obedience training with the canine equivalent of musical dressage. It is technically precise, but fluid and creative. And, unlike obedience and agility, canine freestyle is "free"—you establish your own routine rather than work through a prescribed order of exercises.

Freestyle takes obedience to a new level,

and requires your dog's complete attention for success. Rather than having your dog continually at your left side (as in obedience), in freestyle, he can be in front of you, backing away from you, weaving through your legs like weave poles, or even heeling on your right. Many different movements are allowed, and your job is to make them flow along with your chosen music.

If you want to try canine freestyle, contact the Canine Freestyle Federation, Inc. (www.canine-freestyle.org) for more information.

Conformation

Are you fascinated by televised dog shows, such as the Westminster Kennel Club Dog Show or the AKC-Eukanuba National Championship? Is *Best in Show* one of your favorite movies? This is conformation—what most people think of when they hear "dog show." Although conformation events may look like beauty pageants for dogs, they are not.

Breed Standard

Each breed of purebred dogs has a parent club—in the case of the Siberian Husky in the United States, this is the SHCA. The parent club and its members work toward national recognition of their breed. As part of that process, the parent club develops a breed standard, which is, in writing, a description of the ideal dog of that breed. The original Standard for Siberian Huskies described actual imports (such as Kreevanka and Tserko), and the Serum Run dogs (such as Togo). The Siberian Standard describes the ideal long-distance, high-endurance working sled dog from Siberia. It describes the structure and movement of the ideal Siberian, as well as the more cosmetic aspects of the breed. However, even the so-called "cosmetic traits" are needed for the Siberian Husky to perform his job in his environment. The double coat, for example, is both beautiful as well as functional, as it keeps the arctic athlete warm and dry.

How Dog Shows Work

Each breed has its own standard, and it is against these standards that each dog is judged in a dog show. The Siberian Husky judge evaluates each dog and compares each to his mental image of the Siberian standard, thus determining the dog who best exemplifies that Standard, and if other dogs are also good representations of that ideal dog.

Because the original and ultimate purpose of conformation dog shows is the exhibition and evaluation of potential breeding stock, only intact males and females who have full AKC (or other national kennel club) registration are allowed to be shown in conformation dog shows.

The behaviors for showing are quite different from those in obedience. Because the judge must analyze the structure of the dog, conformation dogs do not sit. In conformation, a dog is expected to stand comfortably, but squarely, without much movement. He must stand nicely while a judge performs a short physical examination, including looking at his teeth. A conformation dog needs to gait alongside his hander at a moderate trot on a loose lead. A conformation handler can entice her dog with treats (bait) and touch her dog to move him into correct position.

Dogs are entered in advance of the show into one of several available classes that separate

In dog shows, dogs are judged against their own breed standard.

dogs by sex, age, level of experience, and other classifications. The male and female from these classes who are judged winners will be awarded points based on the level of competition. A dog must amass a minimum of 15 points, some earned with adequately large competition, in order to complete his Championship. Champions are exhibited in a separate class, and compete for Best of Breed, the Best of the Opposite Sex to the dog winning Best of Breed, and the judge's choice of the next best male and female, called Grand Champion Select. Only champions may compete for points to be awarded their Grand Champion titles. The dogs judged best of each breed compete in groups with similar breeds, and ultimately those group-winning dogs compete for Best in Show.

Many Siberian Husky fanciers enjoy this type of competition, as it helps assure them that their dogs are good examples of Siberian Huskies and share many of the characteristics of those original imports and Serum Run dogs. Conformation shows are held mostly on weekends all over the country. For more information about showing, visit the American Kennel Club's website at www.akc.org.

Rally and Obedience

As an extension of the training you have already done with your Siberian, you might want to become involved with obedience, or its companion sport, rally. Both rally and obedience build on training and the teamwork that exists between handler and dog.

Rally has three increasingly difficult levels of competition, and all allow at least verbal encouragement by the handler. The first level is done completely on leash, and the handler can offer some physical encouragement, such as clapping hands. The exercises are basic obedience exercises, such as heeling, calling

your dog, stand, and others.

Each team of handler and dog performs the same routine, which is marked by signs. A judge scores and times each routine. Handlers and dogs earn their titles by receiving a minimum number of points in three trials with different judges. Many handlers view each level of rally competition as a good first step to the corresponding obedience competition level.

Obedience is similar to rally in that there are three levels of increasing difficulty, and in order to complete a title, a dog must receive a minimum number of points on three different occasions, with three different judges. Although they are both scored by judges, obedience differs from rally in that there are no signs. To complete the required tasks, the obedience handler receives directions from the judge.

Even at its lowest level of competition, obedience requires some of the exercises to be performed off leash. Obedience also takes training to a different level, as it requires a dog to jump, retrieve, and be able to discern his owner's scent on an object. Achieving the highest obedience title, Utility Dog, is a very significant accomplishment.

Sledding

If you are interested in encouraging your Siberian to do what he does best—sledding—there are a number of activities you can pursue. As a general rule, Siberian Huskies do not

Multi-Dog Tip

The easiest way to train a Siberian to be a sled dog is to put him on a team with other dogs.

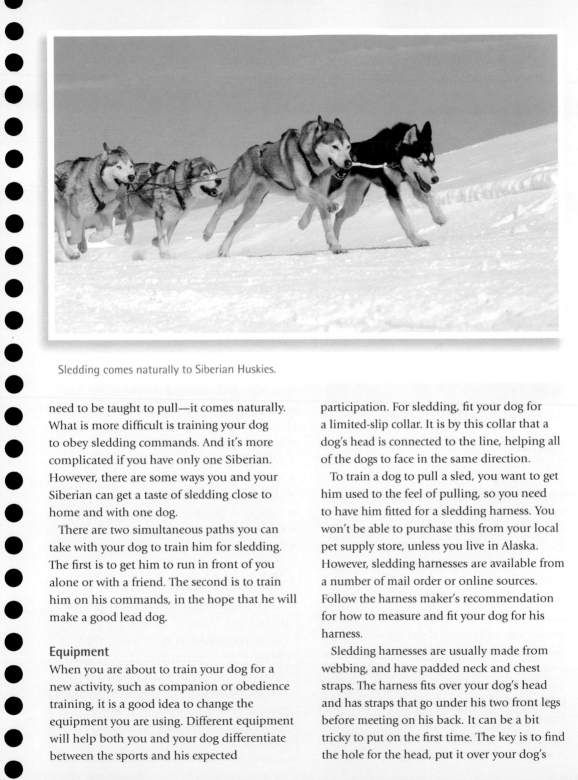

Sledding comes naturally to Siberian Huskies.

need to be taught to pull—it comes naturally. What is more difficult is training your dog to obey sledding commands. And it's more complicated if you have only one Siberian. However, there are some ways you and your Siberian can get a taste of sledding close to home and with one dog.

There are two simultaneous paths you can take with your dog to train him for sledding. The first is to get him to run in front of you alone or with a friend. The second is to train him on his commands, in the hope that he will make a good lead dog.

Equipment

When you are about to train your dog for a new activity, such as companion or obedience training, it is a good idea to change the equipment you are using. Different equipment will help both you and your dog differentiate between the sports and his expected

participation. For sledding, fit your dog for a limited-slip collar. It is by this collar that a dog's head is connected to the line, helping all of the dogs to face in the same direction.

To train a dog to pull a sled, you want to get him used to the feel of pulling, so you need to have him fitted for a sledding harness. You won't be able to purchase this from your local pet supply store, unless you live in Alaska. However, sledding harnesses are available from a number of mail order or online sources. Follow the harness maker's recommendation for how to measure and fit your dog for his harness.

Sledding harnesses are usually made from webbing, and have padded neck and chest straps. The harness fits over your dog's head and has straps that go under his two front legs before meeting on his back. It can be a bit tricky to put on the first time. The key is to find the hole for the head, put it over your dog's

This Siberian is waiting for the command "Hike!"

head, then bring each foreleg up and through its hole. Pull the rear point of the harness toward your dog's tail. It is from this rear point that your dog will do his pulling.

Pulling

When you begin training your Siberian to be a sled dog, there are a variety of skills to learn and ways to teach them. If you can add your dog to an existing dog team, he will learn what to do very quickly. Otherwise, you will want to work on a number of skills: pulling, getting out in front, and learning commands.

To begin training your dog to pull, you will need a long piece (about 7 feet [2 m]) of strong cord with a secure clip on one end and a weighted object that you want your dog to pull. This weight could be a tire or a piece of wood, but should not be anything that could shatter or that has sharp edges. The idea is to have a slight weight that causes some resistance for your dog to pull, but not so heavy as to be a hazard.

Find some place where you and your dog can walk (with his tire) that is reasonably flat, gives you some distance to walk, and is not heavily populated. Put your dog's harness on. Securely tie the tire to the strong cord, and attach the clip to the end of your dog's harness. Put your dog's lead on, give him the command to heel, and walk briskly forward. Encourage him when he meets resistance from the weight. Given time and practice, your dog will soon become accustomed to the weight he is pulling.

Commands

You can begin command training at any time you are out with your dog. There are several basic commands:

- *Hike*! To get your dog to go.
- *Whoa*! To get your dog to stop.
- *Gee*! To turn to the right.
- *Haw*! To turn to the left.
- *Come Gee*! To make a U-turn to the right.
- *Come Haw*! To make a U-turn to the left.
- *Trail*! To keep your dog on the trail.

What About "Mush"?

It is disappointing, but most people do not use "Mush!" (although you can if you wish). It is believed that "Mush!" is a corruption of the French "Marche!" to go or march, used by French Canadian fur trappers. Today, most people use "Hike!" or even "Let's go!" to get their teams in motion.

• *On By!* To get your dog to pass another team.
You can train your dog on his sledding
commands any time you are on a walk or a
hike. Just make sure that you always use the
commands when you are about to accomplish
the task. When you turn left, say, "Haw"; turn
to the right, say, "Gee." Some of the commands
are best understood when your dog is in front
of you, because there is a difference between
"Heel" and "Hike."

Go Out in Front

If your dog is well trained to walk nicely with
you on a leash, training him to go out in front
of you may take a bit of time. If you are a
jogger, this process may be somewhat easier.
To begin, use a long leash, an extending lead,
or a jogging line. Connect the long line to your
dog's limited slip collar. Then, in an area where
you will not encounter other dogs and people,
set off for a walk. Do not use the command to
heel, as that is not what you want him to do.
Just start walking. Slowly, as your dog moves
a bit ahead of you, let out more leash, so it
allows him freedom, but will not trip anyone.
When he is about 10 feet (3 m) ahead of you,
pick up your speed, and encourage him to do
so, too. If possible, begin to jog with him.

With your dog that far away from your
immediate control, you will have to pay careful
attention to any hazards or obstacles both he
and you may encounter. If you want him to
stop, say, "Whoa." If you encounter a turn, give
the proper command. And, when you want
him to return to you, use leash pressure in
one direction or the other, and give the proper
command. As your dog starts learning the
commands in the context of walking in front of
you, you can put on his harness and attach the
line to the harness.

When you have good control of your dog in
these training activities, you might consider

Safety

Participation in sled training
requires the same common-sense
practices that apply for all the other
sports mentioned here. Have your
veterinarian clear your dog for the
type of physical activity you are
attempting. Start things slowly, and
consistently monitor your and your
dog's health and progress, as well as
check for strain and injury. The idea
is to make sure that both you and
your dog are safe and having fun
working together as partners.

using a bicycle so that you can pick up the
pace, or try using one of the single-person
wheeled carts available for urban mushing.
Then, contact local Siberian Husky or sledding
clubs and see if you can get your dog pulling a
sled on the snow. You never know, you might
turn into a musher in the process!

Tracking

When it comes to tracking, one usually
thinks of Bloodhounds or even Foxhounds;
rarely does a Siberian Husky come to mind.
However, anyone who has ever been on a sled
behind a team of Siberians, especially on an
unmarked trail or in poor visibility, knows of
the remarkable ability of the Siberian Husky
to track. Unlike the normal scent hounds,
Siberian Huskies do not usually have their
noses to the ground trying to trap the scent.
Rather, Siberians are air scenters—they catch
the scent of what they are tracking in the air.

Reading the accounts of those teams of
sled dogs transporting the diphtheria serum
to Nome in 1925 proves that these are dogs
with amazing air-scenting abilities. The dog
team relay was needed because of storms

CT Savitar's Pipe Down Otis is the first (and only) Champion Tracker Siberian Husky.

that grounded airplanes. In near white-out conditions, the dog teams managed to find the trail and eventually reach Nome. All current Siberians are descendents of these dogs, and they, too, have great scenting abilities.

Tracking is completely different from the other activities previously mentioned. In agility and obedience, the dog is responding to the hander's commands. In tracking, the dog is working basically alone—another perfect role for the Siberian Husky.

The AKC offers a series of tracking tests that dogs can enter to receive titles. Three increasingly difficult levels of tracking tests differ in length, aging of the trail, complexity of the trail, number of articles found, and surface of the track. Due to the requirements of space and time, there is great demand for participation in these tracking tests. For information about tracking, visit the AKC's website at www.akc.org.

THERAPY

If your preferred activity level runs less to the athletic and more toward the sedate, you might consider sharing the human–dog bond with others. Siberian Huskies, especially those more reserved adults, make wonderful therapy dogs. Hospital- and home-bound children and adults may be even more in need of canine companionship than others, and Siberians can make excellent canine ambassadors.

A number of organizations certify therapy dogs. The certification programs often include all of the AKC Canine Good Citizenship tests, with the inclusion of some specialized tests to make sure the dogs are comfortable around medical equipment, children, and those with infirmities. If you are interested in pursuing therapy certification for your Siberian Husky, contact Therapy Dogs International, or another therapy certification program.

TRAVEL

Siberian Huskies become so much a part of your life that it is only fitting he joins you on vacation.

Travel by Car

As a general rule, Siberians usually are fine car riders. However, if your dog seems anxious in the car, practice with him. Put him in the car with you without the engine running. Bring some treats and toys, and just play together for a short time. Next, start the engine but do not go anywhere, and play in the car. Or, if possible, drive him up and back in the driveway. If your dog still is anxious, ask your veterinarian for some suggestions.

If you plan on taking your dog in the car for any length trip (even to the veterinarian), do not let him ride unsecured. Just as children need car seats and people need seatbelts, dogs need to be protected in case of an accident. At a minimum, fit your dog with a pet restraint that attaches to the seat belt and use it at all times. Or, better yet, put your dog's crate in the car and have him ride in it.

Travel by Plane

Occasionally, there may be the need to travel by plane with your Siberian. Dogs can fly safely, and yours can too—with a few pointers. Siberian Huskies, due to their size, must fly in crates in the cargo area of the plane. This is a pressurized space that usually is fairly small, so there is a limit to the number of dogs each plane can carry. Therefore, you must call the airline and add a "dog" reservation to your own flight reservation. Try to book a non-stop ticket, so the flight will be as short as possible and will not require moving your dog from one plane to another.

Requirements include:

- Dogs must fly in USDA- and airline-approved crates that have enough room for them to stand comfortably and turn. For a Siberian Husky, this is generally a 400-size crate for females and either a 400- or 500-size crate for males.

- There must be absorbent material in the bottom—a towel or shredded newspaper will do.

- Two food/water dishes must be provided inside the crate; ones that attach to the crate door work well.

- A health certification from your veterinarian is required within a certain number of days before the flight. The length of time may vary among different airlines, so check with your carrier for its requirements. When getting the health certification, consider the date of your return flight to make sure the certification date meets the return flight time requirement.

- Once you get to the airport, you will need to fill out some forms, and "Live Animal" stickers will be applied to the crate.

Airlines may have other requirements, so contact your carrier for any additional restrictions.

Car Safety

Never leave your dog alone in a car, even in the shade with the windows slightly open. A few minutes in a hot car can cause severe damage or even death. Your Siberian is a member of your family, so please make sure he is always as safe as you are.

Before your travel date, make sure your dog feels at home in his crate. Don't feed him immediately before getting on the plane, and give him water, but not too much. Make sure he has a good-fitting collar with current contact information, including your cell phone number or the numbers both of home and your destination. Do not sedate him unless your veterinarian recommends it. Dogs tend to fly better without sedation. Tape a bag of food to the top of your dog's crate, and make sure your name and contact information are on the crate. Exercise your dog prior to putting him in the crate. Make sure you have a leash and an extra collar in your bag, along with more food or treats. Once you are on the plane, watch for your dog to be loaded and/or ask the flight attendant to verify when your dog has been loaded onto the plane.

When you arrive at your destination, locate the airport's dog exercise area—most airports have one. Bring some water with you, as your dog will be thirsty and happy to see you upon arrival. You'll be amazed at what a good traveler your Siberian is!

Lodging

When traveling with your pet, you will find that a number of nationwide hotel chains accept well-behaved pets. This information is generally available through hotel websites or by asking reservation agents. For your own

Brush up on your manners training before you travel with your Siberian.

convenience, you may wish to request a room on the first floor or near the door.

When staying with a dog in a hotel, follow the basic rules of canine courtesy:

- Do not try to sneak your dog in to avoid a pet deposit or to a hotel that does not allow pets.
- Bring a large plastic garbage bag to put under his crate in case of spilled water.
- Keep your dog in his crate when you are not in the room.
- Keep him quiet at all times.
- Keep your dog out of non-dog areas at all times.
- Use only approved exercise areas, and clean up after your dog.
- Do not allow him to do any damage to your room or any common areas of the hotel.

- If he should have an accident, notify the hotel staff immediately.
- When vacating the room, clean up any pet hair or debris.

Pet Sitting/Boarding

Occasionally, you may not be able to take your Siberian with you when you leave town. If this is the case, a number of options are available for his care. You can have a neighbor feed and take care of him, you can hire a pet sitter to come to your house and stay with him; or you can board him somewhere. Any of these can be a good solution depending on your situation.

Often one of the easiest solutions is to have a family member or friend stay in your house with your dog while you are gone. This person can also take care of your plants, pick up your mail and papers, and keep things going in your absence. If you do not have a friend who can help in this way, hire a professional pet or house sitters to provide this service. Recommendations from your veterinarian, breeder, or other dog friends are a good place to start, but you and your dog should both meet any potential pet sitter before engaging her services. You should also ask for references and ensure that the sitter is bonded.

Depending on your situation, you may also be able to ask a neighbor to feed and care for your dog while you are away. That way, your dog can stay in his own environment while you are gone, and his schedule will not be too disrupted. However, unless your neighbor will spend time with your dog, this may be a lonely and potentially dangerous option.

If you opt for a solution in which someone cares for your dog at your house, write out thorough directions, which include veterinarian contact information, and walk through your rules and care guidelines in advance.

The other option is to have your dog cared for at a facility. If your breeder is close by and can take your dog back for a short vacation, you will know he'll be well cared for by someone who knows Siberian Huskies. This can be a great solution.

However, if you must find a boarding kennel, ask your veterinarian, breeder, and friends for recommendations. Call each kennel to ask them about their rates, availability, physical setup, and services offered (some offer doggy day care, which would keep your Siberian entertained). Visit each kennel on your short list—it is better if a kennel does not force you to make an appointment for the visit. Ask for the kennel's affiliations or certifications. Watch the staff interact with the dogs in their kennel. Bring your dog to meet the kennel staff. Ask for recommendations. If you are concerned about your dog's diet, consider bringing your own food. Remember that boarding kennels require proof of current vaccinations, so get copies from your veterinarian. Before leaving your dog at a new kennel for a week or more, try a short two- or three-day visit. See what condition your dog is in when you return.

Although finding a good boarding kennel may take some effort, when you find one, you'll feel secure knowing that your dog is safe with professionals while you are gone. And, if it is a good boarding kennel, your Siberian will think he has gone on vacation, too!

If you need to travel, hire a pet sitter come to your house and stay with your Siberian.

PART III

SENIOR YEARS

CHAPTER 12

FINDING YOUR SIBERIAN HUSKY SENIOR

The American Kennel Club (AKC) considers dogs to be "veterans" at 7 years of age. The Siberian Husky Club of America (SHCA), however, does not consider Siberians to be "veterans" until they are 9 years of age. This is due to the expectation that a Siberian will be active, in good health and shape, and able to do his job long into his twilight years.

Siberian Huskies have a life expectancy of 12 to 13 years, which is average for dogs. Giant breeds live shorter lives, and small dogs tend to live longer lives. So, it is not unusual that your medium-sized dog lives medium-length life. Due to the overall health of the breed, Siberians are quite vibrant and vital long into old age. It is not uncommon that semi-retired sled dogs spend their twilight years running on dog teams, helping to train the youngsters. The old sled dogs may have lost some of their speed, but they have a lot of experience and desire to keep working; plus, they run at the perfect pace for puppies.

WHY ADOPT A VETERAN?

These elder statesmen of the breed, while still vital, usually have lost some of the wanderlust of their youth and have developed some dignity and reserve. They are a pure pleasure to have in your home. In fact, a veteran might be the perfect dog to bring into your life. If you are looking for a companion who is trained and polite, an older dog might be perfect for you.

In addition to temperament and good health, adopting a veteran may be a good solution for someone who has some concerns about making the 12- to 13-year commitment required when getting a puppy. By adopting a senior, you may be getting the best 5-plus years in the dog's life. When you bring a veteran into your home, you are providing him with a new experience, which may energize him. And, if you find your senior in a shelter or rescue, you may be saving his life.

Training Tidbit

Sometimes it *is* difficult to teach an old dog new tricks. Before adopting a senior, make sure he is tolerant of the children and other pets in your household.

Occasionally, rescue organizations receive veteran Siberians for placement.

hand, some veterans may get a new lease on life with a puppy in the house. You must rely on the knowledge of the person placing the senior with you to know what is best for the dog. If you have other pets and children in your family, make sure to discuss the senior's background and tolerance for children and animals.

Realize, also, that senior dogs are prone to the health issues of age, such as arthritis, hearing loss, or blindness. And, although the breed is a relatively healthy one, your veteran could develop cancer or some other medical problem that could hasten his death. There are no guarantees in any dog's life, though, and accidents or unforeseen medical conditions can strike a younger dog, too.

WHERE TO FIND A VETERAN

Occasionally, rescue organizations receive veteran dogs for placement. Breeders may also look for retirement homes for their good producers and retired show dogs who are of a certain age. Both of these groups pay close attention to finding the perfect home for a senior.

Adopting a veteran requires a family who is aware of the plusses and minuses of an older dog. If you are considering bringing an older dog into your home, be prepared to discuss your expectations with the person placing the dog. She will want to be certain that you are

Siberians, due to their inherent temperament, are not generally one-person dogs, but rather are gregarious and loving toward everyone. This makes them the perfect dog for later adoption, as they will generally be very adaptive to a new environment and loving toward their new families.

Adopting a veteran can be a wonderful choice, but there are some concerns to think about. Although Siberians are vital into old age, as dogs age they may become less tolerant. It may not be a good idea to place some seniors in homes with other pets, young dogs, or children. Although, on the other

Multi-Dog Tip

Some seniors thrive with other, younger dogs in the home—they keep the veteran young at heart.

prepared for the senior, and that it will be a successful placement. Old dogs occasionally have trouble adapting to change, and being adopted and subsequently returned might be difficult for the veteran.

If you are considering adding a veteran to your home, ask the rescue worker or breeder about the dog. Learn as much about him and his background as possible. Find out about the longevity of his family. Ask if any familial tendencies for disease or cancer are present. Find out about his temperament and current life: Is he housetrained, is he good with children? Ask for a geriatric blood panel and complete physical examination prior to adoption. This will let you know if any existing conditions or lurking problems are present.

By the Numbers

- **7:** The age that the American Kennel Club considers a dog to be a "veteran."
- **9:** The age that the Siberian Husky Club of America, Inc. considers a Siberian to be a "veteran."
- **12 to 13:** The average life expectancy for a Siberian Husky.
- **17 to 18:** It is not unheard of for Siberian Huskies to live to this age.

PREPARING TO ADD A VETERAN TO YOUR HOME

Seniors may require some additional considerations inside your home. Occasionally, older dogs urinate more frequently. They may have some stiffness that would make significant stair climbing difficult. They may be more prone to feeling the cold. You will want to evaluate your home to make sure it is appropriate for a senior dog. A high-rise apartment with an elevator trip to get outside might not be the best location for a veteran. However, a rooftop garden or deck could make that high-rise a fine choice.

You may find that a few changes in your home will make a world of difference for your senior. The installation of a doggy door will give him the opportunity to come in and go

out as needed without needing to disturb you every time. A soft bed in a warm corner of the family room might ease his cold and tired bones. An insulated dog house might provide both coolness in the summer and a toasty den in the winter. The addition of a ramp to get into the car might make it easier for him to take rides with you.

After due consideration of all these issues, if you are still interested in the veteran, bring him to your house for a trial visit. Prepare your house for your guest, and see how he fits in with your family. Remember that this will be a new experience for the dog, too, so be patient. You will probably discover that he has selected your home for his retirement, and you'll never want to give him back.

CHAPTER 13

CARE OF YOUR SIBERIAN HUSKY SENIOR

The senior years spent with your dog should be considered a gift. This is the time when you are old friends. Your Siberian knows all of the rules, understands all of your moods, and like old friends, you are comfortable together. Gone is the youngster who would challenge you at every turn (although you still see that spirit in his occasional senior antics). His muzzle and head may be graying, but your hair probably is, too. It is almost as if you and your Siberian can look back on his puppyhood together and wonder how both of you survived it!

In addition to the graying, you will see other changes in your old friend. His coat may become a bit thinner and less shiny, and he may not be shedding as he did in his youth. You may find him a bit stiff when getting up. His breath may be bad due to some increased dental disease. He will have less energy than he did in his youth. You may find that he drinks more water and urinates more frequently. He may seem to come when called even less frequently than before—this time, however, it is not selective hearing, but hearing loss. His eyes may appear cloudy, and his eyesight may be a bit dim.

All of these signs are the normal changes of aging. Siberian Huskies should not begin to show these signs until they are between 7 and 10 years of age. If you start to see these earlier, it might indicate a problem. Pay attention to the severity of the change. Significant, severe, or sudden changes could be a sign of a more serious problem than the simple passage of time.

FEEDING

One way to keep your dog as healthy as possible is to make sure he is still getting optimum nutrition for this new stage in his life. As you have been providing good nutrition for your dog throughout his life, you understand his nutritional needs up to now. But with a senior dog, you may discover that his nutritional needs change a bit. He will most likely be less active, so his caloric needs will drop. In response to changes in seniors' nutritional needs, most commercial dog food manufacturers have developed special foods for aging dogs.

You have probably been feeding your Siberian a food that is fairly high in protein and fat to provide him with optimum fuel for his body. As he ages, your dog's need for fat is

Siberian Huskies don't show signs of aging until they are between 7 and 10 years of age.

somewhat reduced, but he still needs a fairly high percentage of protein. Most good-quality senior dog food formulations are between 27% and 30% protein (probably similar to what your dog was eating in his youth). However, the fat level of senior foods is usually between 11% and 14%, which is probably less than in his puppy and adult foods. Senior dog foods may increase the level of omega fatty acids, which are good for the aging dog's coat. And senior foods also include a supplement of

glucosamine and chondroitin, which are added for bone and joint health.

Changing Foods

When your Siberian starts showing some of the signs of aging (around 7 to 9 years of age), it is time to talk with your veterinarian. This is probably the time to consider changing his food. If you have been happy with the food you have been feeding, especially the protein and carbohydrate source, check if the manufacturer offers a similar senior product. Often, the easiest food transition is a gradual one from a manufacturer's adult food to that same manufacturer's senior food. This change in formulation often allows you to feed the same quantity of food, while keeping the calories lower.

Changes in Appetite

Siberian Huskies are not necessarily known for being picky eaters. So, your senior will most likely continue eating with the enthusiasm he has always shown for food. However, if you find that he is leaving some of his food or is slow to eat, he may need some encouragement. If your Siberian is having dental problems, chewing his food might be difficult. Try soaking his kibble in warm water prior to

feeding to make chewing easier. If you have other animals, sometimes eating in proximity to another pet may encourage a reluctant eater to eat faster. If you have traditionally fed your dog once a day, it might help if you break his food portion into two meals, morning, and afternoon/evening, to see if he is just having trouble eating the quantity of food in one sitting. You also may find the need to entice him to eat. The addition of a protein supplement, fatty acid supplement, or small bits of meat or gravy might encourage your dog to eat.

When a dog who has been a good eater changes to a picky eater, this may indicate a significant health issue. In such a case, please consult your veterinarian for advice. Also be aware that, if your senior has some health

Some seniors suffer from a loss of appetite.

problems, his feeding schedule and process may need to change. He may have additional nutritional needs; he may need to eat more frequent, smaller meals; his food intake may need to be closely monitored; or your veterinarian may recommend any number of other suggestions. As your dog ages, a good relationship with your veterinarian will help to keep your dog as healthy as possible long into old age.

GROOMING

As your Siberian ages, he might be less tolerant of being groomed. This could be for a variety of reasons, including difficulty standing, pain, or the prerogative of old age. Whatever the case, he stills need grooming, and some aspects are even more important for the senior Siberian. You will need to be creative in how, where, and when you groom your Siberian.

In addition to keeping your senior Siberian clean and comfortable, grooming allows you the best opportunity to check his body frequently for growths, injuries, and pains. You will also want to continue nail trimming, as a senior's nails may get brittle, may not be worn down due to diminished activity, and if left to grow too long, are in danger of snagging and ripping. Dental disease is also a significant problem with seniors, so you need to continue your tooth-brushing regimen.

Because bathing is often difficult with a senior dog, especially one who is sensitive to temperature changes, the best way to keep your old Siberian in good condition is to keep up on his periodic grooming, but reduce the

Good genetics and your veterinarian will help keep your aging Siberian healthy.

number of baths. The coat of a frequently groomed dog should remain fairly clean and in good condition with just the occasional bath. You may find, however, that your dog's tolerance for the length of each grooming session or its location has diminished. If this is the case, it might be time to develop a new, senior grooming regimen.

Try to take advantage of 10 to 15 minutes each day while your dog is relaxed on the family room floor or in some other comfortable location. Have your grooming tools at hand, and spend the time rotating through the grooming tasks of trimming, grinding, and filing his nails, gently combing his coat (while performing your complete examination of his body), and brushing his teeth. (Some of these routine grooming tasks may be done outside or in some place where toothpaste splatter would be acceptable.)

You may also wish to evaluate your grooming tools with your senior Siberian in mind. Make sure that your rake and comb are not too sharp, and that you use them gently on your dog's skin. This might also be the time to only use the wide-tined tools. If you are finding it difficult to draw the rake or comb through your dog's coat, use a spray-on conditioner or detangler to make this an easier process. And, if all else fails, rather than pull your senior's coat to remove a snarl, use a small blunt-nose pair of scissors to remove

the problem. A small hair cut is preferable to causing pain.

To keep your senior Siberian's coat in the best condition possible, make sure to apply a light conditioner to his coat and a spray on sunscreen. The healthier his coat, the easier it is to comb, and the less pain you will cause him. Just remember what a good companion your dog has been, and make sure you keep him as comfortable and beautiful as he can be in his old age.

SENIOR HEALTH CARE

As your keep your aging Siberian Husky beautiful, good genetics and your veterinarian will help keep him healthy. When a dog reaches 7 to 9 years of age, and periodically thereafter, veterinarians often recommend running a group of geriatric tests. These tests, along with your observations of your Siberian's health and behavior and the veterinarian's physical examination of your dog, will help identify any existing problems or potential medical issues. These tests usually include a complete blood count (CBC) to provide indications of anemia, infection, cancer, and some autoimmune problems. Your veterinarian may also do a T4 test to check thyroid function. He may order a urinalysis to check for diabetes, kidney disease, and bladder infections. Finally, a chemistry panel will check organs such as kidneys, liver, and pancreas.

Arthritis is not reversible, but its damage can be slowed and the symptoms and pain controlled.

In partnering with your veterinarian to support your aging Siberian, your significant role is to monitor any symptoms. Often, veterinarians will want to see their older patients every 6 months, instead of annually, to keep a closer eye on any changes in their condition. Frequent grooming and physical examination will help locate pain, swelling, weight gain or loss, and growths. Pay attention to your dog's mobility, how often you need to fill his water bowl, how frequently he urinates, if he is incontinent, how active your dog is, if his appetite changes, if he is coughing.

Although these can simply be signs that your dog is aging, pay careful attention to changes. All of these symptoms could be signs of more serious conditions.

Arthritis

If you notice that your dog seems unusually stiff and slow to move, his joints seem swollen or tender, or he is in pain, it may indicate that he has osteoarthritis or degenerative joint disease. In these diseases, loss of cartilage causes bone-on-bone contact and stiffness and pain for your Siberian. Arthritis is not reversible, but its damage can be slowed and the symptoms and pain controlled. The non-prescription method is to supplement with glucosamine and chondroitin, which are added to most commercially available senior dog food. Your veterinarian will be able to determine if additional supplementation is indicated.

Your veterinarian may also prescribe one of several possible non-steroidal anti-inflammatory drugs (NSAIDs), including aspirin. However, *never give your dog acetaminophen in place of aspirin*, and only give your dog aspirin upon instruction from your veterinarian. In addition to the medication, make sure your arthritic dog is not overweight. Providing him with a warm soft bed may also help. And regular walking will help keep him from becoming stiff. However, avoid strenuous and high-impact exercise.

Want to Know More?

For more information about keeping your Siberian healthy, see Chapter 8: Siberian Husky Health and Wellness.

Canine Cognitive Dysfunction

Apparent changes in your Siberian's personality, such as disorientation, anxiety, pacing, incontinence, vocalization (barking, whining, etc.), not paying attention, and other personality changes, could indicate a number of possible issues. These could be symptoms of blindness, deafness, arthritis, or canine cognitive dysfunction (CCD)—somewhat similar to Alzheimer's disease in humans.

Since these symptoms could be caused by a number of different diseases, your veterinarian will want to eliminate the other possible causes, and make some additional tests. If CCD is diagnosed, there is no cure, but a few medications are available to reduce some of the symptoms. The addition of antioxidants to his diet may also help. Work with your veterinarian to try to make your dog as comfortable as possible.

Cataracts

Blindness and deafness frequently occur with old age. Blindness is usually caused by old-age cataracts, which give a cloudy appearance to the eye. Cataracts are not reversible, but surgery can be performed to replace the cloudy lens. The surgical prognosis can be determined by a canine ophthalmologist. Whether or not your senior Siberian is a good surgical risk can best be determined by your veterinarian.

Should you choose not to perform surgery, you may find that the blindness will progress. As your dog's vision continues to fail, survey his yard and home for potential hazards and remove them. Consider restricting his access

Although many Siberians instinctively avoid water, if yours enjoys it a low-impact exercise like swimming can be good for your senior.

Just because your dog is getting older does not mean that his training should end.

to certain areas of the house. Try not to move furniture or add new potential obstacles to his world; don't change his routine. A blind dog in a familiar world succeeds quite well.

Cushing's Disease

If your dog is drinking more water and urinating more frequently, combined with an increase in appetite, apparent swelling of the abdomen, and hair loss, he may be suffering from Cushing's disease—the overproduction of glucocorticoid. Your veterinarian can perform tests to complete the diagnosis. Although rare in Siberian Huskies, this disease cannot be cured, although some treatments are available that may improve the quality of a dog's life.

Deafness

If your Siberian loses his hearing, you must become vigilant on his behalf for potential dangers. You will not be able to warn him of hazards or call him from danger. Consider restricting his area to keep him out of danger. And, have patience when you want to get his attention—instead of calling, you may have to go get him.

Liver and Kidney Disease

Liver disorders and kidney diseases are sometimes diagnosed in seniors. These two disorders often have similar symptoms. Symptoms of liver disease include jaundice, increased drinking and urinating, distended abdomen, decreased appetite, and weight loss. Symptoms of kidney disease include increased drinking, either increased urination or lack of urination, decreased appetite, and weight loss.

Your veterinarian can order a number of lab tests to check for the cause of the symptoms. If kidney disease is diagnosed early enough, it can be reversed. If not, other treatments can make your dog more comfortable. If the problem is liver disorder, your veterinarian can use additional tests to determine the cause and treat it.

Other Problems

Other health issues, such as diabetes, respiratory disease, or heart disease, although not all that common in Siberians, are not unseen in a senior dog. The key to catching them early is to pay close attention to your dog and his symptoms and work closely with your veterinarian. In many cases, late-onset health problems may be irreversible. However, by partnering with your vet, your old friend's quality of life can be improved.

TRAINING

Just because your dog is getting older does not mean that his training should end. Occasionally, you will discover that your senior Siberian Husky conveniently forgets some of his lessons, and a bit of a refresher is in order. But don't forget about his age and possible physical limitations. Your dog may no longer be able to go for long walks or participate in marathon training sessions.

Although walking is good exercise that should continue, your Siberian may have trouble sitting down and getting back up. In this case, be more lenient with the requirement that he *sit* when you stop. Instead, a command to *stand* may be a very welcome one.

If your Siberian has enjoyed his training sessions throughout his life, there is no reason that he should be deprived of them in his twilight years. Just remember to make the sessions appropriate to him and his health needs, and make sure you are both still having fun!

CHAPTER 14

END-OF-LIFE ISSUES

The final chapter in your dog's life will be the hardest for you to bear. Your Siberian has been your companion, friend, therapist, child, and partner since the minute he entered your life. And that life was clearly not long enough—no matter when it nears the end. Even as his health is failing, when you look into his eyes you can still see his noble heritage, reflecting the close relationship between these dogs and man, thousands of years ago in the most desolate corner of Siberia. For he is a direct ancestor of those dogs who saved Nome in 1925, and also of those dogs who have been part of their human's lives for thousands of years—just as he has been part of your life.

Your Siberian's life may end naturally. If not, it is your job to give him the final gift and not to let him suffer. This decision is not always easy.

WHEN IS IT TIME?

When your pet is ill, ask your veterinarian all of the questions you'll need to help you make the decision. What is the prognosis? What is the treatment? What is the chance of recovery? What can be done to manage his pain?

Realize that you will also need to understand how the treatment will affect you. What will it cost? How long will it last? Where do you have to take your dog for treatment? Can you handle the necessary care and treatment alone? Is there someone to help?

The answers to these questions will help you understand the options available. You will understand the quality of life your dog is and will be experiencing. And at the end, it is the quality of his life that must be of most concern to you. Does your dog still enjoy doing the things he has always liked to do? Is he still eating and drinking? Can he get up? Does he acknowledge you when he sees you? Is he in pain?

HOSPICE

If you determine that it is not time for your dog to go, he will most likely need some special care, including pain management. This is the canine equivalent of home hospice care. In some cases, you and your family may need help in providing the type of care that is required. Many veterinary practices or specialized veterinary services offer home hospice services for their clients.

Your schedule may require in-home help. Or, the care your dog requires may be beyond

Your Siberian may let you know when it's time to let go.

your capabilities. In either case, veterinary technicians can help make this difficult time easier on both you and your Siberian, while still respecting your desire for your pet not to suffer.

EUTHANASIA

If and when you make the decision that it is time to say goodbye to your dog, the most important thing is not to feel guilty because of your decision. If your dog has been diagnosed with a terminal illness, or his organs are failing due to old age, or even if your decision is partially based on financial considerations—do not feel guilty. Not everyone can afford the expense of special treatment, and it's not likely to change your pet's condition—it will merely prolong the inevitable. You made the decision

to end your dog's suffering from a position of love. He has been a good companion, and you can give him one last gift to ease his pain. This decision shows how much you do love him. If he could tell you himself, he would not want to be in any more pain or suffer any longer.

Once you have made the decision, make sure that all of your family members have the opportunity to say goodbye.

The process of euthanasia is fairly easy and is pain free. Your veterinarian will insert a catheter into a vein in your dog's leg and inject a drug. Often, a mild sedative will be injected first, followed by the euthanasia drug. This injection works quickly, and your dog's suffering will end soon.

It is a very personal decision whether or not to be with your dog as he is euthanized. It's not necessary for you to be there, and if you choose not to be present it does not make you a bad owner. Do not feel bad about whatever decision you make. Whether or not you want children present is also your decision. Realize that, during the euthanasia process, muscles may involuntarily contract, and your dog's eyes will most likely remain open. Anyone who is present should be prepared for that.

If you do not wish to be present, but wish to say good bye to your dog after the process is over, let your veterinarian know. Veterinary staff will do whatever they can to support your wishes.

You may wish to bring your pet's collar home, and some veterinary offices will make a cast of his pawprint as a remembrance. Some owners opt for burial, while others for cremation. Your veterinarian will be able to outline the options available, including the local ordinances about burial at home and individual cremation. The choice is yours, and your veterinary staff will help however they can. Remember that your beloved Siberian has been their good patient for years, and they want what is best for you.

GRIEF

After the death of your pet, grief is normal. You will go through all of the stages of grief: denial, bargaining, anger, sorrow and sadness, and resolution. Often people who have trouble showing grief at the loss of a family member or friend are much more demonstrative at the loss of a pet.

It will be difficult to explain the loss of

Many veterinary practices or specialized veterinary services offer home hospice services for their clients.

your pet to the children in your house. Depending on the age of the children, the concept of euthanasia may be beyond their understanding. It is fine to say that the pet was given medication so he would not suffer and died peacefully.

Your home will not feel the same for some time. Just as with the passing of people, you may wish to develop a ritual for the entire family to say goodbye to your dog. Children might find some comfort in telling favorite stories about your Siberian, mounting a favorite photograph, or drawing a picture.

The other pets in your household may be subdued upon the death of your Siberian. Whether it is a result of the actual loss of the pet or in response to your grief is not known.

However, as Siberians are pack animals, the loss of a member of the pack does require a shifting of roles. Make sure not to avoid your other pets—being with them will not only help them get through the loss, but will also help you work through your grief.

ANOTHER SIBERIAN?

The decision about if or when to get another Siberian is a personal one. You will never find a dog to replace the one you just lost. Rather, you will begin a new friendship with another descendent of Togo, Kreevanka, and Fritz. Whatever your decision, do not rush through the grieving process for this departed friend. You will know if and when you are ready for another Siberian. When you are, contact your breeder.

One solace Siberian Husky owners may take from the death of a dog is the ancient Chukchi belief that Siberian Huskies guard the gate to heaven and decide who is allowed to enter and who is not. The dogs make their decision based on how well the people cared for their own dogs during their lives. As a Siberian Husky owner, you not only know who will be awaiting you at the gates of heaven, you know that you will be allowed to enter.

You will know if and when you are ready for another Siberian.

1. True Siberian Husky fanciers never call the breed "Sibes" or "huskies." Always refer to them as Siberians or Siberian Huskies.

2. True appreciation of the Siberian Husky is in the knowledge of this noble breed's heritage. Take pride in the knowledge that your Siberian is a direct descendent of those original imports who helped save the children of Nome in 1925.

3. Never, ever shave a Siberian Husky; his coat insulates him from heat as well as from cold.

4. Siberian Huskies were bred to run. Therefore, if allowed freedom, they will run—run for fun, run out of curiosity. For their safety, like all dogs, Siberians should be kept in adequately fenced yards or on leash.

5. Siberian Huskies are the "Atkins diet" dogs. They tend to do better on a food with a higher protein and fat content and lower carbohydrates.

6. Siberian Huskies have a significant prey drive, so it is probably better to bring a puppy, rather than an adult dog, into a house with cats. Even if a Siberian shows his manners with his own cats, do not trust him with other cats or small animals.

7. Nothing about the Siberian Husky (the noun) should be husky (the adjective). The Siberian Husky is a long-distance, endurance sled dog, and any huskiness will adversely affect his ability to do his job.

8. To a Siberian Husky, humans are members of his pack, but not always the most important members. You must earn your position as pack leader.

9. Siberians are very intelligent, but very independent. They will learn behaviors quickly, but often will not show you what they know. Frequently, however, they are open to negotiation, and may demonstrate their knowledge in exchange for a biscuit.

10. It is believed that the generic word "husky," when used to mean an Arctic sled dog, is actually a corruption of the word "esky" or Eskimo dog.

11. When initially imported into Alaska, the Siberian Husky was called a Siberian "rat," due to his significantly smaller size than the native dogs.

12. Siberian Huskies were originally domesticated by the Chukchi natives of the most northeastern area in Siberia.

13. The name Leonhard Seppala is forever linked with the breed of Siberian Husky, as he trained and raced teams of original imports and their offspring.

14. The first Siberian Huskies were brought into Alaska during the early 1900s, with the last group of four dogs arriving in the late 1920s.

15. The record set in the 1910 All-Alaska Sweepstakes race was by a team of Siberian Huskies driven by John "Ironman" Johnson. That record held until it was broken in 2008.

16. The 1925 Serum Run relay consisted of 20 mushers and 150 dogs, who carried the serum 674 miles from Nenana to Nome in five days, seven hours.

17. The statue commemorating the 1925 Nome Serum Run is in New York City's Central Park, not far from the Children's Zoo. Although it is a statue of Balto, Togo was the true hero of the Serum Run, having led his team a total of over 250 miles.

18. The inscription on the Balto statue is: *Dedicated to the indomitable spirit of the sled dogs that relayed the antitoxins 660 miles over rough ice, across treacherous waters, through Arctic blizzards from Nenana to the relief of stricken Nome in the winter of 1925. Endurance • Fidelity • Intelligence*

19. All present-day Siberian Huskies can directly trace their lineage back to five sires: Togo, his sire Suggen, and Kreevanka, Tserko, and Fritz.

20. Although Siberian Huskies love their families, they are generally not fiercely loyal, one-person dogs. Their gregarious and curious nature will let them easily leave you for another friendly person.

21. Siberian Huskies generally shed their coats once to twice each year. During their shedding season, their loose fur will fill a couple of large trash bags.

22. Siberian Huskies love their crates. They have strong denning instincts, so their creates become their dens.

23. Crates are the way to make sure your Siberian is safe in any situation, including in the car.

24. Many Siberian Huskies have what Siberian owners refer to as "selective hearing." Although a Siberian's hearing is usually fine, his independent nature isn't always interested in listening to you and following your commands.

25. Siberian Huskies, although great sled dogs, should not be allowed to pull you when taking a walk. They should be trained to walk nicely on a lead with you.

26. The parent club for the Siberian Husky is the

Siberian Husky Club of America, Inc. (SHCA), which owns the standard for Siberian Huskies, a written description of the ideal Siberian.

27. Most mushers use "Hike!" to get their teams started.

28. "Mush!" is thought to be a corruption of "Marche!" used by French-Canadian fur trappers, meaning "Go!"

29. The SHCA has a program to recognize accomplishments of Siberians in sled races.

30. The SHCA has a program to recognize accomplishments of Siberians used as working pack dogs.

31. Throughout the years, several teams of purebred Siberian Huskies have competed in the Iditarod Trail Sled Dog Race.

32. The Iditarod Trail Sled Dog Race, begun in the 1970s, commemorates the 1925 Serum Run to Nome. It begins in Anchorage on the first Saturday of March and the dog teams mush to Nome, a distance in excess of 1,049 miles.

33. The first Siberian Husky to win Best in Show at an all-breed kennel club show was Ch. Alaskan's Bonzo of Anadyr, CD, bred and owned by Earl and Natalie Norris of Alaska.

34. The first Siberian Husky to win Best in Show outside of Alaska was Ch. Monadnock's King, bred and owned by Lorna Demidoff of New Hampshire.

35. The first Siberian to complete the title of Obedience Trial Champion was OTCH Storm King of the Yukon, owned by Weldon Fulton of California.

36. The first Siberian Husky to complete the title of Champion Tracker was CT Savitar's Pipe Down Otis, owned by Carol Clark of Missouri.

37. Never use a heated air dryer to dry a Siberian's coat; you could damage the coat and burn the dog.

38. Never use a metal grooming tool on a dry coat, as this could damage the coat.

39. Always use shampoos and grooming products developed for a dog's pH.

40. The first Siberian Husky to win Best in Show at the Westminster Kennel Club Dog Show was Ch. Innisfree's Sierra Cinnar, bred by Michael Burnside and Sally Higginbotham, owned by Kathleen Kanzler, and handled by Patricia Kanzler.

41. Siberian Huskies can be nearly any color (from pure white to black) with any type of markings, and can have any eye color or combination of colors. No color, eye color, or markings are better than any other or "worth more."

42. A bored Siberian Husky can be a destructive Siberian Husky. Make sure to keep your Siberian occupied and well exercised so he does not think of things to do on his own.

43. Siberian Huskies are ingenious dogs who are capable of digging under, climbing over, or getting through most fences, if they wish to get free. Because of this, Siberians require owners who may need to be a bit more creative about securing the yard.

44. Siberian Huskies are often thought to cause the "potato chip syndrome"—their owners can't just have one.

45. The SHCA annually holds a national dog show only for Siberian Huskies. The location moves around the country to make it accessible to more people, and the event occurs at some time in the month of September or October. Siberian owners from around the world are encouraged to attend the near-week-long event.

46. The Siberian Husky has an unusual metabolism that is similar to that of other dogs while at rest. However, when a Siberian needs extra energy at work, there appears to be a metabolic adaptation that provides them great endurance.

47. Although Siberia covers a vast area (approximately 10% of earth's land mass), the Siberian Husky comes from a small corner of that vast region: the northeastern area known as the Chukchi peninsula.

48. The Siberian Husky is probably among the most ancient of domesticated dogs, thought to be part of the "primitive" group of dogs from Asia and Africa.

49. The Siberian Husky is closely related to the wolf, as well as to the other spitz-type dogs, such as the Akita, Alaskan Malamute, Samoyed, and even Pomeranian.

50. The Chukchis believe that Siberian Huskies guard the gates of heaven and decide who gets to enter based on how well people treated their dogs in life.

ASSOCIATIONS AND ORGANIZATIONS

Breed Clubs

American Kennel Club (AKC)
5580 Centerview Drive
Raleigh, NC 27606
Telephone: (919) 233-9767
Fax: (919) 233-3627
E-Mail: info@akc.org
www.akc.org

Canadian Kennel Club (CKC)
89 Skyway Avenue, Suite 100
Etobicoke, Ontario M9W 6R4
Telephone: (416) 675-5511
Fax: (416) 675-6506
E-Mail: information@ckc.ca
www.ckc.ca

Federation Cynologique
Internationale (FCI)
Secretariat Général de la FCI
Place Albert 1er, 13
B – 6530 Thuin
Belqique
www.fci.be

Siberian Husky Club of America,
Inc. (SHCA)
www.shca.org

SHCA Trust
Benefitting Education, Health &
Recue of the Siberian Husky
www.shcatrust.org

United Kennel Club (UKC)
100 E. Kilgore Road
Kalamazoo, MI 49002-5584
Telephone: (269) 343-9020
Fax: (269) 343-7037
E-Mail: pbickell@ukcdogs.com
www.ukcdogs.com

Pet Sitters

National Association of
Professional Pet Sitters
15000 Commerce Parkway,
Suite C
Mt. Laurel, New Jersey 08054
Telephone: (856) 439-0324
Fax: (856) 439-0525
E-Mail: napps@ahint.com
www.petsitters.org

Pet Sitters International
201 East King Street
King, NC 27021-9161
Telephone: (336) 983-9222
Fax: (336) 983-5266
E-Mail: info@petsit.com
www.petsit.com

Rescue Organizations and Animal Welfare Groups

American Humane Association
(AHA)
63 Inverness Drive East
Englewood, CO 80112
Telephone: (303) 792-9900
Fax: 792-5333
www.americanhumane.org

American Society for the
Prevention of Cruelty to Animals
(ASPCA)
424 E. 92nd Street
New York, NY 10128-6804
Telephone: (212) 876-7700
www.aspca.org

Royal Society for the Prevention
of Cruelty to Animals (RSPCA)
RSPCA Enquiries Service
Wilberforce Way, Southwater,
Horsham, West Sussex RH13
9RS
United Kingdom
Telephone: 0870 3335 999
Fax: 0870 7530 284
www.rspca.org.uk

Sports

International Agility Link (IAL)
Global Administrator: Steve
Drinkwater
E-Mail: yunde@powerup.au
www.agilityclick.com/~ial

The World Canine Freestyle
Organization, Inc.
P.O. Box 350122
Brooklyn, NY 11235
Telephone: (718) 332-8336
Fax: (718) 646-2686
E-Mail: WCFODOGS@aol.com
www.worldcaninefreestyle.org

Therapy

Delta Society
875 124th Ave, NE, Suite 101
Bellevue, WA 98005
Telephone: (425) 679-5500
Fax: (425) 679-5539
E-Mail: info@DeltaSociety.org
www.deltasociety.org

Therapy Dogs Inc.
P.O. Box 20227
Cheyenne WY 82003
Telephone: (877) 843-7364
Fax: (307) 638-2079
E-Mail: therapydogsinc@
qwestoffice.net
www.therapydogs.com

Therapy Dogs International
(TDI)
88 Bartley Road
Flanders, NJ 07836
Telephone: (973) 252-9800
Fax: (973) 252-7171
E-Mail: tdi@gti.net
www.tdi-dog.org

Training

Association of Pet Dog Trainers (APDT)
150 Executive Center Drive Box 35
Greenville, SC 29615
Telephone: (800) PET-DOGS
Fax: (864) 331-0767
E-Mail: information@apdt.com
www.apdt.com

International Association of Animal Behavior Consultants (IAABC)
565 Callery Road
Cranberry Township, PA 16066
E-Mail: info@iaabc.org
www.iaabc.org

National Association of Dog Obedience Instructors (NADOI)
PMB 369
729 Grapevine Hwy.
Hurst, TX 76054-2085
www.nadoi.org

Veterinary and Health Resources

Academy of Veterinary Homeopathy (AVH)
P.O. Box 9280
Wilmington, DE 19809
Telephone: (866) 652-1590
Fax: (866) 652-1590
www.theavh.org

American Academy of Veterinary Acupuncture (AAVA)
P.O. Box 1058
Glastonbury, CT 06033
Telephone: (860) 632-9911
Fax: (860) 659-8772
www.aava.org

American Animal Hospital

Association (AAHA)
12575 W. Bayaud Ave.
Lakewood, CO 80228
Telephone: (303) 986-2800
Fax: (303) 986-1700
E-Mail: info@aahanet.org
www.aahanet.org/index.cfm

American College of Veterinary Internal Medicine (ACVIM)
1997 Wadsworth Blvd., Suite A
Lakewood, CO 80214-5293
Telephone: (800) 245-9081
Fax: (303) 231-0880
Email: ACVIM@ACVIM.org
www.acvim.org

American College of Veterinary Ophthalmologists (ACVO)
P.O. Box 1311
Meridian, ID 83860
Telephone: (208) 466-7624
Fax: (208) 466-7693
E-Mail: office09@acvo.com
www.acvo.com

American Holistic Veterinary Medical Association (AHVMA)
2218 Old Emmorton Road
Bel Air, MD 21015
Telephone: (410) 569-0795
Fax: (410) 569-2346
E-Mail: office@ahvma.org
www.ahvma.org

American Veterinary Medical Association (AVMA)
1931 North Meacham Road, Suite 100
Schaumburg, IL 60173-4360
Telephone: (847) 925-8070
Fax: (847) 925-1329
E-Mail: avmainfo@avma.org
www.avma.org

ASPCA Animal Poison Control Center
Telephone: (888) 426-4435
www.aspca.org

British Veterinary Association (BVA)
7 Mansfield Street
London
W1G 9NQ
Telephone: 0207 636 6541
Fax: 0207 908 6349
E-Mail: bvahq@bva.co.uk
www.bva.co.uk

Canine Eye Registration Foundation (CERF)
VMDB/CERF
1717 Philo Rd
P O Box 3007
Urbana, IL 61803-3007
Telephone: (217) 693-4800
Fax: (217) 693-4801
E-Mail: CERF@vmbd.org
www.vmdb.org

Orthopedic Foundation for Animals (OFA)
2300 NE Nifong Blvd
Columbus, Missouri 65201-3856
Telephone: (573) 442-0418
Fax: (573) 875-5073
Email: ofa@offa.org
www.offa.org

US Food and Drug Administration Center for Veterinary Medicine (CVM)
7519 Standish Place
HFV-12
Rockville, MD 20855-0001
Telephone: (240) 276-9300 or (888) INFO-FDA
http://www.fda.gov/cvm

PHOTO CREDITS

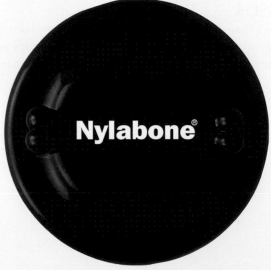

ACKNOWLEDGMENTS

In thanks to three generous women who, over the past 35 years, shared their knowledge and dogs: Phyllis Brayton, Natalie Norris, and Judy Russell. To four gentlemen who taught me much about the Breed: Hiberian Suski, our first Siberian, Alaskan's Jonah of Anadyr, who taught me about sled dogs, and Rushmore, Ch. Karnovanda's North By Northwest, and Ted, Ch. Karnovanda's Your Teddy Bear, for the fun ride. And, last to the non-dog person who joined me on this dog life journey, my husband, Ric.

ABOUT THE AUTHOR

Donna Beckman has over 35 years of experience with Siberian Huskies. She is active in her local Siberian Husky club as well as the Siberian Husky Club of America, Inc., and is currently their Delegate to the American Kennel Club. Donna has been a breeder and exhibitor of Siberians, including of a number of top-ranked, multiple-group-winning, and Best in Show Siberians in the US and abroad. She is approved by the American Kennel Club to judge Siberians and the other Working Arctic breeds.

VETERINARY ADVISOR

Wayne Hunthausen, DVM, consulting veterinary editor and pet behavior consultant, is the director of Animal Behavior Consultations in the Kansas City area and currently serves on the *Practioner Board for Veterinary Medicine* and the Behavior Advisory Board for *Veterinary Forum*.

BREEDER ADVISOR

Judith M. Russell is owner of Karnovanda Kennels, which has produced many Siberian Husky bench show champions, group placers and winners, and Best-in-Show dogs, as well as a number of obedience-titled dogs. Judy won the Siberian Husky Club of America's Working/Showing award five consecutive years.